The Travelers' Guide to
Middle Eastern
and
North African
Customs and Manners

Also by the authors

The Travelers' Guide to European Customs and Manners
The Travelers' Guide to Asian Customs and Manners
The Travelers' Guide to Latin American Customs and Manners

The Travelers' Guide to
Middle Eastern
and
North African
Customs and Manners

Elizabeth Devine

and

Nancy L. Braganti

St. Martin's Press · New York

THE TRAVELERS' GUIDE TO MIDDLE EASTERN AND NORTH AFRICAN CUSTOMS
AND MANNERS. Copyright © 1991 by Elizabeth Devine and Nancy L. Braganti.
All rights reserved. Printed in the United States of America. No part of this
book may be used or reproduced in any manner whatsoever without written
permission except in the case of brief quotations embodied in critical articles or
reviews. For information, address St. Martin's Press, 175 Fifth Avenue, New
York, N.Y. 10010.

Library of Congress Cataloging-in-Publication Data

Devine, Elizabeth
    The travelers' guide to Middle Eastern and North African customs and
manners / Elizabeth Devine and Nancy L. Braganti.
        p.   cm.
    ISBN 0-312-05523-4 (pbk.)
    1. Middle East—Description and travel—Guide-books.   2. Middle
East—Social life and customs.   3. Africa, North—Description and
travel—Guide-books.   4. Africa, North—Social life and
customs.   I. Braganti, Nancy L.   II. Title.
DS43.D45   1991
915.604'53—dc20   90-19223
                                                                CIP

10 9 8 7 6 5 4 3 2

Contents

●

Acknowledgments
✸

We wish to thank those who assisted but prefer to remain anonymous, and we wish to thank the following for helping us to prepare this book: Abdul Rahim Abu Romman, Hamed Alnawafleh, Dr. Assem Badawy, William Bartley, Béatrice Bastiani, NourEddine Benakezouh, H. Bruce Boal, Tanya Braganti, Samir Bustany, Elizabeth Corella, Barbara Croken, Benjamin Dyal, Sahar El-Huneidi, Nancy Esposito, Catherine Essoyan, Kate Fallon, Elizabeth Fernea, William Flemmer, Nancy Galvin, Dr. Carney Gavin, Dr. Maureen Giovannini, Christine Helms, David Herman, Talia Herman, Dr. Ernest Johnson, Helen Johnson, Jean Johnston, Eric Karlstad, Arthur Kemelman, Mary E. King, James Kostaras, Edna Kutai, Ann Lesch, Tamsen Lord, Andrea Lorenz, Alain McNamara, Syham Manns, Dr. Robert Meagher, Evelyn Menchoni, Elaine Metzler, Minou Modabber, Lawrence Murphy, Teresa Muxie, Thomas O'Donnell, Cate Olson, Darrah Ostrander, Mary Ellen Peebles, Dr. Diana Reynolds, Nash Robbins, Michelle Hadj Salem, Salem Hadj Salem, Wafa Salman, Erlinda Samonteza, Heidi Sawyer, Annabel Seligman, Laura Stanley, Dennis Sullivan, Katherine Sullivan, Sally M. Swartz, Patricia Walsh, Alexzandra Zallen.

Introduction

From Humphrey Bogart and Ingrid Bergman in *Casablanca* to Bob Hope and Bing Crosby in *Road to Morocco* to Peter O'Toole in *Lawrence of Arabia*, filmmakers and film audiences have responded to the mystery, adventure, and romance of the Middle East.

In this book, we want to take some of the mystery out of traveling in the area so that your adventures are those of your own choosing. For romance, you're on your own.

We've departed a bit from the arrangement of our previous *Travelers' Guide* books. Since all but one of the countries is an Arab nation whose dominant religion is Islam, we have provided a brief overview of the effects of Islam on daily life and the behavior common in all the countries of the Arab world.

Whether you are a traveler who wants to see some of civilization's most ancient monuments or a businessperson who wants to take advantage of the burgeoning markets in the Middle East, this book will advise you what to expect of others and what others expect of you.

To make this guide easy to use, we have divided the information about each country into the following topics:

Greetings: We all know that first impressions count and that meeting someone from another culture can make us feel awkward. We'll tell you what the appropriate gestures of greeting are, as well as the appropriate words. Pay special attention to the way that a foreign man should greet an Arab woman. In some countries, touching between unrelated members of opposite sexes is taboo.

Conversation: The subjects you choose to discuss can make or break a potential friendship or business deal. *Never, never, never* mention religion, politics, the conflicts between Israel and Arab countries, or the Palestinian situation. If a Middle Eastern person introduces one of those subjects, call on all your diplomatic resources. Be noncommittal and nonjudgmental.

This advice is so important that we'll repeat it over again. Don't get drawn into a conversation about possible political changes as a result of the Gulf War of 1991. Don't offer opinions on the war and its aftermath, and don't ask questions about possible political liberalizations (e.g., "Do you think women will be given more freedom?")

A reliable source of conversation can be TV shows and sports from the West. The introduction of cable television in many Arab countries has made people conversant with many sports and TV series popular in Western countries. One Chicago investment banker said that he was pleased to find his city no longer identified with Al Capone and gangsters but with the Chicago Bears (whose games people had seen on cable TV).

Telephones: You'll learn where to look for public telephones and in which countries and areas you won't find any.

In some places, you may find it easier to fax messages abroad than to try to telephone.

In Public: We'll acquaint you with the appropriate forms of behavior in public. Pay special attention to how you should treat members of the opposite sex and to the special meaning certain gestures have in the Middle East.

Dress: Here you'll find advice on what to wear for both casual wear and business. We'll also advise about appropriate dress for visiting religious sites. Remember that—especially in the Arab world—you can't err by dressing conservatively. Women should take special note of this, because much of what the Western world regards as acceptable casual wear is considered offensively immodest by Muslims.

The climate in the Middle East and North Africa can be incredibly hot (many people say that you never get used to the heat, however long you're in the area). Therefore a bit of advice: Bring garments made *only* of natural fabrics. Synthetics are murderously hot. Men should not bring seersucker suits under the mistaken impression that seersucker is a natural fabric.

The best strategy is to bring layered outfits. For very hot weather, you can remove layers. In air-conditioned places or on chilly nights, you can add layers.

Meals: Here we cover when you'll eat, what you'll eat, and how you'll eat it. In some places, eating will be just as it is at home—around a table set with knives, forks, and spoons. In other places, you'll sit on the floor and use slices of bread instead of utensils. In some cases you'll find unfamiliar eating arrangements, such as men and women eating in separate rooms.

We also provide information about eating in restaurants and about the special dishes of each country. (A quick scan will show that lovers of lamb are in for a treat in the Middle East.)

Hotels: The exploration for oil in the Middle East led to the construction of many excellent, Western-style hotels, where you will find the same level of comfort as you do in Chicago, Toronto, or London. However, you'll also learn about the levels of accommodations available outside the urban centers of the Middle East, and, in many cases, you'll find them somewhat primitive.

Tipping: Check individual countries to discover how much to tip and to whom you should give a tip. In some countries, it's appropriate to tip people we ordinarily don't in North America and Europe—gas station attendants and cinema ushers, for example.

Private Homes: Whether you're planning a short social visit or are invited to stay with a family, you'll want to know the accepted customs as well as the gifts people in the Middle East and North Africa appreciate.

As dress should be conservative, behavior in private homes should be discreet and modest. A woman staying with a family must be particularly careful, because her behavior will reflect—for good or ill—on her host family.

Business: Before doing business, you'll want to know about the hours that businesses, government offices, and banks are open and also about the country's currency.

Under "Business Practices," we offer information about which countries require a foreign company to have an agent to do business there, and how to go about finding both agents and contacts in Middle Eastern countries.

We'll take you through the negotiating process. Among the many tips you'll find will be information about scheduling meetings (when and where), identifying the decision makers, and getting a *written* contract.

You'll also find information about two important subjects: (1) those countries (the preponderance) in which developing a close personal relationship is absolutely essential to doing business; and (2) those countries in which foreign businesswomen will be taken seriously—and those in which they won't.

We also comment on business entertaining and the issue in much of the Middle East about whether spouses are included in business dinners.

Holidays and Special Occasions: In Israel and the Arab world, each year has periods associated with religious observances as well as secular holidays. Travelers may wish to include some of these observances in their itineraries, while people on business trips may want to avoid them, since little or no business is done.

Transportation: We cover the methods of public transportation in the countries—buses, trains, taxis—as well as driving. Some transportation, particularly local buses, is *very* primitive, while some trains offer every type of luxury.

In almost all cases, we recommend hiring a car and driver, rather than renting a car and driving yourself. Should you decide to drive in the desert, *please* pay close attention to the discussion of desert driving in "Customs and Manners in the Arab World."

Legal Matters, Safety, and Health: We've all read tales of people unwittingly falling afoul of the law in foreign countries and, in some cases, spending time in prison there. In this chapter, you'll find information on some legalities of which you may be unaware.

To further ensure a healthy trip, follow the advice about what you should or shouldn't eat. Also observe the warning not to swim in most of the waters of the area—for fear of the parasitic disease bilharzia. The disease can lead to fatigue, extreme exhaustion, and even death.

To ensure a healthy trip, in the U.S., call the Centers for Disease Control in Atlanta, Georgia—(404) 639–3311—to learn about required immunizations and about any special health problems. Or you can call the office of the U.S. Public Health Quarantine Station nearest you: Chicago: (312) 686–2150; Honolulu: (808) 541–2552; Los Angeles: (213) 215–2365; Miami: (305) 526–2910; New York City: (718) 917–1685; San Francisco: (415) 876–2872; Seattle: (206) 442–4519.

Canadians should write or call for the brochure "Travel and Health," which gives information about health precautions to take when traveling outside Canada. Address: Health and Welfare Canada, Fifth Floor, Brooke Claxton Building, Tunney's Pasture, Ottawa K1A OK9. Phone: (613) 957–2991.

British travelers should ask their travel agents about health conditions, since the agents are updated frequently by the Department of Health and Social Security. Travelers may also telephone the Department at (01) 407–5522 and ask for "Public Inquiries," to learn of any updated health forecasts, and to request a copy of their booklet, "Protect Your Health Abroad."

Another health tip if you're going to a country where you should not drink the water: About 45 minutes before your plane lands, ask the flight attendant for a canned soft drink (e.g., soda water, Coca Cola, 7-Up, etc). Hold on to it. You'll probably be very thirsty when you land, since plane trips are dehydrating. Have your drink while you're waiting for your baggage or in the taxi on the way to your hotel.

For most of us, safety is important to our enjoyment of travel. To make sure you're not venturing into an unsafe environment, if you're planning a trip from the U.S., call the Citizens' Emergency Center Division of the State Department to find out about any particular trouble spots in the Middle East. The phone number is (202) 647–5225. Call Monday through Friday, 8:15 A.M. to 5:00 P.M., or Saturday, 9:00 A.M. to 3:00 P.M., Eastern Time. In Great Britain, call the Consular Advice to the Public, a division of the Foreign Office at (01) 270–4129. Canadians should phone the Consular Operations Division of the Department of External Affairs at (613) 992–3705.

In individual cities or towns, ask friends, business colleagues, and hotel staff which areas are safe and which you should avoid.

Key Phrases: At the end of the book, we've provided a list of useful words and phrases in Arabic and Hebrew. Learning the basic courtesies, numbers, and words for common terms and places will stand you in good stead.

SOME GENERAL ADVICE

Before you go, read as much as you can about the area and its history. People in the Middle East are rightly proud of their area as the cradle of civilization. The only survivor of the Seven Wonders of the Ancient

World—the pyramids of Egypt, begun by Cheops in 2700 B.C.—are a short drive from modern Cairo. Jordan includes the ruins of Petra, "the rose-red city half as old as time."

Some recommended reading: *The Arab World: Personal Encounters*, by Elizabeth Warnock Fernea and Robert A. Fernea (Garden City, NY: Anchor Books, 1987, $9.95); Jonathan Raban's *A Journey through the Labyrinth*, a British journalist's account of his journey through the Arab world (New York: Simon & Schuster, 1980, $7.75); *Baghdad Without a Map*, Tony Horowitz's amusing and informative account of his "misadventures in Arabia" (New York, Dutton, 1991, $19.95); the chapters on Islam and Judaism in Huston Smith's marvelous *The Religions of Man* (New York: Harper and Row, $4.95). Smith writes for the layperson, and he gives excellent insights into the two religions.

Remember that different means different; it doesn't mean better or worse. People who eat with knives and forks are not inherently more civilized than people who use bread to scoop their food. They are just different in their approaches to eating. Never make negative comparisons by saying, for example, that some action is accomplished more quickly or more efficiently in your country.

PACKING LIST

This list doesn't cover everything you'll want to bring along, but let us suggest some important items. If your visit is limited to cities, you can count on finding toiletries and aspirin, but if you prefer a particular brand, bring it with you. If you're venturing into rural areas, take along everything you'll need. Wherever you are traveling, pack a hat to ward off the intense sun.

Medical Supplies: Be sure to bring a more-than-adequate supply of any prescription drugs (in their original containers, if possible) you may be taking. If you run out, you could be in trouble, since drugs are known by different names in different countries. Your best bet is to ask your physician to provide you with a detailed list—with generic names and dosage amounts—of all prescription drugs you are taking, plus duplicate prescriptions for those items. Always pack your medication in your carry-on bag for safety.

If you use birth control, bring an ample supply. In the Arab world, you may be able to get contraceptives, but it won't be easy. Birth control is against Islamic beliefs, and you will have to find a physician to give you a prescription.

If you wear glasses, bring an extra pair as well as a copy of your prescription. Be sure to pack a pair of sunglasses.

Besides any medication you may be taking, bring an antidiarrheal medication and a broad-spectrum antibiotic to combat bacterial infection. You'll need a prescription for both.

Other items to consider bringing: aspirin or your favorite headache-fever remedy, an antacid, a laxative, a motion-sickness remedy, insect repellant, lotion for insect bites, sunscreen, a cream to relieve sunburn, an antibiotic ointment for cuts, Band-Aids, a mentholated decongestant, cough medicine, a remedy for muscle pains. It's also wise to bring a thermometer. Women may wish to include remedies for menstrual cramps and vaginal yeast infections.

Toiletries: Shampoo, deodorant, toothbrush and toothpaste, soap powder or liquid for washing clothes, a portable clothesline that can be strung over a bathtub, a shower cap, tissues (always carry some, as public washrooms often do not have toilet paper), and moist towelettes.

Supplies: A flashlight with batteries and a hair dryer (one that works on both 110 and 220 volts if possible); a collapsible plastic cup.

SOME SPECIAL WORDS FOR WOMEN

If you're traveling alone, whether for business or pleasure, you might want to invest in an inexpensive wedding band. When people ask about your husband, say that he'll be joining you shortly. If you prefer a fib to a lie, respond to questions about your marital status by saying that you're engaged.

To avoid appearing to make eye contact with men (a taboo in Arab countries), women may want to wear dark sunglasses.

Wherever you are in the Middle East, you won't err by being conservative, whether in dress or behavior.

At the end of *Casablanca*, as Rick and Captain Reynaud (Humphrey Bogart and Claude Rains) walk into the darkness, Rick says, "This could be the beginning of a beautiful friendship." We hope that this book will be your first step in a beautiful relationship with one of the world's most entrancing areas.

Customs and
Manners in the
Arab World
☙❧

The term "Arab" describes not a race but a cultural association. Arab people are descended of several racial stocks of the Mediterranean area. People whose mother tongue is Arabic and who consider themselves Arabs are Arabs. When relating to Arabs, keep the following in mind: (1) a person's honor is of the utmost importance; (2) loyalties are ranked in a hierarchy—first, the extended family, then friends, then the Arab Islamic community, then their country, and then non-Arab Muslims; and (3) status is based on social class and family background.

Enough customs are common to the Arab countries that we decided to provide an introduction with customs applicable to all the Arab world and to present distinctive customs under individual countries.

GREETINGS

• Try to learn a few phrases of greeting in Arabic (See "Key Words and Phrases"—Arabic, page 227). You'll make a favorable impression with just a few words.

• Expect first names to be used immediately. Precede an Arab's first name with Mr., Miss, or Mrs. If Doctor or Professor is the appropriate title, use it with the first name. Arab men and women have a first name, which is followed by their father's first name, and then family names (Example: Ahmed Abdallah Haddad). From the first time that they meet you, people will call you by your first name preceded by Mr., Miss, or Mrs.

• Remember that an Arab woman does not change her name when she marries.

• Note that a Western-sounding name usually means that the person is a Christian.

• If you would like to address people with the Arabic version of their titles, use the following: *Duktoar* (male) or *Duktoara* (female) for a Ph.D. or an M.D.; *Ma'ali* (Excellency) for a government minister; *Sa'ada* for a senior official; *Shaykh* (male) or *Shaykah* (female) for members of the ruling families of the Gulf.

• Note that a sign of sincerity in greeting is to shake hands and then place the right hand on the chest near the heart. If you see other people doing this, follow suit.

• Realize that people shake hands and hold hands in greeting longer than Westerners do. Let the Mid-East person withdraw from the handshake first.

• When a Western man is introduced to an Arab woman, he should wait to see if she extends her hand. If she does not, he should not shake hands.

• In greeting Arab men and departing from them, shake hands. Some Arabs use both hands to shake hands—four hands clasped into a ball. This is usually used with close friends. If your host clasps your right hand with both of his, cover them with your left hand.

• Mid-Eastern women kiss on both cheeks if they haven't seen one another for a long time or if there is going to be a long separation.

CONVERSATION

• Expect a *great deal* of conversation when you visit the Arab world. It's the most popular form of entertainment.

• Ask people about their children, a subject they enjoy.

• Seek advice about sights to see and local food specialties to try. People especially enjoy answering questions about food.

• Don't be surprised when asked very personal questions, even in a first conversation: Are you married? Why not? What is your salary? . . . People often don't understand an adult's not being married. If you're a woman, say that you're engaged in order to avoid a barrage of questions.

• Never discuss or ask about an Arab's wife, sister, or daughter.

• Be prepared for Arabs to bring up Islam frequently and even try to convert you. To avoid committing yourself, say that it would offend your family if you did. Admitting that you are an atheist or an agnostic would shock Arabs, and they will lose respect for you.

• Don't bring up politics, even though Arabs enjoy discussing it. Never bring up the Arab-Israeli conflict, but be prepared to be pressed for your country's views on the issue. If you're from the U.S., try saying that the press is doing its best to present a balanced view of the problem. Mention PBS programs that have presented the Palestinian viewpoint and David Shipler's book and film presenting both sides. It would be helpful to read Shipler's *Arab and Jew: Wounded Spirits in the Promised Land* (New York: Penguin, 1987, $8.95) before your visit to the Arab world.

• Expect Arabs to refer to Israel as "The Occupied Territories," both in conversation and on the maps they use.

• If you mention your family, be sure to be positive. Never mention a relative with low moral standards, and never express animosity toward any of your family members.

• If you've come from a "humble" background, don't bring it up.

• Expect to hear many euphemisms when Arabs talk about misfortune, illness, or death. They believe that discussing the matter makes the situation worse. Therefore, they will refer to someone who is seriously ill as being "a bit tired."

• Remember that Arabs regard praise of their children as bad luck. Pay the compliment indirectly, attributing the children's good qualities to God; for example, "What beautiful children you have. God has been very good to you. How blessed you are."

• Refrain from paying a compliment about a specific object. If you say "I love that painting," an Arab will feel obliged to give it to you. However, you could offer general praise, "Your home is so beautiful. You've chosen things so well."

• Never use "swear words," even "damn." Such words are very offensive throughout the Arab world.

• Don't attack a man's honor by criticizing him in public—for example, "That was a stupid thing to do." Such an assault is unforgivable by Arab standards. By the same token, never criticize one of your own countrymen, either in his presence or in his absence.

• Be sure that you don't phrase questions in an aggressive manner. Arabs won't respond well.

• Don't use the word "Mohammedan." Use "Muslim" or "Moslem."

• To avoid offending Arabs, use the term "Arab nation" rather than "Arab nations."

• In referring to changes in the Arab world, use "modernize" rather than "Westernize."

• A Western woman conversing with Arab women should discuss fashion, cooking, and travel.

• Don't keep glancing at your watch while you're talking with someone. It's insulting and considered a rejection of the person you're with.

• Avoid ending a conversation abruptly. Say something such as "I hope you will have a peaceful weekend with your family" or "Stay in good health." Never say that you have to be somewhere else.

IN PUBLIC

• Don't back away when an Arab stands very close while speaking to you. He won't be more than two feet away. Arabs constantly stare into other people's eyes, watching the pupils for an indication of the other person's response. However, foreign men should never stare directly into a *woman's* eyes, either in speaking to her or in passing on the street. He should avert his eyes or keep his eyes on the ground.

• Remember that the giving and receiving of favors are the foremost bases of friendship. Arabs will always say "Yes" when asked to do a favor, because they believe that one can never refuse a friend's request. If an Arab asks you for help or a favor, say that you will try. Your willingness *to try* is much more important than whether you ultimately succeed. If you later report that you were unsuccessful, your Arab friend won't expect a reason or ask for one.

• Realize that there is no concept of privacy in Arab culture. People will feel free to comment on your weight, your marital status, etc., and they will ask about your salary and how much you paid for various things.

• Be aware that people are easily offended if you constantly refuse invitations, excusing yourself by saying that you're "too busy" or "too tired." Further, don't say, "I hope to see you later this week," if you don't really mean it. Arabs would regard this as a total lack of sincerity.

• If men sit on the floor, they can cross their legs or put them to the side. Feel free to shift your position to be more comfortable. Women should kneel with their legs under them, or, if their skirt is long enough to cover the soles of the shoes, with legs at the side. Don't cross your legs in the presence of royalty.

• Never point the sole of your shoes or feet at an Arab, since this action signifies contempt.

• If you need directions, ask a policeman. Other people may tell you what they think you want to hear. For example, don't say "Is the train station down that way?" because they will respond "Yes," whether it is or not. If you ask "Where is the train station?" you may get an accurate response.

• Expect to be offered cigarettes frequently. If you don't smoke, you might want to carry a supply of hard candies so that you will have something to offer others.

• If you do smoke and are in a group, always offer a cigarette to other members of the group. However, keep in mind that smoking in the presence of people in authority (including royalty, of course) or older people is disrespectful. Another smoking tip: Don't light your cigarette from the bowl of a water pipe while the pipe is being smoked.

• Realize that keeping your hands in your pockets or leaning against a wall while talking to someone shows a lack of respect.

• When you hand anything to another person, always use your *right* hand.

• Be aware that use of the right hand for eating has become ingrained in Arabs because when people lived in the desert, there was little water to wash the left hand—the hand used for cleaning oneself after using the toilet. Note: Some left-handed travelers have reported that urban Arabs who have had experience with the West have been tolerant of their eating with their left hand.

• Refrain from any expression of intimacy with a member of the opposite sex in public. Even husbands and wives should avoid any displays of affection, such as holding hands or kissing on the cheek. If you are too familiar with a member of the opposite sex, Arabs will believe that you have low moral standards. Perhaps to discourage familiarity, Arab men and women sometimes separate into two groups at parties.

• Foreign men should *never* touch an Arab woman, even with such a harmless gesture as helping her into a car.

• Note that rules for members of the same sex are very different. They often stand very close to one another and touch frequently during a conversation. Men often hold hands with men and women with women when walking. The action has no sexual implications. Men should note, however, that certain familiarities with Arab men aren't acceptable. Don't slap an Arab on the back or call him by a nickname.

• Be advised that it is *very* important to learn to read Arabic numerals. Knowing them will be necessary when taking a bus or shopping.

• Prepare for major crushes in lines. Try talking to people around you and establishing a brief, personal contact; you will probably avoid people pushing you out of line. People have different manners for friends and for strangers. Don't take it personally when you're jostled or pushed.

• Remember that upper-class Arabs never do manual work of any kind in front of others, because such work is considered beneath their status.

• When someone leaves you—whether it be at hotel, home, or office—always accompany him to the door.

• These seven gestures have common meanings you should be familiar with: (1) To indicate "What does it mean" or "What are you saying," hold up your right hand and twist it as if you were screwing in a light bulb one turn; (2) all fingers and thumb touching with the palm up means "Wait a minute"; (3) "No" is signaled in one of three ways—either moving the head back slightly and raising the eyebrows *or* moving the head back and raising the chin *or* moving the head back and clicking with the tongue; (4) "Come here" is indicated by holding the right hand out with the palm up and opening and closing the hand; (5) to signify "Go away," hold the right hand out with the palm down, and move it as if pushing something away from you; (6) if you see someone holding the right hand out with palm up and moving it up and down slowly, he means "Be quiet"; (7) holding the right forefinger up and moving it from left to right quickly and repeatedly is a forceful "Never"; (8) "Very good" is indicated by the traditional "thumbs up" sign—right fist clenched with thumb up.

• Never point your finger at anyone.

A Camel Ride: In many countries you will have the opportunity to take a camel ride. The experience will be a bit less daunting if you know what to expect: Get on when the camel is squatting. Quickly take hold of the saddle pommel. This signals the camel to rise. (Another signal might be your guide's making a "zzt zzt" sound.) Quickly throw your leg over the camel and brace yourself. The camel lifts his rear first, then the front legs. Lean backward as he lifts the rear legs so that you won't be over his head. Prepare for a rocky ride, since the camel moves his right front and right rear legs simultaneously and then his two left legs. When the camel lies down again, hold tight. You'll be thrown forward and then backward. Depending on the length of the ride, your legs may feel shaky afterward. (One traveler reported that she simply wanted to have her picture taken while the camel was on the ground. After she got on, the camel driver had the camel stand up. The traveler said, "After my initial screams I loved it. I felt like Lawrence of Arabia.")

DRESS

• Remember that you can't err by dressing conservatively. To a meal in a home, neither sex should ever wear sandals, shorts, or jeans.

• To a dinner in a home, men should wear a suit, while women should wear a long—but not formal—dress or skirt and jewelry. A floor-length skirt is a good idea, since it will allow you to shift your position from kneeling to having your legs to the side without exposing the soles of your shoes.

• Women should not go to beaches wearing skimpy bikinis. Outraged Arab women will confront you (as they did one traveler in Oman).

MEALS

Table Manners

• When sitting on the floor to eat, men may sit cross-legged (yoga style), but women should not. Women sit with their legs folded underneath them—Japanese style. It's okay to shift position. Men may choose to go from the yoga position to putting the legs to one side (or vice versa), being careful not to have the soles of their shoes pointing at anyone. Women may shift from kneeling to putting their legs to the side, provided that the skirt will cover the soles of the shoes.

• Anticipate finding a platter of dip in the middle of the table. Follow others if they break off pieces of bread and dip it directly into the sauce.

• If you are the guest of honor, expect to be served first. Indicate with a slight wave of your hand that your host should start eating first. Your host will decline, and you should then begin to eat.

• Taste everything. Arabs will always make sure that food is abundant to show that they are not skimpy. You may be shocked at the quantity of food—two meat dishes, five vegetable dishes, two fish dishes, etc. Always comment on the diversity of the food.

• Plan to eat a great deal. The enjoyment of meals is a central part of Arab culture.

• Since the temperature of the food may be hot, when you eat with your hands, eat from the periphery of the bowl to prevent getting burned.

• Be aware that your host (or someone else) may cut a choice morsel and put it on your plate. If you don't want it, just leave it.

• *Don't* clean your plate, because you'll signal that you have not had enough to eat. If your plate is clean, your host will continue to fill it.

• Expect Arabs to eat noisily and to belch at the end of a meal. The former signifies enjoyment and the latter that they are full and don't want any more food. (You're not expected to do the same.)

• Realize that custom is that you shouldn't drink more than three cups of coffee at one time. By the way, coffee is often flavored with cardamom.

• When you finish coffee—whether in a home, office, or shop—always hand the cup back to the server. Don't just put it on the table, because that's considered rude and because the cup may then be refilled and handed to another person without being washed first.

• Be patient at the end of a meal. Don't leave the table early.

Eating Out

• In most countries in the Arab world, expect to find only two kinds of restaurants: stylish and expensive, usually found in the best hotels; and dives. Western women should stick to hotel restaurants.

• Keep your voice down in a restaurant. In Muslim countries, people can never hear what is being said at the next table because people speak so quietly.

• Remember that the person who invites pays. Never suggest splitting a check.

HOTELS

• Realize that in some countries, people listen in on phone calls made from hotels as a matter of routine. Don't discuss anything in a phone conversation that you would not want overheard.

• Remember that hotels levy a surcharge if you make long-distance calls, but the cost is often worth it to avoid the crowds and the long waits at the post office.

PRIVATE HOMES

• Consider the words of the pre-Islamic poet Hatem Alta' for an insight into the feelings about hospitality of the Middle Eastern people: "I am never a slave—except to my guest." Arab hospitality came about as a result of the desert environment and people's complete dependence on one another there. One day someone might be in need of food and protection, so he must give both to others when they need them. Now, in cities, because hospitality shows a man's status, much money is spent on entertaining guests. In the countryside, each village has a guest house for visitors who have no families with whom they can stay.

• Realize that it's a tremendous honor to be invited to an Arab's home, because an Arab's home is sacred. Government workers may be reluctant to invite you to their homes because they may not make the same high salaries as their foreign counterparts and may be embarrassed by their homes. Arabs would never invite someone to their home for a purely business reason—to "wrap up" a contract, for example.

• Be aware that Arabs never refuse any guest who arrives at the door. The single exception occurs when a man arrives and a woman is alone in the house.

• Don't be offended if an invitation is verbal. It's not customary to send written invitations.

• Avoid calling or visiting from 2:00 P.M. until after the afternoon prayer (time varies from country to country and season to season).

• When a woman enters a room, men should stand. Everyone should stand when new guests arrive at a party and when a high-ranking person or an elderly person enters the room.

• Show respect for the values of the Arab world—don't have an alcoholic drink the first night you're with your host or business counterpart unless the host is drinking. Even if he says "Are you sure you don't want a whiskey?" refuse.

• When your host or hostess invites you to wash up before and after dinner, always say "Yes."

• Never admire a specific object in a home; the host or hostess may feel obliged to give it to you. Rather than say "That's a lovely vase," offer a general compliment: "You have a lovely home."

• If you feel it's time to leave, say "This was a treat and an honor and an experience that I will cherish forever." If your host protests a great deal, stay a bit longer.

• If you're staying with a family, realize that a guest is an honored person whose every whim must be fulfilled. Therefore, it's insulting to your host family for you to want to do things, for example, sightseeing, on your own.

• If you're a woman alone visiting in a home, feel free to ask the women in the house about almost anything: customs, places to go, recipes and how to cook certain dishes, how to dress, where to have dresses made.

(Draw the line, however, at any questions relating to sex.) Arab women will be pleased and take your questions as a sign of tremendous confidence. They will take you under their wing and take you around to show you things.

• Remember that Arabs consider dogs unclean and never have them as pets in their homes. If you have a pet with you in the Arab world, never allow it near visitors.

• Always pay attention to the children in a family. Children are sacred in Islamic cultures. Kiss young children, and shake hands with older children. If you're staying with a family for a while, you will please your hosts by offering to help the children with their English homework.

• Offer to help in the kitchen, but don't expect your offer to be accepted.

• Be discreet, and be sure to be dressed at all times. Don't go barefoot. Don't run from the shower to your room with a towel draped around you. Wear a bathrobe.

Gifts: When invited to a meal, bring a houseplant. Don't bring roses, as they might be interpreted as directed to the lady of the house.

• Avoid giving any gift that represents the human figure.

• Never give books with a political content.

• Never give a *personal* gift to someone's wife. Silk scarves are always appreciated and are not considered too personal. Women and girls also like posters, especially those with travel scenes.

• Bring children M&Ms, sweatshirts, puppets, games, and books. Older children appreciate university T-shirts, banners, and decals.

• Always give and receive gifts with both hands.

• Remember that gifts aren't opened when they are received.

BUSINESS

Business Practices

• Realize that Arab countries have "mixed economies," with a varying proportion of emphasis on a private enterprise market and a planned public sector.

• If you're fortunate enough to have had contact with Arab businessmen in your own country, ask them to sponsor your visit to their country. They can often arrange meetings with government officials during your visit.

• Try to cultivate a good relationship with an Arab businessman who's in your country. Spend a great deal of time with him, not just a one-hour lunch or one day of his visit. Your attention will be more than repaid when you go to your business colleague's country.

• Prepare to make several trips to accomplish your goal. It takes an average of three visits to accomplish anything. You may visit and make your presentation, but orders may not come in for six months. In the meantime, don't become dispirited and think that the project is over.

• Be aware that you must be *physically* present to do business with Arabs. If you or your representative are not present, nothing will be accomplished.

• Plan on doing business in the Arab world in November through April. Avoid the period of Ramadan, when everything closes down. Work does go on, but people work shorter hours, and they tend to be touchy because they are fasting. Remember also that Thursday afternoon and all day Friday are days of rest.

• Have separate tickets for the two parts of your journey if you are going to both Israel and the Gulf countries.

• Before leaving, check the expiration date of your visa. You may find that you must spend more time in the Middle East than you had anticipated. You might want to renew your visa to allow extra time there.

• Keep in mind that a good way to do business is to choose a local businessman as your agent. Check with your embassy in the country in which you'll be doing business as to the type of agent you should contact. In addition to the Commercial Attache at your embassy, there is a local staff of foreign service specialists (nationals of the country). They know the market because they keep their positions for many years, while the Commercial Attaches stay for just a few years. Another route to an agent: The U.S. Department of Commerce will find agents for you via a computer cross-check on what products you have to offer. They then send your inquiry to the Commercial Attache in the country you're interested in. For a nominal fee (about $25), the Commercial Attache will do preliminary searches and check out names. However, since this work doesn't have top priority with the Commercial Attaches, it may take several months. A third source of contacts in the U.S.: the American-Arab Chamber of Commerce, which has branches in many cities.

• Call the people you want to see about four to six weeks in advance, and tell them when you'll be in their city. However, neither you nor an agent can really fix an appointment until you arrive. (Agents are reluctant to make appointments in advance, because they'll be embarrassed if they have to cancel.) If you'll be dealing with Western companies as well as local companies, arrange to see the Western company on the first day, and then, when you arrive, you can make definite appointments with the local company.

• In making your plans, don't forget that flights are frequently delayed in the Middle East, or that you may be bumped because an important person has arrived at the last minute. When you make a reservation, obtain the computer print-out of your reservation, because that is the only way that you can prove you have a reservation. Try not to make last-minute changes, because you'll find it very difficult. If you are told to be at the airport two hours in advance of your flight, *be there*.

• Try to make appointments in the morning, since that's the time during which most business is accomplished. The afternoon—roughly 4:00 to 6:00 P.M.—is the time for follow-up discussions with your agent or representative.

• Strike up conversations with people you meet on planes, at your hotel, or in restaurants. Networking is extremely important, and you never know when someone can open a door. Any conversation with local people will make you feel more relaxed in the country. One traveler said that he was very nervous on his first trip to the Arab world and was afraid he would freeze at his first business meeting. He struck up a conversation with the cab driver on the way from the airport, asking him what certain buildings were and why streets had certain names. He chatted with the doorman and the bellman at his hotel. By the time he reached his business meeting he had the sense that he could speak to the people of the country.

• Book your hotel room as far in advance as possible, even though there is now a surplus of rooms in most countries (after years of shortage). Despite the surplus, you may find that a room isn't available when you arrive, because a sheik who is part owner of the hotel has taken over rooms for a conference.

• Expect to find fax machines everywhere. You can have information sent to your hotel or to your agent within minutes from your home office.

• Remember that Arabs tend to be late—anywhere from three minutes to five hours—but they don't like it when foreigners are late. Be prepared to wait.

• If you're meeting with an important government person, expect someone to be waiting outside the office with coffee or tea. After you're ushered into the office, he'll serve you and wait to offer refills. If you don't want more, indicate that you've had enough by holding your cup in your right hand and shaking it gently from side to side.

• Remember that the typical pattern of an office is a main desk and then a U-shaped desk. When you're admitted to the room, others may be conducting business. You are expected to sit and listen until they are ready to discuss your business. (If privacy and security are concerned, the behavior may be different.) Though you may think that your time is being wasted, use the opportunity for listening to how others conduct business. Names and access are critical because the general approach to business is all from the top.

• Since all decisions are made by one person, try to identify that person. It will not necessarily be the person who does the most talking at a meeting. One American businessman says that his trick is to find the man with the most expensive watch. Very likely, he'll be making the decisions.

• Keep in mind that protocol and the expected, appropriate behavior within Arab culture are well established. Arabs respect the English because of their courtesy and respect in conducting business. (You may be surprised at how many Englishmen you encounter in the Arab business world.)

• Even though you have an appointment with a person, expect constant interruptions from friends and family members. Try to refocus the person on the main topic for which you have come to the meeting (but never in an aggressive or unpleasant manner).

• Learn several polite phrases in Arabic, especially greetings. Knowing such phrases will make you more successful in business. You are sending a message that you want to please your Arab counterparts.

• Never forget that personal relationships are of the utmost importance in doing business. An American businessman commented, "Remember that friendship is Number One on an Arab's list, and doing business is about Number Seventy-two." (If you come with a letter of introduction from an Arab businessman who is a mutual acquaintance, you will be welcomed warmly.)

• Expect Arabs to weigh your credibility and who you are beyond the product or service you are offering. There will be a great deal of conversation before business. (Never try to steer the discussion to business before an Arab businessman does.) Prepare to discuss your business and how you got into it, your area of the country, your education, and sports. Cable TV has come to much of the Arab world, so Western sports and TV series are good ice-breakers. Many Arabs are very knowledgeable about and interested in the sports of other countries. They have also seen many of the nighttime soap operas, such as *Dallas* and *Dynasty* and are interested in those shows and their stars.

• Be familiar with the political situation in your own country. Arabs are interested in and knowledgeable about political events in other countries.

• Don't ask questions that cover sensitive political areas. People may not be able to answer honestly, and, if they do, they may jeopardize their safety.

• Never bring up any problems in your family (trouble with your spouse, for example).

• Adjust your voice to the situation. In a one-on-one conversation, keep your voice low and don't raise it. In a group, however, you may find that you have to get into a shouting match to be heard.

• Keep in mind that Arabs repeat themselves frequently. If you *don't* repeat yourself frequently, Arabs may believe that you're not telling the truth.

• Don't be offended if Arabs interrupt you constantly. Interrupting is common practice.

• Don't hire an interpreter in advance, since you probably won't need one. Many people in the business world have been educated abroad.

• Realize that you don't need to translate materials about products to be used for business or technical purposes. However, if the products will eventually be used by consumers, any material should be translated.

• Don't denigrate your competitors. However, it's important to know who may be fighting you and what they are offering. The final decision will be based not on technical merits but on how well you have played the political game by establishing a personal relationship with the Arab businessmen with whom you're dealing.

• Provide positive reinforcement and praise frequently. Never openly criticize anyone, because an Arab's sense of self-esteem is easily offended. Always begin with the good qualities of the person or project and then subtly suggest changes.

• Remember that Arabs frequently use intermediaries as negotiators or to make requests. Foreigners need contacts with government officials who will act as intermediaries for them.

• Always make constant eye contact with the person with whom you are speaking. If you let your attention wander while talking to an Arab, you're being impolite.

• Don't be upset at the long periods of silence that occur during business negotiations. The silence isn't a sign of rejection or displeasure. Just wait patiently. You can tell that the meeting hasn't ended because more coffee will be served at the end.

• Expect a bid bond and a performance bond to be required in most Arab countries.

• Never pressure anyone. For example, don't say "I can give you a special price, but you've got to act by the end of the month." Such a strategy won't succeed.

• When a high official makes a proposal, respond by suggesting that you both think it over. You can then be in touch with your main office for approval. This tactic doesn't cause the Arab to lose face by implying that he's dealing with someone in a lower position than he is.

• Be prepared for delays. You won't get anywhere if you set a deadline and press Arab businessmen to adhere to it.

• Keep your planned departure date to yourself. If your Arab counterparts know that you plan to leave on a certain date, they'll make their decision at the last minute, and you probably won't get the price that you want.

• Note that written contracts are very common. After you've submitted a proposal, the Arab businessmen will study it and make changes. The signing of the contract will be followed by the Arabs issuing a letter of credit to you.

• If you are planning to return several times to be dealing with the same people, ask them if there is something they would like you to bring them from abroad.

• Western women should know that many Muslim countries show a certain indulgence for Western women, who are not expected to behave as Muslim women do. There is an undercurrent of chivalry and protectiveness, which may allow them to be more successful than men (especially in journalism and broadcasting). Recently the top Citibank official sent to Bahrain was a woman. On the other hand, an American businessman said that he would never send a woman to do business in the Arab world unless he were selling jewelry.

• Keep in mind that you cannot err by taking an Arab business associate to the restaurant of a top-class hotel.

• Since lunch is the main meal of the day, suggest a noon meal for a business discussion.

• Should you be traveling with your wife, feel free to ask an Arab colleague if your wife could meet his wife. He may set a date, but don't press the issue if he doesn't.

• If you're being entertained at a dinner and your hosts are very Westernized, feel free to ask, "Should I bring my wife?" However, if you are the host, don't say to an Arab, "Would you care to bring your wife along to the restaurant?" Let the Arab make the initial overture. When you've known a person for a period of time, you might say, "I would be honored to have your wife and children join us for dinner."

• If an Arab wife comes with her husband to dinner in a restaurant, the foreign businessman should not engage her in lengthy conversation. Let her take the initiative. If she does, ask about her children.

• Don't forget that appearance and decorum are important. For example, the wife of a foreign businessman should not go to the hotel pool in a skimpy bikini. In fact, it would be best if she didn't go to the pool at all unless the hotel is very Western, with primarily Western clientele. Word spreads quickly, and a wife's behavior could have a significant effect on her husband's business.

• When invited to a home, the wife of a foreign businessman should take a cue from the host as to whether she should stay with the men or join the women in another room. If she stays with the men, she should never initiate a conversation, nor should she break into a conversation. In fact, unless the host is very tuned in to Western ways, he may not talk to her at all. The woman should not be insulted. A woman who accompanies her husband has the same status as an Arab housewife, while a businesswoman who is alone is expected to join the men and take the initiative.

HOLIDAYS AND SPECIAL OCCASIONS

The holidays below are Muslim religious holidays and are celebrated throughout the Arab world. Individual countries have other observances.

• *Ramadan*—name of the ninth month of the Muslim calendar, which is a lunar calendar. It occurs eleven days earlier each year. During the month, Muslims do not eat, drink, or smoke between sunrise and sunset. If you are in a Muslim country during Ramadan, refrain from eating, smoking, or drinking in the presence of those who are observing the fast.

• *Id al-Fitr* (Feast of Breaking the Fast)—at the end of Ramadan and lasting three days, during which children receive gifts, alms are given to the poor, and people wear new clothes.

• *Id al-Adha* (Feast of the Sacrifice)—celebrated at the end of the pilgrimage to Mecca. It commemorates Abraham's willingness to sacrifice his son Ishmael. People kill a sheep, camel, or goat, and share it with the poor.

TRANSPORTATION

Public Transportation

• Be aware that many Middle Eastern airlines do not enforce "No Smoking" regulations in economy class. If smoke really bothers you, you might want to fly first class. One problem: First-class plane tickets are horrendously expensive.

• Women traveling alone should know that Arabs may be shocked to see a woman traveling by herself. Bring photos of your family (children, nieces, nephews, siblings), since people will always be interested in family.

• Women alone may wish to fly first class, since there are many, many workers flying back and forth to jobs in the Gulf. They are very aggressive about grabbing seats and space for luggage in overhead compartments. The men won't harass you.

Driving

• If you're going to be in a country for a short time, hire a car and driver. In many countries there are no signs and no good maps available (so it's very easy to get lost), and the drivers are very aggressive.

• Note that you can usually rent a car with an American or British driver's license. Be sure to take all the insurance available; if you're in an accident and someone is injured, you will be considered guilty since you're a foreigner.

• Be especially alert to avoid camels when driving at night. They are probably the major hazard of night driving, since you can't see them because they're the same color as the landscape. (They also have the right of way—camels came before cars.) If you drive at night, don't go over 80 kilometers per hour.

• Study the laws of the road before you begin driving. Pay special attention to who has the right of way in various situations.

• Should the police stop you, don't even consider offering a bribe.

Driving in the Desert: Take all possible precautions. Use a four-wheel-drive vehicle. Have a destination, and let the desert police know where you are going and when. If you get lost or have a breakdown, don't leave your car. It will provide shade and protection. Before you set out, get information about the terrain, since flash floods during the rainy season can be dangerous. Writing in *The New York Times*, Eric Sandberg-Diment also recommends perforated steel plate, which comes in four-foot aluminum sections that are laid under the wheels of vehicles trapped in the sand. He also suggests reconditioned steel jerrycans for carrying gasoline and plastic jerrycans for your water supply. (Don't transport gasoline in the plastic jerrycans.)

• Additional requirements for driving in the Sahara—also advisable for any desert driving: snake-bite serum, scorpion serum, food for two days, special tires, a spade, a compass, a medical kit, a red smoke bomb, and a black smoke bomb.

• *Never* drive in the Sahara in the summer. The heat is intolerable.

LEGAL MATTERS, SAFETY, AND HEALTH

• Don't forget that if you visit Israel and then want to visit an Arab country other than Egypt, you won't be allowed in the Arab country if your passport has an Israeli stamp on it. Ask the Israeli customs official to stamp a separate piece of paper. It is then slipped into your passport, and when you go to an Arab country you can simply throw it away.

• General dietary advice: Drink only bottled water. Don't use ice cubes. Drink fruit juices only if you're sure that they have not been mixed with ice or water. Avoid dairy products. Don't eat fruits or vegetables that aren't peeled.

• Pay special attention to the discussions of requirements for AIDS tests in the chapters on Iraq, Kuwait, Qatar, Saudi Arabia, and the United Arab Emirates. If the country you plan to visit will accept results of a test done in your home country, phone the Arab country's embassy in your country to find out which laboratories in your country they'll accept results from. Since AIDS testing policies change frequently, before you travel to the Middle East call the U.S. State Department's Bureau of Consular Affairs: (202) 647–1488. The Bureau keeps its information on AIDS testing policies up to date, and someone may unofficially tell you how rigorously a specific country enforces its policy.

• ALWAYS keep your prescription drugs in their original containers. Don't, for example, take them out to put them in moisture-proof pill boxes. When you enter a Middle Eastern or North African country, you could be suspected of attempting to smuggle drugs into the country. Remember, also, that drugs available over the counter in these countries may be available only by prescription in your home country. Bringing such medicine (even something as seemingly innocent as cough medicine) with you when you come home may subject you to arrest.

Some Special Words for Women

• Work at becoming a kind of "third sex." Arabs generally accept professional women and take them seriously. Western businesswomen are often invited to all-male professional meetings or gatherings. At a wedding or a party, Western women will have an advantage in that they have access to both men and women.

• Morocco has the worst reputation for the harassment of foreign women, with Tunisia the second worst. Egypt has the best record. One way to minimize harassment is to travel in a group or with a male escort.

• When making your hotel reservations, ask for a room above the ground floor or one near the lobby. This sends the message to the hotel staff that you're a serious person and are not there to use the hotel to meet men.

• Avoid jogging in public places.

• Don't go out after dark, even in a taxi.

• Be aware that sanitary napkins are available in shops everywhere, and tampons can be found in supermarkets, pharmacies, or hotel shops. Bring a supply of whatever form of birth control you use. Though birth control is anti-Islam, you can get it through a doctor, since many people in the Arab world practice birth control.

• Both businesswomen and women tourists should ask their hotel manager to arrange for a trustworthy driver whose charge is reasonable. If you plan to return to the country, you can notify the driver in advance, and he'll be ready for you. Once you've established rapport, the driver can be a real asset—with advice on restaurants, etc. One businesswoman reported that she asked her regular taxi driver for advice about appropriate dress for an occasion to which she had been invited.

Islam and the Arab World
૭૧૭

Islam (which means "submission to the will of God") is at the center of life in Muslim countries. The traveler should be sensitive to and show respect for the often deeply held religious beliefs of people in Muslim countries.

The belief that God has direct control over everything that happens tends to make Muslims—especially the older, more traditional ones—fatalistic. A word you'll hear constantly is "*Insha'allah*," meaning "God willing." Example: Two travelers hired a driver to take them from Fez to Marrakesh, a trip of about six hours. Whenever one asked, "Is there a bathroom in this town?" or "Can we stop at such-and-such a restaurant?" the answer was always "*Insha'allah*." The driver never responded directly to a question.

In Muslim countries, the constitution and legal systems are frequently based on Islamic law. A Muslim has five duties:

1. Prayer (usually private) five times daily. On Friday, the Muslim Sabbath, men gather at mosques at mid-day for prayer.

2. Giving alms to the poor.

3. Fasting during Ramadan.

4. Making a pilgrimage to Mecca.

5. A profession of faith—stating in front of two male Muslim witnesses that there is no God but God.

The call to prayer sounds five times each day from the minarets of mosques: *Fajr*—one hour before sunrise; *Dhuhr*—at noon; *Asr*—mid-afternoon; *Maghreb*—sunset; and *Isha*—about 90 minutes after sunset.

One of the holiest periods in the Muslim calendar is Ramadan, which lasts for one month. Since Muslims use a lunar calendar, Ramadan falls eleven days earlier each year. During Ramadan, people abstain from food, drink, and tobacco from dawn until sunset. Muslims believe that fasting trains one in self-discipline and that it quiets the spirit, subdues the passions, and gives one a sense of unity with all Muslims. People often spend much of the day in mosques, praying and reading the Koran. A cannon is fired to announce the rising and setting of the sun. It is also fired two hours before sunset to give people time to prepare a meal. (The meal is eaten after sunset.)

On the 29th night of Ramadan—when the new moon appears— Ramadan is over. The breaking of the fast begins, and for three days everyone stops working. On the first morning after Ramadan, families dress in their finest and go to mosque. Then they have a special mid-day meal at home (their first mid-day meal for a month). There are special foods associated with Ramadan: *saiwiyan*—noodles cooked with milk, sugar, and coconut; and candy made with nuts, honey, and sesame seeds. Many cities hold fairs at which children paint their sheep in bright colors. The third day is spent visiting relatives and friends. Children, who receive a great deal of attention during the post-Ramadan period, get gifts and coins from relatives and visitors.

If you are in a Muslim country during Ramadan, be sensitive to the feelings of people observing the holiday. No one will expect non-Muslims to observe the ban on drinking, smoking, and eating. They will, however, appreciate your sensitivity if you eat in your hotel dining room and refrain from eating, smoking, and drinking in the presence of Muslims.

Some other things to know about Islam:

• The letters A.H. stand for *Anno Hegirae*, the year of the Hegira, Mohammed's flight from Mecca to Medina, which took place in 622 A.D. A.H. is the equivalent of A.D. in the Gregorian calendar. To get the number of the Arab year, subtract 622 from the Western year. Note that the Muslim calendar follows lunar cycles and is therefore eleven days shorter than the Gregorian calendar's year.

• Eating pork and drinking alcohol are forbidden by Islamic law. Don't do either in the presence of a Muslim.

• Don't step on a prayer mat on which someone is praying or walk in front of or photograph someone who is praying. During a period of Muslim holy days, wear clothing in subdued colors.

• Never place the Koran on the floor or put anything on top of it.

• Keep in mind that, since giving alms to the poor is an important part of Islam, begging is an Islamic institution. Whether or not to give something to a beggar is an entirely personal decision. If a horde of

begging children surrounds you, and you don't want to give them anything, say *"Mafi flus"* (mah-fée flóos), which means "I have no money."
One traveler said that if she and her husband see a few maimed people
standing in a doorway, they give money. However, if they stop their car
in a little village and a crowd of kids surrounds it, they don't get out
and they don't give anything, because the situation is too scary.

• Women should be sure to dress modestly at all times. Long sleeves
are the rule. Check individual countries to learn in which ones mid-calf
skirts are acceptable and in which ones the skirt must come to the ground.
Women should bring a shawl and make it part of their regular costume.
Fold it and drape it over one shoulder. For going into a mosque, or in
the presence of conservative people, it can be used to cover shoulders
and/or head. Another useful item of clothing for women is a long, loose
caftan-style dress; it can be worn in the company of conservative people
or in a mosque.

• Women should *never* go topless on beaches in Islamic countries.
Muslim fundamentalists will be outraged.

• For most Arabs (royalty are in a different league), wealth is down-
played, because lavish displays of wealth are thought to be in bad taste,
and they may be offensive to God, who may bring misfortune to someone
who is ostentatious about his wealth.

• Because everything is in God's hands, Arabs think it is bad luck to
talk too much about the future. They consider it unlucky to announce
anything (e.g., an agreement or a contract) before it is truly final. You
won't impress a Muslim businessman with long-range forecasts or pre-
dictions. He'll think that you've taken leave of your senses.

EGYPT

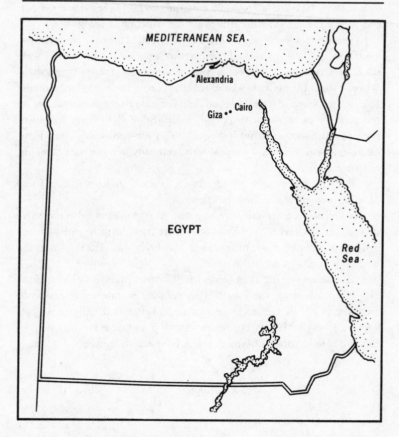

If any country has captured the world's imagination, it is Egypt. Cleopatra fascinated two of the English language's greatest playwrights —Shakespeare and Shaw—and two of its most famous actresses—Vivien Leigh, whose kittenish Cleopatra ensnared Julius Caesar, and Elizabeth Taylor, whose sultry Cleopatra caused Marc Antony to renounce an empire for her. Further, record crowds flocked to museums when the treasures of the tomb of Tutankhamen made the rounds of the Western world. The only known cure for the flights of fancy inspired by Egypt is a personal visit to the Pyramids, the Great Sphinx, and the Valley of the Kings.

GREETINGS

• When introduced, use titles —President (for the president of the country or of any organization), Doctor (for both M.D. and Ph.D.), Engineer, or Mr., Miss, and Mrs. plus first names. Some people use French forms of address for women—*Madame, Mademoiselle*. Example: A Fulbright student at the University of Cairo was told, "Madame Mona will be your professor." (For titles in Arabic, see "Key Words and Phrases—Arabic," page 227.)

• Egyptians don't use first names without titles immediately. Continue to use first name plus appropriate title until an Egyptian invites you to stop using the title.

• Don't be surprised if people change their form of greeting, depending on the setting. Good friends use first names in informal settings, but may revert to title plus first name in more formal settings such as business meetings.

• Note that men shake hands with men and with women when introduced. Women also shake hands with other women. Close friends kiss members of the same sex in greeting. However, men and women shake hands but don't kiss.

• If a foreign man is kissed by an Egyptian man in greeting, he (the foreigner) should not withdraw. This form of greeting (usually reserved for good friends) is traditional, and the foreigner will offend if he withdraws.

CONVERSATION

• Don't discuss the accomplishments of Anwar Sadat. Egyptians don't like him. People may make jokes about Hosni Mubarak, but, as a foreigner, you shouldn't criticize him.

• Feel free to ask Muslims about important Coptic sites or synagogues. They will be happy to tell you about them.

• Note that Egyptians love to discuss, argue, and debate—especially about politics. However, allow an Egyptian to initiate any political discussion.

• Avoid personal questions in a first conversation. For example, don't ask a person if he/she is married or has children. However, if you know a family, be sure to ask about each of the children individually.

• Don't make a direct reference to your host's wife unless you've had a long friendship with the family.

• If you're planning to visit Israel, don't mention it in Egypt.

• Don't take personally any attacks on the U.S. government. Egyptians like Americans but often criticize the government's policies.

• Realize that it's regarded as impolite to relate bad news on a social occasion.

TELEPHONES

• Look for telephone booths at railroad stations, tobacco stands, kiosks, main town squares, and large hotels. Many shops will allow you to make local calls if you pay them.

• If you use a telephone directory, remember that names of Egyptian individuals and companies are indexed under the initial letter of the first name, while names of non-Egyptians are listed under the initial letter of the last name.

• Dial *very slowly*, because the system is erratic and overloaded. It's often faster to seek people out in person than to telephone them.

• Remember that local calls cost 10 *piastres*. Deposit that amount in the public phone. The operator will tell you when to put in more money.

• Note that there's no such thing as a collect call in Egypt.

• Make international calls from your hotel or from a telephone office, which you can identify by the sign with a telephone dial on it. Main telephone offices are open 24 hours a day—even on Friday, the Muslim Sabbath, and during Ramadan—while branches are open from 7:00 A.M. to 9:00 P.M. While there is a huge surcharge to make international calls from hotels, the cost may be worth it. At the telephone office, you pay for your three-minute international call in advance and are cut off when the three minutes are up. Keep your receipt in case no one answers.

IN PUBLIC

• Two gestures to know: (1) The right hand held up with the palm facing away from the body and the fingers waving up and down means "Come here." (In Western countries the same gesture means "Good-bye.") (2) The hand and palm facing toward you with all fingertips touching and the hand moving up and down means, "Wait a minute" or "Shut up!" or "Take it easy."

• When you enter an elevator, always greet the people in it.

• Don't be surprised if you're accosted by perfect strangers asking where you are from, what you are carrying, etc.

• Realize that people posing as guides will approach you. Use only a licensed guide, one you find through the Tourist Office or your hotel.

• Expect to find children begging, especially in upper Egypt. If you're alone, don't give anything or there will be swarms around you. If you're with a guide,

let her/him deal with the situation. *If* you decide to give something to begging children, bring inexpensive ballpoint pens to hand out. This strategy works only if there are a few children and you have enough pens to give one to each. (Note that you won't find adults begging in the cities.)

• If you're in a small town and need directions, head for the local pharmacy. Almost all pharmacists speak English.

• Be aware that Egyptians don't keep a distance between themselves and others as Westerners often do. They deliberately choose places near others. For example, in an almost-empty movie theater, an Egyptian will sit next to the only other person in the theater; on a beach, Egyptians deliberately sit very close to others, rather than finding their own space a distance away.

• Realize that foreigners are allowed to visit mosques (even during Ramadan) when people are not at prayer.

• If you visit a mosque, speak softly. Remove your shoes when you enter and put on the slippers provided at the entrance. Don't walk in front of praying people. Women should have their arms and backs covered, and men should not wear shorts.

• Don't plan to visit mosques between noon and 1:00 P.M. on Fridays. They may be restricted to

Muslims, and you won't be allowed to enter.

• Note that credit cards are accepted in major hotels, restaurants, and shops. However, you can't be sure of the rate of exchange that you will receive since the exchange rate is not locked in until the transaction reaches the credit card company. You won't know what rate you've paid until you receive your statement—after you've returned home. To avoid the possibility of the rate going up after you've made your purchase, use traveler's checks or cash.

• If you're using cash, keep a supply of small bills, since Egyptians won't give change (even if they have it), and you'll lose less if a merchant refuses you change for one Egyptian pound rather than five.

• Feel free to photograph in temples and mosques (but not people at prayer) and at historical sites. There is a fee for using video or movie cameras at historical places, as well as a fee to photograph inside Cairo's museums. To photograph tombs, you must have permission from the General Authority of Antiquities.

• Remember that you're not allowed to photograph military installations, bridges, dams, power stations, airports, or radio and television buildings.

• Always ask permission before photographing a person. Some people will demand a fee. Don't

photograph beggars. Egyptians are sensitive to people recording negative aspects of the country.

• Be aware that prices are not negotiable in department stores, but they are in souvenir shops and bazaars. The best technique of bargaining is to praise the items in the shop without showing special interest in any one item. Ask the price of several items, and then ask for a lower price on the item that you really want. You and the dealer will then go back and forth. Sometimes leaving the shop will cause the merchant to follow you and accept your last offer. On most items, settle for a third to a half off the asking price.

• Remember to compare prices in several places before making a purchase.

• Note that if you are buying gold jewelry, it will be sold by weight with a fee added for craftsmanship. Offer 25% less than the requested price. If you're buying glass, brass, or wooden objects, ask for 50% off.

• If you're interested in gambling, keep your passport handy. There are casinos in major hotels, but they are only for foreigners (hence the passport as I.D.), and you must use foreign currency.

• There are two kinds of beaches: At public beaches you will find no tourists—mainly Egyptian women who bathe fully clothed; for private beaches, where you will find both Egyptians and tourists in bathing suits, there is a small fee.

• Women should avoid direct eye contact with men and should avoid crowds, where men may try to touch. If a man makes a comment, ignore it.

• Don't look for public bathrooms. There aren't any. Use those in a hotel or restaurant. The bathrooms there will be Western style, so you don't need to bring toilet paper with you. However, in the desert or countryside, the toilets will be Turkish style (simply a hole in the floor), so you should carry a supply of tissue.

DRESS

• In planning their traveling wardrobes, women should be aware that Islamic fundamentalism has become much more prevalent in Egypt of late. Dress conservatively, and you'll be treated with respect.

• When visiting pyramids and monuments, women can wear pants. Men, however, should not wear shorts. Sneakers are the best footwear for visiting pyramids and ruins.

• Women should feel free to dress casually in Luxor or in Aswan; if you're touring with a group there, halters and shorts are acceptable, but if you're on your own, wear a skirt and a short-sleeved top. In other areas foreign women should avoid wearing halter tops, shorts, or miniskirts. In general, women should dress modestly. Long skirts or dresses are *not* necessary, but avoid tight pants, miniskirts, sleeveless blouses, or shorts. To show great respect for Muslim tradition, women should wear their hair tied in a scarf.

• Don't bring your blue jeans. They're much too hot for the climate.

• When visiting a mosque, women should wear a head scarf, a top that has sleeves below the elbow and that doesn't expose the back, and a skirt that comes below the knees. (Never wear pants to a mosque.)

• For mosque visits, men and women should wear shoes that are easily removable. At some mosques, for a small fee you'll receive slippers to put on over your shoes. To be safe, carry light-weight slippers or socks to put on when you remove your shoes. Leave your shoes at the door of the mosque. You'll find someone there to watch them.

• Men should take their cue for business attire from upper-class and middle-class men, who wear suits in winter and pants and shirts in summer. Women should also follow the practice of Egyptian businesswomen who wear elegant Western clothes. A simple and elegant suit or dress is the best business costume. (Men of modest means wear a *galabiyyah*, a long loose garment, and women wear a veil.)

• To a dinner in a home, men should wear a suit and tie and women a dress or skirt and blouse.

• For an upper-class gathering such as a wedding, men should wear a dark suit or tuxedo and women should wear a silk dress that is below the knee but not floor-length.

MEALS

Hours and Foods

• The staples of the Egyptian diet have changed little over the centuries. The walls of tombs show paintings of garlic, beans, leeks, and rice. These remain the basics for Egyptians today.

Breakfast: About 8:00 A.M. In a middle- or upper-class home, the meal will be French style, with pastry, coffee, or tea. In a working-class home, there will be beans, rice, macaroni, and strong tea.

• At 9:00 or 10:00 A.M., expect a snack break—usually a salad or fruit and tea.

Lunch: The main meal, lunch is served at 2:00 or 3:00 P.M. As a guest, expect several types of meat, which is your hosts' way of showing generosity and abundance, since the main diet of Egyptians consists of vegetables. The meal might include whole roast lamb with head on; roasted pigeon, duck, or goose; fried liver; rice with walnuts and raisins; vegetable dishes such as okra, spinach, beans, or eggplant cooked in a tomato sauce; dessert of fruits and very sweet pastries; and coffee.

• Prepare for another break at 5:00 or 6:00 P.M., when most people take afternoon tea.

Dinner: In a home it's a light meal at about 7:00 P.M. and will consist of leftovers from lunch, or yogurt, cheese, and vegetables, or salad and bread. Other possibilities are falafel or shish kebab.

• For festive occasions, there might be *ferakh bel'borghul*, chickens stuffed with rice and cooked *inside* a turkey or lamb, followed by a dessert of *baklava*, which is light sweet layers of flaky pastry with nuts and honey syrup.

• Look for olives on the table at all meals—as salt and pepper are in Western countries.

Beverages: With meals people drink sodas of varying types; Egyptian beer—Stella, a light lager, and Stella export, sweeter; *zibib*, an anise-flavored liqueur, similar to French Pernod, served with ice or diluted with water; *karkade*, a nonalcoholic beverage made from plants.

• While you can find imported beers and liquors in hotels and nightclubs, they will be extremely expensive there. You are allowed to bring one bottle with you into the country. You're also allowed to buy one more duty-free bottle after passing through customs at the airport; you must pay for it in foreign currency.

Table Manners

• Before you go to dinner in a home, have a snack. You'll probably be invited for 9:00 P.M. but won't be served until 10:00 or 11:00 P.M.

• Don't expect appetizers before a meal. However, don't be surprised to be served appetizers in an upper-class home.

• In traditional homes, be prepared to sit on carpets. Platters of food will be placed on low wooden tables. There will be no plates or cutlery. Eat food with your *right*

hand or scoop it up with Arabic bread. Servants will pass bowls of scented water between courses. Turkish coffee and water pipes (*nargila*) will be offered after the meal.

• Be aware that upper-class homes will have Western-style furniture for dining and will use knives and forks.

• Be sure to eat any finger foods with the right hand.

• Note that the male guest of honor will be seated to the right of the host.

• If you dine in the home of a family of modest means, don't be surprised to be offered the only chair, table, and silverware. You can accept or tell them that you're comfortable eating the way they eat.

• Anticipate all courses being placed on the table at once, and helping yourself. You don't have to eat everything, but try to taste each dish. If you don't want to eat something for hygienic reasons (such as salad), say that you've been having stomach problems and perhaps you shouldn't have the offered dish.

• If water is served with a meal and you don't want to drink it for hygienic reasons, request a soft drink.

• Never add salt to food that is served to you in a home.

• Don't eat everything on your plate. It's considered rude, because left-over food is a symbol of abundance and a compliment to the host.

• Expect talking, joking, and discussions during the meal.

Eating Out

• Look for restaurants of many different nationalities, especially Japanese, Indian, Korean, and German.

• If you want to stop for a cocktail, go to a bar in a hotel, where cocktails are usually served between 7:00 and 9:00 P.M. Hard liquor is available only in hotel bars; restaurants offer beer and Egyptian wine.

• Stop at an outdoor cafe called a *casino* (kah-zee-no), where both men and women are welcome. There are some cafes just for men. If a woman goes into one alone, she wouldn't be told to leave, but she would probably feel uncomfortable. If a woman sees only men in a cafe, she should probably avoid it.

• Keep in mind that restaurants usually serve lunch from 1:00 to 3:00 or 4:00 P.M. and dinner from 8:00 P.M. to midnight. Most people don't go to dinner at a restaurant before 8:30 or 9:00 P.M.

• There is usually no difference between prices at lunch and dinner.

• If you dine in a restaurant on the Mediterranean, expect to order fish by the kilo. Choose the fish from an ice-filled tray, and it will be cooked—usually grilled—for you. The meal's price usually includes bread, salad, and either tahini or *hummus*.

• Remember that Egyptian coffee (*ahwa turki*) is very strong and is served in small cups. Since it is prepared with sugar, state whether you want it *zaida* (zee-eh-dah), which is sweet; *mazbout* (mahzboot), which is moderately sweet; or *sada* (sah-dah), which is without sugar.

• Realize that if you go to a restaurant for the working class, there won't be silverware. You must scoop up the food with bread.

• Women traveling alone should not have a problem dining alone in most restaurants. However, if you're in the bazaar and see a small restaurant with only men eating there, avoid it.

Specialties

• The national dish is *molochaia*, "green herb" cooked with chicken broth, tomatoes, and garlic. The green herb is the young shoots of the jute plant, viscous like okra, and similar in taste to spinach or sorrel. A main course, it's served with rice or bread. Another staple is *ful*—fava beans with oil and lemon.

Appetizer Specialties: *Batarikh*—Egyptian caviar served in small slices with bread or crackers; *baba ghanouzh*—eggplant mashed and mixed with lemon, garlic, olive oil, and sesame paste, served as a dip or as a first course; *leban zabadi*—thick yogurt; *mish*—dried cheese with spices made into a paste; *turshi* or *bickley*—mixed pickled vegetables; *waraq anab*—stuffed grape leaves; *mahshi*—vegetables (eggplant, zucchini, peppers) stuffed with meat and rice; *fiteer*—a cross between a pastry and a pizza, filled with ground meat or eggs or white cheese or sometimes with raisins and powdered sugar.

Bread: There are two types—*aysh baladi* (pita) and *aysh fransawi* (French bread).

Cheese: Again, there are two main types—*gibna beyda* (like Greek feta cheese) and *gibna rumi* (hard and sharp cheese).

Main dishes: *hamam meshwi* —pigeon broiled on a grill; *roz bel khalta*—fried rice mixed with nuts, raisins, meat, and liver; *gamberi mashwi*—grilled shrimp; *tamaya*—fried chick-pea balls; *koffa*—grilled cylinders of spiced chopped meat; *bamia*—stew of okra, vegetables, and meat.

Desserts: *Umm ali*—hot bread pudding topped with milk and pine nuts; *kanafa*—shredded wheat pastries with nuts, rosewater, and syrup; *mihallabia*—rice pudding; *babousa*—a semolina cake over which a sugar syrup is poured.

HOTELS

• Reserve well in advance if you wish to stay at one of the better (and correspondingly expensive) hotels during high season—October through March. They tend to be fully booked.

• If you choose a small hotel, ask to see the room before you check in, and make *sure* that the air-conditioner works.

• Note that you'll pay a larger surcharge on long-distance calls in the best hotels than you will at smaller hotels.

• When you register, don't be surprised if you're asked to leave your passport at the desk for 24 hours. It will be registered with the authorities. If your stay at the hotel will be just for one night, be sure to tell the desk clerk. Otherwise, you might not be able to get your passport.

• At a major hotel, expect a huge buffet breakfast to be offered at a very reasonable price. Most hotels provide a continental breakfast (toast and rolls; butter; jam; strong, French coffee or tea) that is served in your room at no extra charge.

• Ask your hotel to arrange for a taxi to stay with you for a day while you visit monuments or mosques or while you go between business appointments. It's less expensive and both easier and *much* safer than renting a car. A bonus: The driver will speak English and can serve as a tour guide.

• When checking out, expect to be approached by many of the hotel's serving people. Tip only those who served you directly, giving them between 50 *piastres* and 1 Egyptian pound (1LE).

TIPPING

• Carry lots of small change with you for tipping.

• Porters: 10 to 25 *piastres* per bag.

• Cafes: Leave 10 to 20 *piastres* per person.

• Restaurants: Usually service is included; give another 5% to the people who have served you.

• Ushers: 50 *piastres*.

• Taxis: For a trip costing 1 or 2 Egyptian pounds, give 10 *piastres*; for longer distances, tip 25 *piastres*. If you hire a driver for the day, offer him lunch. It's not common to tip drivers hired by the day.

• Gas station attendants: 50 *piastres*.

• For the person who cleans your hotel room, leave 10 *piastres* per day.

• Tour bus drivers: 1 Egyptian pound per day.

• Guides at historic sites who show you something off the beaten track: 50 *piastres* to 1 Egyptian pound.

• Mosque attendants who give you slippers: 50 *piastres*.

• If you stay with a family for a week, tip the maid 5 to 10 Egyptian pounds.

PRIVATE HOMES

• Be aware that if you are staying with friends you must register at the Passport Office in Cairo or Alexandria.

• If you're visiting in an older apartment building, be sure that the elevator doors are shut tightly. If not, the current is disconnected, and the elevator won't work.

• When visiting, expect to be offered a drink and usually some food. If someone asks what you'd like to drink, ask what's available. Your hosts may not drink liquor for religious reasons, and you may cause embarrassment if you request an alcoholic drink. If you don't want to drink the water for hygienic reasons, ask for soda.

• Remember that in winter, temperatures in Cairo range from 40 to 65 degrees Fahrenheit (4 to 18 degrees Centigrade). It can be very cold inside homes because many are unheated. Dress warmly.

• Realize that Egyptians equate privacy with deprivation. If you're staying with a family, you won't

be allowed much privacy or independence, because family members will try to anticipate your every need. Westerners tend to feel smothered, but they must adapt. Egyptians are not invading your privacy but trying to be helpful.

• If you're a young, single Westerner (of either sex) staying with a family, expect them to want you to be home at a certain time of night. Otherwise, their reputation will be affected by your behavior—and reputation is extremely important. For example, if a young, single woman wanted to go alone to a discotheque at night, the family probably would not allow it.

• If you're staying with a family and want to turn on a butane gas heater in the bathroom, never light it when the tap is on. It could explode.

• Note that in upper-class homes, toilets are Western style. In middle-and lower-class homes, there are usually holes in the floor. You'll find a bucket with a spout, which functions as a bidet. Cold water shoots out. Sit on it, and clean yourself after using the toilet.

• Ask when it's convenient for you to have a bath, as there may not be constant hot water. If there's a shower, don't spend a long time in it, or you'll use up everyone's share of the hot water.

• Since there's a shortage of water, don't be surprised if the water is cut off without notice or warning. Some people keep buckets of extra water for such emergencies.

• When staying with a family, ask whether they have a special telephone for calling outside Egypt. If not, you can *receive* long-distance calls, but you can't call out. To make a long-distance call, you'll have to go to the Telephone Office.

• If you stay with a family for several days, tip the maid and the cook 5 to 10 Egyptian pounds per week. They may initially refuse, but you should insist that they accept it.

Gifts: When invited to a meal, bring cake or candy. Don't bring flowers, since they're only suitable for illness or a wedding. If you know in advance that someone drinks, bring good-quality whiskey.

Good gifts from abroad are digital watches; gadgets (such as a musical cup, which plays a tune when you lift it to drink); battery-operated radios; picture books of your city or area of the country; and calendars of your country.

• Always present a gift with both hands or with the right hand alone, *never* the left hand.

BUSINESS

Hours

• In general, banks, government offices, and Muslim businesses are closed on Friday. Certain businesses are closed on Saturday.

Banks: Monday through Thursday, 8:30 A.M. to 1:30 P.M., and Sunday, 10:00 A.M. to noon. Closed Friday. Foreign banks usually close on Friday and Saturday. Some banks close Saturday and Sunday. Some banks have additional hours, 4:00 to 8:00 P.M. on Sunday.

Businesses: Saturday through Thursday morning in summer, 8:00 A.M. to 2:00 P.M.; in winter, 9:00 A.M. to 1:00 P.M. and 4:30 or 5:00 to 7:00 P.M.

Government Offices: Sunday to Thursday, 8:00 A.M. to 2:00 P.M. Closed Friday and either Thursday or Saturday.

Shops: In summer, 9:00 A.M. to 1:00 P.M. and 4:30 to 7:30 or 8:00 P.M. In winter, 10:00 A.M. to 5:00 or 6:00 P.M. Many close on Sunday and some close on Friday.

• Remember that many government and business offices are closed on Sunday instead of Friday.

• Note that the Western (Gregorian) calendar—as opposed to the Muslim calendar—is used for business and government.

Currency

• The basic unit is the Egyptian pound, abbreviated LE (*livre Egyptienne*). One Egyptian pound equals 100 *piastres*, abbreviated PT.

• Coins: 1, 5, and 10 *piastres*. Coins of 25 and 50 *piastres* exist but are rarely found in circulation.

• Bills: 1, 5, 10, 20, 50, and 100 Egyptian pounds.

• Realize that it is illegal to pay for any purchases with foreign currency, and it is illegal to import or export more than 20 Egyptian pounds, and it is illegal to change money on the black market.

Business Practices

• Remember that Egyptian law requires that a foreign company have an Egyptian agent. Sources of agents/contacts: the Commercial Attache of the Egyptian Embassy or Consulate in your country; the commercial section of your country's embassy in Cairo. In the U.S.: the Egyptian-American Chamber of Commerce in New York; the Department of Commerce, Near East Bureau. If you've dealt with bankers or lawyers that regularly do business in Egypt, they may be sources for an agent. The agent will be a person who is on good terms with government officials and who is familiar with regulations, permits, etc. The Commercial, Economic, and Political Offices of your embassy can also provide you with materials and briefings.

• Be aware that both private and public companies act as agents. The private company may be more aggressive in taking care of a foreign company's interests.

• If you're doing business in both Cairo and Alexandria, retain an agent for each city.

• Don't worry about cultivating political contacts. Political power doesn't have the same influence in Egypt as in other Middle Eastern countries.

• Don't load your luggage with copies of materials you plan to use. Most five-star hotels have secretarial, translation, and photocopying services. Expect fax machines in large businesses and in the business centers of the best hotels.

• Expect no language problems. Most educated Egyptians speak both English and French.

• Find out in advance the work hours of the organizations with which you'll be doing business, since some government offices in Cairo close on Thursday and others on Saturday. Most embassies and some businesses close on Friday and Saturday, others on Saturday and Sunday.

• Don't plan a business trip to Egypt during the month of Ramadan, a religious period during which people fast.

• Try for business appointments about 10:00 A.M.

• For appointments in Cairo, consider walking to your destination rather than taking a taxi. It may well be faster.

• Realize that the structure of business is very different in Egypt from that in Western countries. People don't separate their personal life from their work. Supervisors, bosses, and directors play the role of father to their employees. They provide advice, listen to problems, and mediate. Employees take on the role of sons performing services for their bosses— paying bills or seeing to repairs. Try to avoid the frequent Western judgment that the relationship is authoritarian and paternalistic.

• Always begin by talking about your Egyptian counterpart's family, office, and your hotel. Inquire after her/his health. Compliment the city and the accommodations at your hotel. Bring up something you've noticed in the country in relation to your business. For example, if your business relates to energy, mention an energy project you've seen and inquire about the people involved. This will lead to a natural exchange regarding your work.

• Always accept the tea or coffee that will be offered, and sip a bit, even if you don't want it. If Egyptians come to your office, *always* offer them something to drink, and join them with a drink. An Egyptian doing business in the U.S. finally asked his host what he had done to offend him. The host replied that there was absolutely nothing wrong. The Egyptian then said, "But I've been here for three hours, and you haven't offered me anything to drink."

• Don't try to do business too quickly, since Egyptians will take such behavior as a personal insult. They want others to think that their business merits deliberation and time. Westerners may regard swift decisions as efficient, but Egyptians will consider them demeaning. If you push too hard for a decision, you may be turned down.

• Expect Egyptians to drive a hard bargain. Be sure to support your presentations with hard facts and to research your competition.

• Don't be surprised if negotiations take a great deal of time. The reasons are probably bureaucratic. Most projects are in the public sector, and the final decision will be made by the Ministers of the appropriate department. The Chairman of the Board will make decisions for a private company.

• Never show anger. It's a certain way to lose a deal.

• Remember that once an agreement is reached, you must deliver products and services as promised.

• If your project is high among the government's priorities, ask for a waiver of customs duties on imported machinery and supplies.

• Since telephone service to other countries can take a very long time, arrange to have your home office (and family) call you in Egypt at specific times.

• Women should expect to find Egypt a relatively comfortable place to do business. Both Cairo and Alexandria are sophisticated and cosmopolitan. Women take a major part in social and business life. When entertaining, invite clients, associates, and their spouses to a European-style restaurant.

• If women have a problem with the bureaucracy, they should enlist the assistance of women who work at their country's embassy.

Women at embassies deal with the bureaucracy daily.

HOLIDAYS AND SPECIAL OCCASIONS

• Note that the Muslim calendar governs religious holidays, while the Western calendar governs secular holidays. Secular holidays are celebrated with parades and displays by the Armed Forces. These observances are not taken so seriously as those of religious holidays.

• The secular holidays: New Year's Day (Jan. 1); Labor Day (May 1); Evacuation Day (June 18); Revolution Day (July 23); Armed Forces Day (Oct. 6); Popular Resistance Day (Oct. 24).

TRANSPORTATION

Public Transportation

• Cairo has an almost interminable rush hour so it will almost always be difficult to get around. The morning rush hour is from 6:00 to 11:00 A.M.; the afternoon rush hour is from 2:00 to 6:00 P.M.

• Don't ride a city bus unless you're with an Egyptian. Buses are packed so tightly that you won't be able to get off at your stop without some help. Another minus: There are many, many pickpockets.

• Consider using Cairo's new subway. There are two fares—one for within the city and another for the longer distances outside the city. Unlike buses, subways are not crowded, are air-conditioned, and tend to have fewer pickpockets.

• It is difficult to find taxis in Cairo during business hours and at any time in residential areas. Arrange with a taxi firm to pick you up at a specific time, or walk to the nearest hotel, where taxis will be dropping off passengers.

• Most taxis are metered, but rates are so low that drivers expect you to pay more. Negotiate the fare before you get into the taxi.

• If you're staying at a major hotel in Cairo, Alexandria, Aswan, or Luxor, consider using cars and drivers available by the hour. Be sure to agree on a price before hiring one.

• Even if you think that you know the direction to your destination, ask someone at your hotel to write the directions in Arabic, and ask that person to explain to the taxi driver how to get to your destination, since many taxi drivers speak only Arabic.

• Consider hiring a limousine at the airport or at your hotel. They are more expensive than taxis, but are controlled by the government and therefore adhere to the rules about fares.

• If necessary, ask Tourist Police to find a taxi for you. They will write down the name of the driver and the number of the taxi, an especially good protection for women traveling alone.

• Be aware that there are taxis between cities. They are station wagons which hold up to seven passengers. The cost is so low that you may want to buy two seats so that you'll have more room. Fares are fixed. The starting points for these taxis are usually near railway or bus stations.

• If you're having problems buying a ticket in Cairo's main railroad station, look for the Tourist Police Office. These police usually speak some English and can direct you to the correct ticket window.

• Realize that there are three classes on trains: third is one that travelers shouldn't use; second is acceptable for short trips, such as Cairo–Alexandria; it's not air-conditioned, but it's not as crowded as third class. First class is air-conditioned with comfortable seats and beverages and snacks available. For long distances (e.g., the 12-hour trip down the Nile), first class offers air-conditioning, sleeping compartments (called *wagons-lits*) with private baths, dinner service, a bar, and breakfast served in your compartment.

• There is an overnight train from Cairo to upper Egypt with *couchettes*. You can make reservations at a major hotel or at the train station, where you will find separate lines for men and women (the women's line is always shorter).

• Expect trains to leave and arrive on time.

• Consider taking a bus between Cairo and Alexandria. Buses on that route are air-conditioned, have toilets, and offer food. There are several departures a day for the three-hour trip. Make your reservation at the bus station, where you'll receive a seat assignment. Book your return trip when you arrive at your destination. (You can't buy a round-trip ticket.)

Driving

• Don't rent a car if you will be staying only in Cairo. Traffic is chaotic. Even for long distances, hiring a taxi or car for a day may be cheaper than renting a car. In repair places, people don't speak English; if you have a breakdown, you may be in a difficult predicament.

• If you decide to drive, remember that driving is on the right and that gas is sold by the liter.

• Keep in mind that outside of major towns, gas stations are few and far between.

• Check with the Automobile Club in Cairo for information about the special permits sometimes required for driving in desert areas.

LEGAL MATTERS, HEALTH, AND SAFETY

• Declare your currency on a special form (Form D) when arriving. All exchange transactions should be recorded on this form and presented to customs officials when you leave the country.

• If you bring in an item such as a lap-top computer, put it in your suitcase. If you show it to the customs official, you will have to pay a deposit. When you leave the country, there may be difficulties, and your money might not be refunded.

• Keep in mind that you will have to pay a tax in Egyptian pounds at the airport when you leave the country. Don't change all your currency beforehand. You can change unused Egyptian currency into the currency of your country when you leave Egypt.

• It is against the law to take authentic antiquities out of the country.

• Note that it is legal to drink alcohol in Egypt.

• Don't drink, swim in, wash in, or stand in water from the Nile or the Nile Delta. You risk contracting bilharzia (for specifics, see "Customs and Manners in the Arab World," page 8).

• Never buy food from street vendors.

• Drink only bottled water, and avoid using ice cubes in drinks.

• Avoid milk or cream-based products. In many places, milk is pasteurized, but it's best to be safe.

• Avoid salads, unpeeled fruits and vegetables, and undercooked meats.

• Note that many medicines that require prescriptions in other countries are sold over the counter in Egypt. Pharmacists give injections and recommend medications for minor ailments. Pharmacies carry some American and European drugs, but if you require certain medications, bring an adequate supply with you. Birth control is also available over the counter, and sanitary napkins and tampons are widely available.

• Recognize Tourist Police by a blue stripe on the left chest and a green arm band with "Tourist Police" written in English and Arabic. You'll find them at ports of entry, tourist sites, and bazaars. They will help with directions, with negotiating with cab drivers, with finding lost articles, and, according to the Egyptian Tourist Authority, "generally easing difficulties."

• Don't worry about violent crime. Egypt has one of the lowest crime rates in the world. Outside of family feuds, violent crimes are virtually unknown.

• Women can feel free to take taxis at night and can eat alone in restaurants without fear of being bothered.

THE GULF STATES

Bahrain, Kuwait, Oman, Qatar, United Arab Emirates

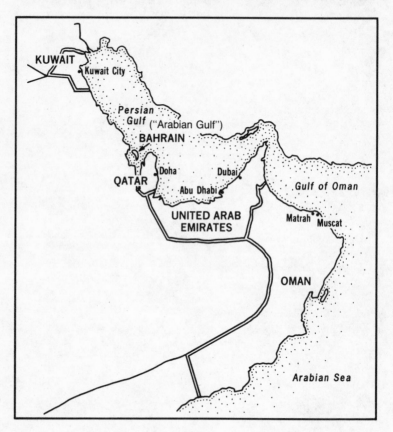

Tucked away on the borders of Saudi Arabia, the Gulf States share many customs, both for social and business occasions. In this chapter, we'll start with a section on common customs in the area and then provide information on distinctive customs for individual countries.

GREETINGS

• Shake hands when introduced for the first time to members of either sex. Some conservative men don't shake hands with women because of their religious beliefs. Usually they will state that they don't shake hands, and then apologize.

• Don't shake hands too vigorously. A strong, pumping grip is considered impolite.

• Realize that men and men as well as women and women greet one another with kisses—one kiss on each cheek, repeated three or four times. Men and women don't kiss in greeting.

• When you see people bowing and kissing someone's hand (in the case of members of the high nobility), don't feel obliged to do the same.

• Note that the only titles used are these: Your Highness for members of royal families; Doctor for physicians; General, Colonel, etc. for high-ranking military officers; Your Excellency for govern-

ment ministers. (See "Key Words and Phrases—Arabic," page 227, for Arabic translations of these terms.)

• Wait until an Arab calls you by your first name before addressing him by his first name.

• As a guest at a party, expect to be introduced individually to each person at the party. Shake hands with each one.

• At the end of a formal visit, shake hands with everyone.

CONVERSATION

• Remember that what many maps identify as the "Persian Gulf" is regarded as the "Arabian Gulf." Be sure to use that term.

• Don't make jokes about harems.

• Never criticize Islam or a country's government.

• Note that the activities of mutual friends are good subjects for conversation.

• To please people, learn a few sentences in Arabic.

• Don't be surprised to hear *very* negative remarks about Indians. There is a great deal of prejudice against them.

IN PUBLIC

• Realize that men often sit, chat, and drink coffee for as long as four to six hours. There may be long periods of silence, and then chat may recommence. The men are just enjoying being in one another's company. If you're included in such a gathering, don't feel you have to fill in the periods of silence.

• Remember that time is less important to Arabs than the obligations imposed by hospitality. Example: One American businessman met an Arab businessman for the first time. The Arab businessman spent six hours showing the American his city. Only later did the American learn that the Arab had been scheduled to leave for vacation two hours after they met.

• Women should never enter a room full of men unless invited.

Furthermore, they should not speak unless spoken to.

• In the presence of an older person, don't cross one leg over the other.

• Never put your arm around your spouse or engage in any other demonstration of affection in public.

• Use the right hand for eating and for handing someone a gift.

• Men should never stare at, speak to, or photograph Arab women, and they should not be seen in public alone with any woman who is not a relative. If questioned, you can make up a relationship—sister, wife, etc.

• Always ask permission of people before photographing them.

• Never photograph religious ceremonies. To do so could get you in *serious* trouble. People might hit you or throw stones at you.

• There are few public toilets, and you'll find that the signs are in Arabic. Use toilet facilities in hotels or restaurants.

• When shopping, remember that gold jewelry is sold by weight, and the price changes daily. However, you can bargain in the jewelry shops.

or jacket, since air-conditioned taxis and offices can be cold.

• Even though the national dress is very comfortable, don't wear it. For a foreigner to wear native dress is insulting.

• Don't expect Arab men to remove their headdress inside a building or a home.

DRESS

• For casual wear, women should wear knee-length (or longer) skirts and tops with short or medium sleeves. Do not wear sleeveless tops, halters, or tight pants. Men should wear long pants and a short-sleeved shirt. Neither men nor women should ever wear shorts, bathing suits, or cut-off T-shirts in public.

• For business, men should wear suits and women modest dresses that are not sleeveless.

• To a mosque, women should wear long-sleeved dresses with modest necklines and with skirts reaching below the knees.

• To nice restaurants, women should wear dresses and men should wear suits and ties.

• Note that there are no occasions for which men will need tuxedos or dinner jackets. A dark suit will suffice. Women won't need a floor-length formal—just cocktail-length dresses.

• Women should carry a sweater

MEALS

Hours and Foods

Breakfast: Between 6:30 and 7:30 A.M. The usual breakfast includes boiled or fried eggs, *khoubiz* (a round flat bread like pita), butter, jam, cheese, olives, and tea (with or without milk) or instant coffee.

Lunch: Between 12:30 and 2:00 P.M. It's the day's main meal and always features rice and bread. There will probably be vegetables or meat in tomato sauce, vegetables stuffed with meat, and salads. Beverages: juices and/or soft drinks with the meal and Arabic coffee after the meal.

Dinner: 8:00 or 9:00 P.M. A light meal, it often features cheeses, cucumber, tomatoes, mortadella (salami) or falafel or *ful* (beans cooked with garlic, lemon, and olive oil). The drink is usually tea with milk.

• Note that the main spices used in cooking in the area are cinnamon, hot chili, ginger, turmeric, saffron, nutmeg, and pepper. Dried limes—whole or ground— are often used in cooking.

Beverages: The coffee is strong and bitter, flavored with cardamom, and served in small cups without handles. It is never served with milk or cream. *After* coffee, you may be offered tea, which is served in small glasses.

Table Manners

• At a dinner party, expect juices and soft drinks to be offered before meals since alcohol is not allowed. It's not customary to offer food before dinner, as the meal will be abundant. However, in some homes, small bowls with nuts, potato chips, and cut salad greens are put out on coffee tables as pre-dinner snacks. (Don't eat the salad greens.)

• As a guest, prepare to be seated first, but there won't be a special seat of honor. Wait for your host to seat you.

• Anticipate one of three methods of meal service: (1) guests sitting on the floor at a low table with the food placed on platters from which the guests help themselves; (2) in more Westernized homes, guests sitting at a standard dining-room table and eating with knives and forks after having been served from platters of food; or (3) if there are more guests than seating will accommodate, a buffet.

• Eat with your *right* hand. (If you're left-handed, practice before going to the Gulf States.) In many homes, you'll find that people eat with fingers and bread, rather than with utensils, particularly if they are eating traditional foods.

• Realize that there's no way to tell how many courses will be served, whether at a dinner in a home or a feast in a tent. The first four or five courses may be just the beginning. If you don't taste everything, you'll offend your host. One Chicago banker recalled his experience when a business colleague from one of the Gulf States was entertaining a group in a tent: "We'd had several courses and were standing outside talking when someone said, 'Won't you come in to dinner?' I thought we had finished, and inside the tent were 150 squab on skewers for 25 people. I couldn't insult my host, so I had to eat again."

• If you're the honored guest, expect the host to place a great deal of food on your plate—and you're expected to eat it. It's acceptable to ask your host for a description of an unfamiliar dish. Be sure to taste at least a bit of each dish.

• Both at a dinner party in a home or a business meal in a hotel, leave as soon as you've finished the coffee or tea.

Eating Out

• Look for better restaurants in hotels. Shopping malls usually have cafes and snack bars.

• If you have a yen for a Western-style sandwich (roast beef, tuna, etc.), head for a coffee shop or snack bar. You'll also find Arabic sandwiches, such as falafel and *shwarma* (lamb cooked on a vertical spit, sliced, and served in Arabic bread).

• Note that you'll find both Oriental and European dishes in many restaurants.

• Be aware that local restaurants are usually frequented by laborers and workers. There are also traditional cafes for men where seating is on cushions on the floor. They are like social clubs where men gather to drink Arab coffee and chat. Visiting males are welcome. Women should avoid cafes.

• Don't look for menus to be posted in restaurant windows. It's not the custom.

• Realize that it's not acceptable

to share a table, if a restaurant is full. Doing so is considered an invasion of privacy.

• Call a waiter by raising your hand, making eye contact, or saying "Excuse Me" in Arabic (Law sah-maht). Don't whistle or clap.

• Keep in mind that customs about paying at a restaurant differ. Among older people, the person who issued the invitation or the oldest person pays for everyone. It's offensive if others insist on paying their share. However, younger people have acquired Western habits and may share the bill.

Specialties

Popular Fish: gugurfan—similar to bream; *beyah*—mullet; *chanad*—mackerel; *machbous*—prawns, rice, parsley, tomatoes, coriander, and several other spices; *samak mashwi*—barbecued fish with dates. Fish is usually grilled, baked in the oven, stewed, or fried.

Rice Dishes: muhammar—rice prepared with rosewater, saffron, cardamom, sugar, salt, and butter; *mashkoul*—rice with onions; *muaddas*—rice with lentils.

Chicken and Meat Dishes: machbous ala dajaj—chicken and rice with tomatoes, dried lime, parsley, and spices; *kabab mashwi*

—ground lamb or beef on skewers served on flat bread with tomatoes, cucumbers, onion, and lettuce; *basal mahshi*—onions stuffed with beef or lamb and rice, tomatoes, and spices; *machbous*—spiced lamb and rice; *lahm bil bayd*—hard-boiled eggs encased in ground meat, and the mixture deep fried.

Other Specialties: *shaurabat*—lentil soup; *samouli*—a white bread, similar to French baguettes.

Desserts: *ghi raybah*—shortbread balls with powdered ginger; *nashab*—fried nut rolls; *sabb al-gafsha*—fried sweet puffs with syrup, served warm; *samboosa holwah*—deep-fried triangles of nuts and phyllo dough.

HOTELS

• Make hotel reservations at least one to two months in advance. If you have a local agent or business associate, he can help with the reservation.

• Confirm your reservation with a deposit. Sometimes, even confirmed reservations aren't honored.

PRIVATE HOMES

• Plan to visit in the evening. If you aren't a relative or a close friend of the family, phone before dropping in. The people of the Gulf States are very open with foreigners, and one can make good friends. Don't be surprised to receive invitations to homes and to social events.

• Remove your shoes when entering a private home. Leave them inside the door.

• When you visit a woman in a home, anticipate seeing several bottles of perfume on a table. They are there as a welcoming gesture. Every woman should spray some perfume on herself.

• Expect to be treated as a guest for the first three days of your stay with a family. After that, you're expected to feel at home and offer to lend a hand with chores. If you're staying for a long period, bring a simple gift every once in a while.

• If your stay is long, and you have rented a home and wish to entertain some friends, serve buffet style. People are casual about accepting invitations and may not turn up *or* they may turn up bringing extra friends with them. Dealing with an unknown number of guests is easier at a buffet.

Gifts: When invited to a meal, bring flowers, chocolates, or Arab sweets. People will appreciate your giving something to the children—e.g., toys or stuffed animals.

• Remember that Arab men don't wear jewelry, so don't give them any (for example, gold chains).

• Good gifts for men: a paperweight; an engraved business-card holder; an expensive gold pen; something from your company or university with the official logo on it. For women: silk scarves. Either sex will enjoy a photographic book of your area or a china box with a picture of a famous building on it. People also enjoy food specialties such as smoked salmon. However, don't ever give alcohol or pork products.

• If you will be going back to your country and then returning, ask people what they would like from abroad. They may want a best-selling book or a favorite brand of tobacco.

• Should an Arab admire something of yours (such as, a tie or a pen), consider giving it to him. At the end of the evening, say "I'd like to give this to you."

• Don't expect effusive verbal thanks if you give an expensive gift. You are a vehicle of Allah for the gift's arrival.

BUSINESS PRACTICES

• Plan your trip between October and April. Many businesspeople leave during the summer months (June to September). The weather should be somewhat cooler in the winter—100°F (38°C) as opposed to 120°F (49°C) in the summer.

• Arrive in the Gulf at least a day before your first appointment to get over jet lag and adapt to the heat (although most businesspeople report that they never adapt to the heat).

• Be prepared to make many trips to accomplish your business. Establishing trust—essential to doing business—takes both time and patience.

• Regard business colleagues as potential friends, not as customers or suppliers. Personal relationships must be strong, or you won't accomplish business goals.

• Send your company's C.E.O. to do business, because, when decisions are made, they will be made on the spot, and businessmen in the Gulf want to deal with *one* person from a company—they don't want someone brought in at the last minute when final decisions are being made.

• To deal with the nervousness that is natural on a first business trip to the Gulf, strike up conversations with people you meet before you go to your business meeting. Chat with the taxi driver, the waiter, the bellboy, the concierge, or the maitre d' in a restaurant. If you can get along with them, you'll gain confidence, and, by the time you get to your business meeting, you'll have a good idea of the rhythm and pace of conversation.

• If you bring a letter of introduction from a mutual acquaintance, you will be accepted very quickly as someone to be trusted. (If you violate that trust in any way, you are finished—permanently.)

• For initial meetings—whether with businesspeople or government officials—start six to eight weeks in advance by writing a letter requesting an appointment and offer a choice of dates. State the exact purpose of your visit, so that the Arab businessman will be able to prepare. After a good relationship has been established, you can make appointments by telephone or fax.

• Be aware that some people won't make appointments until you actually arrive in the country.

• Never "drop in" at an office. It's insulting.

• Acquire a sponsor in the country in which you wish to do business; otherwise, you won't be able to obtain a visa. Seek contacts through the Commercial Section of the Arab country's embassy, through your own country's embassy in the Gulf country, or through an international bank with which you may do business.

• Remember that business is conducted primarily with companies that have a "local presence." It's important to have local representatives because opportunities for engineers, contractors, and consultants are not always published.

• If you have several appointments in different places, hire a car and driver by the day.

• Stay in one of the best hotels, because your hotel reflects your status.

• Rather than doing business in an office, try to persuade the Arab businessman to come to your hotel. Most hotel lobbies are laid out so that it's easy to have a meeting of a few people or a conference. This arrangement has two advantages: (1) You won't have to deal with the constant interruptions, both from people and from telephone calls, that will occur in an office. (2) You'll be able to drink Western-style coffee, tea, or bottled water, rather than endless cups of Arab coffee and tea, which, businessmen report, "can take the roof right off your mouth."

• If you meet in an Arab businessman's office, accept the offer of coffee, tea, or a soft drink. (The soft drink is probably the safest bet.) If you're not offered a soft drink, ask for bottled water. Coffee will be served in small cups without handles; they resemble egg cups. To be polite, drink two or three cups of coffee or tea. When you finish, shake the cup gently from side to side. During Ramadan, you won't be offered food or drink.

• To make a really good impression, learn a few polite phrases in Arabic, especially words of greeting. Though most top-level people in business and government are fluent in English, they will appreciate your gesture. Those who don't speak English will have an interpreter.

• Remember, remember, remember not to get involved in a conversation about possible liberalization in a country as the result of the Gulf War. Never say something such as, "Do you think that women will be getting the vote soon?" That's a sure way to ruin a business deal. The people with whom you'll be dealing—those in a position to give out contracts—are members of "the establishment" and tend to be very conservative.

• Avoid colloquial expressions (especially those drawn from American sports), because most people won't understand them.

• Though English is widely accepted in business circles, realize that certain documents, such as company registration papers, must be in Arabic.

• Have business cards printed in English on one side and Arabic on the other. On your card, transliterate the names of companies rather than using a direct translation. Always present the Arabic side. Keep an Arab's business cards, because they may include unlisted telephone numbers and unpublished addresses.

• Be prepared to spend hours—even days—in small talk about the state of your health and that of your male relatives. Serious business may not be discussed until your third or fourth meeting. Let your Arab business associate take the lead in concluding the social phase and moving to the business phase. Don't rush into doing business, because you'll surely fail if you do. In a few cases, people who have been educated abroad will proceed directly to business. (You may be fooled because they're wearing traditional Arab dress.)

• In drawing up any specifications, be sure to use metric measurements.

• Avoid swearing, and never use the word "God" in any negative context.

• Don't put on airs and pretend to be someone you're not.

• Study your competition and its strengths so that you will be well prepared to argue your own case.

• Realize that your most difficult problem will be to distinguish between the gatekeeper, the man who does the analysis, and the decision maker. The gatekeeper has nothing to do except talk to you forever. You must get past him. The person who does the analysis is never the decision maker, but you'll have to work with him so that he will introduce you to the top man. Try to develop a network of contacts so that you can ask, "Who is the person I want to see?" and "Could you introduce me?" An insider has commented that one clue to identifying an influential businessman in the Gulf States is to look at his wristwatch: if it is expensive, he's most likely someone who makes the decisions.

• Expect the following at a business meeting: There will be a Pakistani note-taker and probably a British person who knows the business well. There may also be one or two Arabs (in addition to the main Arab businessman, who has probably studied abroad and is therefore Westernized). One of the Arabs is the decision maker. After you make your presentation, you'll be grilled by the British person or by a very educated Pakistani. The others will sit and drink coffee. The decision maker, who has his role by virtue of being in the family that runs the business or the country, says nothing. He observes how you answer questions. When you finish your proposal, say "Do you have any questions?" and "Is there anything I can answer for you?"

• Be aware that you may make a 45-minute presentation and at the end another man will come in, and you'll have to repeat the whole thing. You may have to repeat the proposal several more times—for hours, in fact. If you display any reluctance to go through the series of repetitions, you won't be successful.

• When you phone a businessperson with whom you've established a relationship, always show that you are interested in his life and welfare— "How was your trip to Yugoslavia?" "Is it a place I should visit?" "Which of our friends have you seen recently?" "How are they?"

• Remember that devout Muslims pray five times each day. They may leave a meeting to go to a mosque, an activity that can interrupt meetings for 30 minutes at a time. It's acceptable to either leave the room or stay if people are praying in the office.

• Avoid using high-pressure tactics. Such strategies may cause you to lose a deal.

• Realize that the Western and the Arab concept of a contract is different. Westerners want precise details and every possibility written into a contract—Westerners want a 30-page contract, and Arabs want a three-page contract. Include only the most important points in the contract. If the contract is too complex, people will suspect that you are trying to cheat them.

• Let your Arab host initiate the end of the meeting. The serving of coffee will signal that the meeting is over. Leave shortly after you've finished your coffee.

• Present a small gift (a book of photographs or an electronic gadget, for example) at the end of your first or second visit. If you neglected to bring something with you, local shops stock items made abroad.

• Don't invite a businessman to a meal until he invites you first.

• Don't offer to entertain an Arab at a nightclub or a bar. Suggest a hotel restaurant. If the group is large, engage a private dining room in the hotel or in a restaurant. Order the dinner in advance.

• Even if an Arab encourages you to drink, don't do it, unless you have seen him drinking in his country. It will upset him, even though he's encouraged you. (The same rule holds true if you meet with Arabs in Europe or North America. Let them take the lead.)

• In a restaurant with an Arab colleague, don't order a dish prepared with wine or liquor, because you may offend your Arab friend.

• If you receive an invitation to a home, *always* accept.

LEGAL MATTERS, SAFETY, AND HEALTH

• Don't bring in any items that could even remotely be regarded as pornographic, because anything vaguely lewd or licentious will cause you trouble at customs.

• If you bring in videotapes, realize that they will be played at customs to make sure that they contain nothing either lewd or political.

• Don't try to smuggle in alcohol.

• Be sure that prescription drugs are in containers labeled with their precise contents.

• Drink only bottled water. Don't eat raw fruits or vegetables that cannot be peeled.

• Avoid food sold by street vendors.

• Be wary of eating shellfish. Be sure to see lobsters and crayfish alive before you agree to eat them.

• Women should not take taxis at night. Always sit in the back seat of a taxi, even if the driver suggests that you sit in the front.

• Unaccompanied women should realize that they will be subject to ogling and propositions. Be polite, but *very* firm. There is no risk of physical harm, but the harassment can be very irritating.

Bahrain

A group of islands, Bahrain has always been a trading society, accustomed to dealing with foreigners. You will find there a more cosmopolitan outlook and more tolerance of Western customs than in neighboring countries.

TELEPHONES

• Bahrain has one of the most efficient telephone services in the Middle East. A call to North America takes only a couple of minutes, and the connections are excellent. Make international calls from the "business centers" you'll find at all major hotels. You can also make calls at the post office or at the arrival/departure lounge in the airport.

• Note that local calls are free. There are no phone booths on the street. You can make local calls from a hotel; if you're out walking or shopping, ask any shop attendant to allow you to use the phone.

IN PUBLIC

• Realize that someone who suggests visiting a garden usually means a small area of land in the country to which families go for picnics on weekends.
• Bahrain is traditionally the most liberal Gulf country regarding women and their behavior. You will find many women employed at all levels of government and in the private sector.
• Bargain in markets, but not in shops.

HOTELS

• Make reservations at least two months in advance for a first-class hotel. The busiest period is from October through May.

• Expect your hotel to provide distilled water.

TIPPING

• Restaurants: If no service charge is included in the bill, leave 10%.
• Porters (at airport and hotels): 200 *fils* per bag.
• Taxis: Tipping is completely optional. Weigh the length of the journey and the level of service.
• Don't tip gas station attendants.
• If you hire a guide for the day, tip 15%.
• Give a hairdresser 15%.

BUSINESS

Hours

Banks: Saturday to Wednesday, 7:30 A.M. to 12:30 P.M., and Thursday, 7:30 to 11:00 A.M.

Businesses: Saturday to Thursday, 7:00 A.M. to noon, and Saturday to Wednesday, 2:30 to 5:30 P.M.

Government Offices: Saturday to Thursday, 7:00 A.M. to 1:00 P.M.

Shops: Saturday to Thursday, 8:30 A.M. to 12:30 P.M., and Saturday to Wednesday 3:30 to 6:30 P.M.

• Note that some shops in the *souk* (old market) are open on Friday morning.

• Remember that during Ramadan, daytime business hours are reduced, but businesses are open from 8:00 to 11:00 A.M.

Currency

• The unit of currency is the *dinar* (abbreviated BD), which consists of 1,000 *fils*.

• Coins: 5, 10, 25, 50, and 100 *fils*.

• Bills: ½, 1, 5, 10, and 20 BD.

• Don't be surprised if a shopkeeper quotes prices in *rupees*. One *rupee* equals 100 *fils*. Ask to have the prices translated into *fils* or *dinars*.

• Realize that currency from Saudi Arabia, Qatar, and the U.A.E. circulates in Bahrain.

• Expect major credit cards to be accepted by major hotels, restaurants, and travel agencies. You can also pay bills in dollars.

Business Practices

• For English translations of laws and regulations in Bahrain, contact the U.S. Department of Commerce. You can be briefed in person in Washington, D.C., by the U.S. Commerce Department's International Trade Administration Office of the Near East.

• To make contacts, have a booth at one of the trade exhibitions in Bahrain. You will gain widespread exposure throughout the Gulf region. Obtain dates of such exhibitions from Bahrain's embassy in your country.

• Remember that, though the official language is Arabic, English is widely spoken in the government and business community. Send letters, cables, telexes, and fax messages in English.

• Realize that it's difficult to get appointments with government officials or businesspeople, since there are few people in either sector assigned to areas of interest to foreign businesspeople. Your contacts will help you get one of these scarce appointments.

• Write a letter requesting an appointment. You may not get an answer. Follow up with a telex, fax message, or telephone call. Don't telex or fax for an appointment from abroad at the last minute.

• Allow extra time in Bahrain, since the opportunity for additional appointments may come up. If you reject an appointment, saying something such as "I have to be in the U.A.E.," you will create resentment on the Bahraini's part. You will alienate Bahrainis by implying that you're just passing through their country on the way to a more profitable deal elsewhere.

• Be sure that all your bids are in English, using metric measurements.

• Never offer a bribe to expedite a deal. Bahrainis are very honest in their business dealings and expect foreigners to be the same.

• Don't be surprised if business is carried out in a social setting, even very early in your dealings. There are fewer traditional rules for business in Bahrain than in other Arab countries.

• Bahrain has neither corporate nor income taxes.

• Be aware that customs duties may be waived on imported machinery, but the machinery must be exported when the project is concluded.

HOLIDAYS AND SPECIAL OCCASIONS

• Other than the holidays governed by the Muslim calendar, Bahrain celebrates New Year's Day (Jan. 1) and Ruler's Accession Day (Dec. 16).

TRANSPORTATION

Public Transportation

• Recognize taxis by orange mudguards and black-on-yellow number plates. All taxis must carry the official price list, but most drivers ignore it. Negotiate the fare in advance. Fares increase by 50% between midnight and 5:30 A.M. Taxis that cruise are less expensive than those that are parked.

• Have someone at your hotel write the address of your destination in Arabic, in case the taxi driver doesn't speak English. It's also a good idea to carry a card with your hotel's name, address, and phone number written in Arabic.

• Never have a taxi driver wait for you unless you know in advance *exactly* what the price will be. Taxis are abundant, so you won't have a problem finding another one.

Driving

• Realize that you can rent a car. You will need an International Driver's License or a U.S. license. Always check out the condition of a rental car before accepting it. Though a car and driver costs a little more than double the charge for a rental, the convenience usually makes the cost worthwhile.

LEGAL MATTERS, SAFETY, AND HEALTH

• Remember that U.S. travelers must have a visa. You can obtain a 72-hour temporary visa at the Bahrain airport if you have an onward ticket.

• Recall that there are no regulations about the amount of U.S. currency you can bring into the country.

• Note that Bahrain is the only Arab country in the Gulf region where you can buy alcohol in retail shops without a permit. Liquor and beer are relatively inexpensive. Hotels and restaurants also serve alcoholic drinks.

Kuwait

Kuwait is a country well tuned to Western ways. Many people have studied or traveled abroad and speak English, French, or both. Only 50% of the population are actually Kuwaitis. The other half is made up of other Arabs, Pakistanis, Iranians, and Indians.

CONVERSATION

• Many Kuwaitis, including women, have traveled abroad, so travel is a good subject for conversation.

• Keep in mind that Kuwaitis are conservative Muslims who do not approve of drinking alcohol. Never mention how much you miss liquor. (The importation of liquor is illegal.)

TELEPHONES

• Expect to find public telephones in booths on the street. Usually, the slots are closed. The phone is not out of order but the closed slots are a reminder that local calls are free. You can also go into a shop and ask to use the phone for a local call.

• Make an international call from the Telecommunications Center, the airport, or your hotel.

• Remember that you can make and receive collect calls.

IN PUBLIC

• Realize that in cinemas there are designated seating areas for unaccompanied men. When a man and woman are together, they sit in the family section. Women should not go to the cinema alone.

• To photograph sites around Kuwait, obtain permission from the Ministry of the Interior.

• Don't photograph the Amir's palace, government buildings, oil fields, electricity plants, or places destroyed by the bombing in the 1991 Gulf War.

• Always bargain—it's a national sport in Kuwait. The only places you can't bargain are in supermarkets or department stores. Bargain everywhere else, including vegetable markets, *souks* (old markets), fish markets, and gold markets.

DRESS

• When local people dress formally, they wear the national dress of Kuwait—called the *dishdasha* or the *thoub*. These are long, loose white robes, made of light cotton for summer and heavy cotton or light wool for winter. For formal occasions—weddings are usually the most formal events—a woman's *thoub* is decorated with sequins. For other functions, women usually wear a shorter dress, but always one that covers the knees.

PRIVATE HOMES

• Don't be surprised if your host—as a sign of welcome—slaughters a sheep on the doorstep. When you arrive, you'll see the bloody corpse.

HOTELS

• Don't forget that men and women use the swimming pool at different hours. There is no mixed swimming.

TIPPING

• Restaurants: If the usual service charge of 10% is not included, leave 10%.
• Porters (airport or hotels): 250 *fils* per bag.
• Taxis: No tipping.
• If you hire a guide for the day, tip 15%.
• Give a hairdresser 15%.
• Don't tip gas station attendants.

BUSINESS

Hours

Banks: Saturday to Thursday, 8:00 A.M. to noon.

Businesses: Saturday to Thursday, 8:30 A.M. to 12:30 P.M. and 4:30 to 8:30 P.M.

Government Offices: In winter (Nov. 1 to Mar. 31), Saturday to Wednesday, 7:30 A.M. to 1:30 P.M. In summer (April 1 to Oct. 31), Saturday to Wednesday, 7:00 A.M. to 1:00 P.M., and Thursday, 7:30 to 11:30 A.M.

Shops: Saturday to Thursday, 8:30 A.M. to 12:30 P.M. and 4:30 to 9:00 P.M.

Currency

• The currency is the Kuwait *dinar* (abbreviated KD), which is made up of 1,000 *fils*.

• Coins: 1, 5, 10, 20, 50, and 100 *fils*.
• Bills: ¼, ½, 1, 5, 10, and 20 KD.

Business Practices

• Don't schedule a business trip at election time. (Check with Kuwait's embassy in your country for dates.) After elections, Kuwaitis celebrate candidates' victories and are not interested in doing business for several days.

• Make an appointment. Never drop in at an office without one. Since Kuwait has a large institutionalized bureaucracy with many officials available to meet with businesspeople, you'll find it easier to make appointments here than in countries such as Bahrain, where there are fewer administrators.

• When suggesting appointment times, remember that government offices are open only in the morning.

• For contacts—whether agents, representatives, or potential partners—go to Kuwait and consult the local commercial attache of your country, the Chamber of Commerce and Industry, the Industrial Development and Consulting Bureau (Ministry of Commerce and Industry), and the local affiliate of your bank. Your agent in the country must be a Kuwaiti.

• Expect to find the latest technology in Kuwait. Companies and hotels will have copiers, telexes, and fax machines. You'll also find copiers at hotels, bookshops, and even in local supermarkets.

• Don't be misled by the extreme politeness and evidence of interest that Kuwaitis display. You may assume that you have a contract, only to learn—months later—that you don't. Kuwaitis are so kind that they may agree to see you in their offices, even if they have no interest in your proposal. In other words, don't believe you have an agreement until you see a written contract.

• Always treat Kuwaitis, who tend to be low-key and quiet, with courtesy and respect. If you lose your temper with one person, you may be cutting off other contacts as well, since Kuwait's business community is a small one.

• Never make derogatory remarks about anyone. You may have inadvertently criticized a member of the royal family.

• Realize that people are somewhat clannish, but you won't meet resistance as an outsider. Americans are held in especially high regard and are warmly welcomed.

• If you need a temporary secretary, arrange for one through your hotel.

• Keep in mind that many middle management positions are held by people from other Arab countries—often Palestinians. Don't express your views on the Israel-Palestine situation.

• Realize that the younger generation takes great pride in the achievements of Kuwait. Praise the country and how much it has accomplished in a short time. Thirty years ago the country was a desert with mud huts. Now there are supermarkets, four-lane highways, schools, universities—and the highest per-capita income in the world.

• Never say "I was sent by So-and-So," unless you know that person well.

• Always send your company's very top people to Kuwait. Kuwaitis admire titles, and they want to deal with a company's top managers. Kuwaitis resent middlemen —i.e., people who take commissions for making introductions. In the past, middlemen often exploited Kuwaitis who didn't have the expertise to handle financial transactions. (These middlemen are different from the agents and representatives described above, who have many functions beyond making introductions.)

• Remember that big decisions are made by one person at the top, but you will have to go through channels to reach that top person.

• Be punctual. Kuwaitis are on time and they expect others to be. If you are even ten minutes late, they may not see you.

- If you're dealing with a private company, expect to conduct business in English. However, any business documents for the government should be translated into Arabic.
- Lavish praise—at great length —on a person's accomplishments, the country, the factory, the equipment, etc.
- Note that promotional materials in English are acceptable, but they will be more impressive if you have them translated into Arabic.
- Make your presentation brief and to the point. Avoid long and detailed expositions since Kuwaiti businessmen tend to lose interest if someone rambles on. (It's to your advantage to keep things short, since you may have to repeat your presentation several times. See general advice on "The Gulf States," page 50.)
- If colorful visual aids fit with your presentation, bring them. You'll impress your audience.
- Know your competitors and what they have to offer. Kuwaitis are very knowledgeable and comb markets for competitive deals.
- Never try to bribe anyone to expedite a deal. You could cause yourself serious trouble.
- Expect Kuwaitis to be very shrewd in negotiations. They have, after all, been traders since the seventh century.
- Realize that, though contract negotiations are in English, the fi-

nal contract must be in Arabic. If there is any dispute as to the two versions of the contract, only the Arabic version has the force of law. From the beginning of your negotiations, present as specific a proposal as possible.
- Don't worry that you'll have difficulty obtaining a written contract. You won't. Once a contract is made, Kuwaitis usually abide by its terms. Business laws are very strict—for example, someone who writes a check that bounces is immediately sent to prison. One problem you may encounter is that people don't always meet deadlines.
- For smaller projects, use "Purchase Orders" rather than contracts.
- Keep contracts simple. If the contract is long and complicated, Kuwaitis may think that you are trying to cheat them in a subtle way. Never imply that you don't trust them, because Kuwaitis are used to accepting a man's word.
- Realize that there is no personal income tax, but corporations must pay tax on income earned in Kuwait.
- Recognize that Kuwait is the only country of the Gulf States where you will find women in business and government. Women own clothing and jewelry businesses, and some hold good positions in journalism and the arts. Top managerial jobs in most areas

are restricted to men. Despite some liberation, women and men tend to lead separate social lives.

• Though women have achieved a certain status in business, don't send a woman to do business in Kuwait.

• If your wife accompanies you to Kuwait, don't expect to be invited to a Kuwaiti home, unless you're dealing with people of the younger, more modern generation, whose wives may be Westernized.

• Lunches are more popular than dinner for business because of the long lunch hour—1:00 to 4:00 P.M.

• If you plan to entertain business colleagues, invite only those with whom you are negotiating.

HOLIDAYS AND SPECIAL OCCASIONS

• In addition to the religious holidays observed according to the Muslim calendar, Kuwait celebrates New Year's Day (Jan. 1) and Kuwait National Day (Feb. 25).

TRANSPORTATION

Public Transportation

• Realize that there are no domestic air or rail services.

• For local buses, enter at the front and buy a ticket from the driver. Fares are based on zones. The usual amount is between 50 and 100 *fils*. Try to have exact change. Many buses don't have conductors, but usually someone will check your ticket.

• Note that taxis aren't easily found on streets. There are two types: (1) orange cabs, which are semi-operated by the government, often shared by a group, and which have negotiable fares; and (2) private-call taxis. Use the private-call taxis, since they are more reliable, cleaner, air-conditioned, and have fixed rates. Drivers speak English and can be helpful as guides. Phone for these taxis, which are readily available.

• Consider hiring an air-conditioned limousine. They are available with or without a driver.

• Remember that there is a nationwide bus system operated by the Kuwait Transport Company. Buy tickets at the bus station. The buses tend to be very crowded and are not recommended for travelers.

Driving

• Rent a car from one of the several international and local agencies located in cities, suburbs, hotels, and at the airport. You'll need an International Driver's License. If you'll be staying in Kuwait for a long time, your original license can be transferred to a local driver's license.

• Expect to find well-developed roads and highways, with signs in both Arabic and English.

• Don't drive after drinking— even a very little. If the police suspect that you have been drinking you can be stopped, given a test for alcohol, and deported immediately (within 24 hours) if you are found to have been drinking.

• Don't park on yellow lines or in "No Parking" areas. If you do, your car will have a "boot" (clamp) affixed to it, and you will be fined heavily. You will have to go to the nearest police station to have the boot removed.

• Wear seat belts, though law doesn't require them. Accident rates in Kuwait are among the highest in the world, primarily due to speeding.

• There are no on-the-spot fines.

For minor infractions, violators are ticketed and pay the fine later. However, committing a greater offense—driving through a red light or driving without a license —could mean arrest and/or deportation.

• *Never* try to bribe a policeman. This would cause you more trouble than the original infraction did.

• Don't argue with a policeman. Be polite; be deferential; don't use harsh words.

• If you are involved in an accident, report it immediately to the police. If there's been an injury, notify your country's consul. As a non-Kuwaiti driver, you will probably be held to be at fault.

LEGAL MATTERS, SAFETY, AND HEALTH

• Keep in mind that the sale and consumption of alcohol is prohibited by law. You aren't allowed to bring any alcohol into the country, not even the small bottles served on planes.

• If you bring videotapes with

you, don't be surprised if they are confiscated by customs officials, who will view them to see if they contain any lewd material. If they don't, they will be returned to you at a later time.

• Don't hesitate to stop a highway police car and ask for assistance. The highway police are very helpful.

• Realize that traffic police have the right to confiscate your driver's license. If that happens to you, have the policeman write down his name, personal number, and car number, so that you can follow up and retrieve your license if it has been taken unfairly.

• Women should know that there are separate beaches for men and for families. Go to the family beach. Even better, go to the beach at your hotel, since hotel beaches are well guarded. Women are not allowed to wear bathing suits, and men must wear boxer short-style bathing suits.

• Note that in restaurants there are separate seating areas for single men and for families. Women should sit in the family area.

• A Western woman alone is thought to be "asking" for advances—whistles, remarks, cars stopping. You are physically safe, but you'll have to put up with harassment. To avoid such situations as much as possible, never walk or jog alone, always dress modestly, and avoid eye contact.

• Women should not stroll in towns or on beaches at night, even with a man. Local people will think that the man accompanying you is trying to sell your services.

• Women should not drive alone.

• Women alone shouldn't use an orange taxi, either during the day or night. They should use call taxis at night.

• If you plan to stay in Kuwait more than six months, you must have an AIDS test. Results of tests from U.S. laboratories are acceptable.

The Gulf War of 1991 wreaked havoc on Kuwait. For a time, buildings, utilities, and amenities may not be up to the country's previous levels. However, many experts predict that rebuilding the country will take less time than has been generally predicted.

Oman

Many visitors find Oman the most pleasant of the Gulf States, in part because of its lovely scenery and in part because of its relaxed social atmosphere. Omanis, who are a blend of Arab, African, and Indian, wear a distinctive national costume. Men wear a long white robe called the *dishdasha*; on their heads they wear a wool Kashmiri scarf. For formal occasions, they wear a curved silver dagger in a belt at the waist. Women wear colorful print pantaloons with a long, loose, long-sleeved, high-necked print dress. On the head they wear a loose, colorful printed scarf. The face is uncovered.

TELEPHONES

• Book an international call at least one to two hours in advance.

IN PUBLIC

• Women can go to public beaches, but they must wear a one-piece bathing suit.
• Note that Oman is more lib-eral than many other Gulf countries. For example, a woman can order a drink in the company of Omani men (and, of course, with Western men). However, she should wait to see if her Arab host orders an alcoholic drink. If he doesn't, she should not.

HOTELS

• Be sure to observe the rules for the hotel swimming pool. Women and men swim at separate times. There is no mixed swimming.

HOLIDAYS AND SPECIAL OCCASIONS .

• In addition to the Muslim holidays, celebrated according to that religion's calendar, Oman celebrates the Accession of the Sultan (July 23), National Day (Nov. 18), and the birthday of the Sultan (Nov. 19).

TIPPING

• At restaurants, the service charge is included.
• Give porters at airports and hotels 200 *baizas* per bag, with a maximum of 500 *baizas*.
• Don't tip taxi drivers.
• If you hire a guide for the day, tip 15%.
• Give a hairdresser 15%.

• Don't tip a gas station attendant.

BUSINESS

Hours

Banks: Saturday to Wednesday, 8:00 A.M. to noon, and Thursday, 8:00 to 11:30 A.M.

Businesses: Saturday to Wednesday, 8:00 A.M. to 1:00 P.M. and 3:00 to 6:00 P.M. *or* 4:00 to 7:00 P.M.

Government Offices: Saturday to Wednesday, 7:30 A.M. to 2:00 P.M., and Thursday, 7:30 A.M. to 1:00 P.M.

Shops: Saturday to Thursday, 8:30 A.M. to 1:00 P.M. and 4:00 to 6:00 P.M.

Currency

• The currency is the Omani *riyal* (abbreviated RO), each of which consists of 1,000 *baizas*.
• Coins: 5, 10, 25, 50, and 100 *baizas*.

• Bills: 500 *baizas*; RO 1, 5, 10, 20.

Business Practices

• Expect English to be widely spoken in the business community, although Arabic is the official language.

• Obtain permission to enter the country from the Omani authorities. You must be sponsored by an institution or by a person resident in the country. Your sponsor must give a reason for the trip when making the application.

• Realize that the British manage many major Omani firms and have had close political and commercial ties with Oman. American companies face stiff competition from other foreign interests.

• To export to Omani, be prepared to satisfy Omani concerns regarding shipping time, price, and availability of spare parts for any equipment.

• If you hold the title Ph.D., have it printed on your business card. Omanis will hold you in high regard. Prior to 1971, Omanis were not allowed to have an education. They now tend to trust the degree more than an individual's competence.

• Keep in mind that women in Oman are forward looking and that many are educated. Many foreign women who are geologists and doctors work in Oman. Your company could send a woman representative if you are selling cosmetics or books, but there would be resistance if you sent a woman to close a major business deal in an area such as oil.

TRANSPORTATION

Public Transportation

• Regular taxis, painted orange and white, operate from 5:00 A.M. to midnight. They don't have meters, so arrange the fare in advance. Service taxis, which carry up to five passengers, run on fixed routes. Each person pays a share of the total fare. Negotiate the fare in advance for both regular taxis and service taxis.

Driving

• Remember that a four-wheel-drive vehicle is essential for desert travel. Ordinary cars can be used up to the edge of the desert. (See the section on "Desert Driving" in "Customs and Manners in the Arab World," page 8)

• If you're going to be in the country for a month or less, use a U.S. driver's license to rent a car. An International Driver's License can be used indefinitely.

• Remember that driving regulations are enforced more strictly than in some other countries.
• Women should note that it's okay for them to drive alone.

Qatar

Like the Saudis, Qataris are Islamic fundamentalists and very conservative. The emir, who rules the country with an advisory council, runs Qatar like a family business.

When speaking of the country, pronounce its name "Katrr."

IN PUBLIC

• Don't smoke or cross your legs in front of a senior member of the royal family.
• Never photograph any religious activity.
• Women should never go alone to the beach, cinema, *souk* (market), or any place where there will be large crowds. People will stare, and you may be harassed.
• If people suggest visiting a garden, expect a family to take you to their place in the country where they picnic on weekends.
• Don't wear a *thobe* in public. People consider it insulting to see foreigners in their national dress. They would not think you were paying a compliment to the comfort of the *thobe*.
• Remember that prices are fixed at large department stores, but you may get a discount for paying cash for large purchases. Bargain in small shops or in *souks*.

MEALS

Table Manners

• Never offer liquor to a Qatari. Drinking is illegal. Qatar differs from other Gulf States such as Bahrain and the U.A.E. in that it has no bars or licensed hotels.

• If you're invited to dinner, don't expect food to be offered immediately. People usually chat first.

• Don't expect conversation during a meal. People eat quickly so that other guests—junior in position of age—can take their places. Hosts don't always eat with guests. If they do, they eat slowly so that guests will be spared the embarrassment of eating after the host has finished.

• Don't be surprised if a number of people drink coffee from the same cup. Be sure to finish the last drop of coffee before handing the cup back to the server. Otherwise the next person—to whom the server will hand the cup without cleaning it—may have to empty the cup on the carpet before pouring a cup. Be sure to hand the cup

back to the server; don't put it on the table.

HOTELS

• Note that there are several first-class, five-star hotels, but there are also three- and four-star hotels that offer an acceptable standard of comfort and service at a reasonable price.

TIPPING

• Restaurants include a service charge, so no tip is necessary.

• Give porters at airports and hotels QR 2 per bag.

• Don't tip taxi drivers.

• There's no need to tip hotel staff, since a 10% service charge is added to your bill.

• Tip 15% if you hire a guide for the day.

• Give a hairdresser 15%.
• Don't tip gas station attendants.

PRIVATE HOMES

• Recall that invitations from Qataris do not usually include wives. If wives are to be included, they will be mentioned in the invitation.

BUSINESS

Hours

Banks: Saturday to Wednesday, 7:30 to 11:30 A.M., and Thursday, 7:30 to 11:00 A.M.

Businesses: Saturday to Thursday, 7:30 A.M. to noon and 2:30 to 6:00 P.M.

Government Offices: Saturday to Thursday, 6:00 A.M. to 1:00 P.M.

Shops: Saturday to Thursday, 8:00 A.M. to noon and 4:00 to 7:00 P.M. (Markets often stay open until 8:00 P.M.) Though Friday is the weekly holiday, some shops open for a few hours in the morning.

Currency

• The unit of currency is the Qatari *riyal* (abbreviated QR), which is made up of 100 *dirhams*.
• Coins: 5, 10, 25, and 50 *dirhams*.
• Bills: QR 1, 5, 10, 50, 100, 500, and 1,000.

Business Practices

• Make your initial contacts with the Ministry of Commerce in Qatar, after a preliminary discussion with Qatar's embassy in your country. After that, discuss your project with Qatar's Country Officer in the Department of Commerce at your embassy in Doha.
• Don't expect to visit Qatar once, find an agent, leave, and then continue your business via correspondence. Continued personal contact is important to Qataris.
• Be aware that all foreign com-

panies must have a local representative or agent who is a Qatari citizen. The agent makes contacts in the government on your behalf and works with you from the beginning to the end of your project, including the negotiating of the contract.

• Submit bids in both Arabic and English. Use the metric system for any specifications. All official documents must be authenticated in Arabic with a translator's signature.

HOLIDAYS AND SPECIAL OCCASIONS

• In addition to the religious holidays governed by the Muslim calendar, Qatar celebrates the Accession of Shaikh Khalifa (Feb. 22) and Independence Day (Sept. 3).

TRANSPORTATION

Public Transportation

• Taxis are the only form of public transportation; there is no rail or bus service in Qatar. Taxis are orange and white with a Taxi sign on the roof. They have meters, but drivers often don't use them. Ask at your hotel what the fare ought to be, and negotiate the fare in advance. If you don't tell the driver not to, he may pick up passengers during your trip. Women should be sure to forbid the driver to pick up passengers—and should always sit in the back seat.

Driving

• Avoid driving. Qatar is one of the worst countries in which to drive. Drivers are often arrogant, don't obey traffic signals, and may try to run your car off the road.

• Be aware that to rent a car you must have an International Driver's License, a passport, and a letter from a Qatari associate stating the length of your stay.

• Note that street signs and instructions will be in both English and Arabic.

LEGAL MATTERS, SAFETY, AND HEALTH

• Realize that all non-Muslims must have permission to visit a mosque. Ask at your hotel where to obtain permission.

• Qatar has *very* strict regulations regarding alcohol: (1) It is an offense for a foreigner to give or sell liquor to a Qatari. (2) Only a few permit holders are allowed to buy alcohol. (3) Hotels serve liquor to hotel guests only.

• To avoid the risk of bilharzia, a parasitic disease, don't wade in, swim in, or drink water from streams, ponds, or lakes.

• Be aware that anyone entering Qatar to work or study must have an AIDS test. Tests made in the U.S. within the previous six months are acceptable.

United Arab Emirates

Tucked between Oman and Qatar along the Gulf coast, the United Arab Emirates (U.A.E.) consists of seven states, each of which regulates its own business affairs.

CONVERSATION

• Be conscious that women are more sophisticated and more widely traveled than women in many other countries. Use travel as an "ice breaker" in conversing with a woman.

TELEPHONES

• To make operator-assisted calls, go to the central post office organization (ETISALAT), which has branches in every area of every city throughout the Emirates. All staff can communicate in English. International calls (all International Operators speak English) can be made by using locally purchased, unit-based cards for pay phones, or you can pay directly at the ETISALAT branch upon completing the call. The unitary cards are very efficient and can be used anywhere in the seven Emirate states.

• Look for pay phones accepting the unitary cards on nearly every major road or shopping area in large cities and towns. You can dial directly using these phones and the card, or you can go through the operator. The cards are available at most major supermarkets, at stores advertising their availability, or at ETISALAT branches.

• Note that public phones also accept coins of 50 *fils*, Dh 1, and Dh 5. Since local calls are free,

shop owners will often allow you to use the phone for a local call.

• Remember that telephone numbers are changed frequently, and the incidence of wrong numbers is high.

IN PUBLIC

• Foreign men should never stare at, speak to, or photograph an Arab woman. Further, they should not be seen alone in public with a woman to whom they aren't related.

• Realize that there are no mail deliveries within the U.A.E. All mail must be sent to a post office box, which people wanting to receive mail must rent. (Don't plan to get mail at your hotel.)

• A woman can order an alcoholic drink in a hotel if her Arab host orders one. The U.A.E. is more liberal about drinking than some other Arab countries.

• Never whistle in public.

• Bargain in bazaars and shops, but not in large stores or boutiques (more elegant than regular shops).

• Women can feel free to go to public beaches. However, they should be sure to wear a one-piece bathing suit, never a bikini.

DRESS

• Note that native men wear a white *dishdasha* at all times, whether the occasion is casual or formal. For major public functions, leading figures will wear a dark robe called a *bisht* over the *dishdasha*.

MEALS

Eating Out

• Expect alcohol to be available in some restaurants in Abu Dhabi. In other areas, only hotels—no restaurants—can sell liquor.

HOTELS

• Realize that hotels are luxurious, but very expensive.
• Book a room well in advance, and ask for a telexed or faxed confirmation.

TIPPING

• Tip 10% at restaurants.
• Don't tip taxi drivers.
• If an office boy runs an errand for you, give him Dh 10 to 20.
• If someone washes your car in a parking lot (they probably won't ask you first if you want your car washed, but they will expect to be paid): Dh 10.
• For a day's service, tip a guide 15%.
• Give a hairdresser 15%.
• Don't tip gas station attendants.

BUSINESS

Hours

Banks: In Abu Dhabi, Saturday to Wednesday, 8:00 A.M. to noon, and Thursday, 8:00 to 11:00 A.M. In the Northern Emirates, Saturday to Thursday, 8:00 A.M. to noon.

Businesses: In Abu Dhabi, during the summer, Saturday to Thursday, 8:00 A.M. to 1:00 P.M. and 4:00 to 8:00 P.M.; in winter, Saturday to Thursday, 8:00 A.M. to 1:00 P.M. and 3:30 to 7:30 P.M. In the Northern Emirates, Saturday to Wednesday, 8:00 A.M. to 1:00 P.M. and 3:00 or 4:00 to 6:00 P.M., and Thursday, 8:00 A.M. to noon. (Though businesses are nominally open on Thursday afternoon, it's difficult to get any business done.)

Government Offices: In winter, Saturday to Wednesday, 7:30 A.M. to 1:30 P.M., and Thursday, 7:30 to 12:30 P.M.; in the summer, Saturday to Wednesday, 7:30 A.M. to 1:30 P.M., and Thursday, 7:00 to 11:00 A.M.

Shops: In Abu Dhabi, during the summer, Saturday to Thursday, 8:00 A.M. to 1:00 P.M. and 4:00 to 8:00 P.M.; in the winter, Saturday to Thursday, 8:00 A.M. to 1:00 P.M. and 3:30 to 7:30 P.M. In the Northern Emirates, Saturday to Wednesday, 8:00 A.M. to 1:00 P.M. and 3:00 or 4:00 to 6:00 P.M., and Thursday, 8:00 A.M. to noon.

Currency

• The unit of currency is the U.A.E. *dirham* (abbreviated Dh), made up of 100 *fils*.
• Coins: 1, 5, 25, 50, and 100 *fils*.
• Bills: Dh 5, 10, 50, 100, 500, and 1,000.
• Note that credit cards are accepted by expensive hotels, restaurants, car rental agencies, and some—but not all—shops. American Express and Diners Club are accepted in more places than Visa and Mastercard.

Business Practices

• Send details of your planned visit ahead of time to the Federal Chambers of Commerce in Abu Dhabi and Dubai. Your letter probably won't be answered, since staffs are very small; however, your letter will acquaint officials with you and your firm. Visit the Chambers when you arrive in the U.A.E.

• Also let the Commercial Attache of your country's embassy know of your impending arrival.

• Plan to send the same person on each visit to the U.A.E. People like to deal with one company and with one person in that company. They tend to stick to a familiar supplier, even if other companies offer lower prices.

• Apply for your visa well in advance, since visa policies fluctuate. If you arrive at the U.A.E. airport without a valid visa, you will be placed on the next plane out of the country. Your only way to avoid deportation would be to be met by a local businessman with an approved letter of sponsorship. Don't take the risk of arriving without a visa in the hope that your contact will arrive and "bail you out."

• For doing business in Abu Dhabi, hire a local agent who is an Abu Dhabi national. (The law requires that you do so.)

• Be aware that Dubai law does not require you to have a local agent to obtain government contracts. However, an agent or partner in Dubai will be an advantage, since he will be able to supply contacts and simplify administrative details.

• Realize that, though Arabic is the official language, English is widely used in commercial circles.

If people don't speak English, they will have an interpreter. Abu Dhabi law requires that bids be in English. Most foreign companies also use English in Dubai.

• Use metric and British imperial measurement systems for specifications.

• Note that the widespread use of English comes about because fewer than 20% of the population are native citizens. Most of the workforce comes from Pakistan, India, Iran, and Western Europe. In general, Iranians and Omanis do the manual labor, Indians are the shopkeepers, Pakistanis the craftsmen, and Palestinians the government officials.

• Acquire a copy of the telephone directory of European and American executives published every two years by the British Bank of the Middle East. It's very valuable, since telephone numbers change frequently. The directory is available at branches of the bank in the U.K. or U.A.E.

• Expect many businesses and better hotels to have fax machines.

• If you're doing business in Dubai or Abu Dhabi, use a middleman to introduce you to those who might go into a joint venture with you and to arrange deals. Your agent should be someone living in the U.A.E. or someone who has had close relationships with the people with whom you hope to do business.

• Note that government officials in the town of Sharjah don't want to deal with middlemen.

• Be aware that business can take a long time, despite the fact that there are fewer formalities (the ritual coffee) than in other Gulf States. Experienced personnel are in short supply, and there are only a few decision makers who handle dealings with foreign companies.

• Be punctual, but don't be surprised if businessmen from the U.A.E. aren't. Westerners are expected to be on time and reliable.

• Go to the U.A.E. with specific proposals for the local market. Don't be surprised if local businessmen don't immediately jump to buy your product or service. Use patience and tactful persuasion.

• Keep proposals, negotiations, and contracts simple.

• Realize that bribery is considered a natural part of doing business. Be very discreet. Never ask how much to give. Ask if the sum you have in mind would be acceptable.

• If you invite someone to a meal, don't be surprised if he doesn't turn up—or if he turns up bringing several friends with him.

HOLIDAYS AND SPECIAL OCCASIONS

• In addition to the holidays celebrated according to the Muslim calendar, people in the U.A.E. celebrate New Year's Day (Jan. 1), Accession of the Ruler of Abu Dhabi (Aug. 6), and National Day (Dec. 2).

TRANSPORTATION

Public Transportation

• Don't expect to find train service.

• Note that buses run within cities and between cities. They can be *very* crowded. (There is a luxury bus service between Abu Dhabi and Dubai.)

• On local buses within cities, women sit in the front and men in the back.

• Look for taxis on the main streets of most cities. In Abu Dhabi, the taxis use meters; elsewhere, negotiate the fare in advance. There will be extra charges for being picked up at your hotel and for night trips.

• Note that most street taxis will make journeys anywhere, and drivers will bargain for fares before starting out. Ask at your hotel what the fare should be. Local taxis cruise the street and stop if you flag them. They have a "taxi hat" in English and are clearly marked. They are usually—but not always —metered.

• As an alternative, go to one of the two major municipal taxi stations. There you can book "local" taxis for a journey anywhere in the country. They look like any taxi on the street, but they run exclusively on long-distance routes. They are a cheap, convenient way to get around.

• Keep in mind that local and long-distance taxis are not marked differently.

• For more comfort on a long trip, arrange for one of the private taxis. They are comfortable and air-conditioned for the long journeys in which they specialize. You'll find them listed in the English/Arabic Yellow Pages and in the daily English newspapers.

Again, your hotel's staff can advise on the service to call. Rates are agreed upon before the trip.

Driving

• Use a U.S. or International Driver's License to obtain a temporary seven-day U.A.E. driver's license at car rental agencies.

• Be aware that there are many hazards in driving in the U.A.E.: (1) You'll find road works at every corner. (2) Bumps have been installed to reduce speeds, but they have only made driving more erratic. (3) Many drivers ignore red lights. (4) Though driving is theoretically on the right, many drivers ignore the correct lanes.

LEGAL MATTERS, SAFETY, AND HEALTH

• If you have a passport that contains evidence of a visit to Israel or South Africa, expect to be denied entry to the U.A.E. If, for example, you traveled to Israel a year before your visit and the Israeli stamp is in your passport, apply for a new passport before visiting the U.A.E.

• Be aware that drinking is legal for non-Muslims. Most hotels have bars, and liquor is freely obtainable in retail stores, and no permit is needed to purchase it. Wine is expensive, but hard liquor and beer are relatively inexpensive.

• Be conscious of the offenses that could lead to imprisonment or deportation: (1) drinking and driving, (2) involvement with narcotics, (3) adultery, or (4) homosexuality.

• Realize that if you want a work or residency permit, you must have an AIDS test on arrival in the U.A.E.

IRAQ

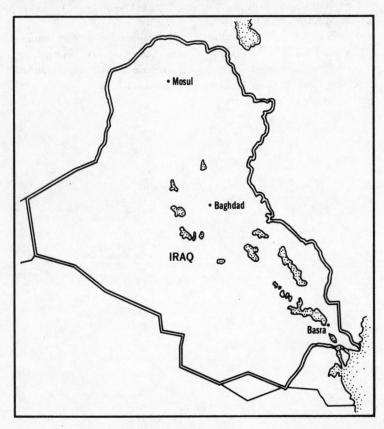

Iraq has been described as a pre-Gorbachev Soviet Union—an authoritarian police state, complete with citizens being followed, having their phones bugged, and not allowed access to foreigners.

As this is written, relations between Iraq and Western nations are almost non-existent. However, as any student of politics knows, things change—sometimes in ways that no one could anticipate.

While the country resonates with names we all remember from ancient (and now modern) history—Tigris, Euphrates, Baghdad, Babylon—its socialist philosophy in the modern era has made it the least traditional of the Arab countries. For example, the country undertook a massive literacy campaign with severe penalties for any man who would not allow his wife to attend classes (his water and electricity were cut off). The population is now 86 percent literate.

GREETINGS

CONVERSATION

• Shake hands when greeting and departing. Good friends of the same sex kiss on both cheeks. Men and women shake hands. When departing, older people often give a sort of salute—first putting the right hand at an angle almost touching the right forehead and then placing the right hand on the heart. Foreigners need not respond with the same gesture—which also means "No, thank you."

• If you're meeting a small group for the first time, expect to be introduced to each person individually. If you know everyone in the group, you can greet the whole group with one "Hello."

• Use first names as soon as you're introduced.

• Remember that the only titles used are Professor and Doctor (for both M.D. and Ph.D.). In introducing a professor or doctor, use the title plus the last name.

• Investigate the rich history of Iraq before visiting the country. The roots of Western civilization and the city as we know it began between the Tigris and the Euphrates. Proud of their cultural heritage, Iraqis are very interested in archeology and architecture (one of the country's flourishing fields).

• Begin conversations with impersonal subjects—sports, books, archeology, or architecture.

• Discuss your work and areas of the country you have visited. With women, bring up clothes, cooking, shopping, and very general questions about the family. Both men and women welcome questions about their children.

• Avoid talking about policies regarding birth control. Because 500,000 men were killed in the war with Iran, Iraq is trying to increase its population. Should you bring up issues relating to birth control, you will be thought of as naive and insensitive to the country's war losses.

• Avoid discussions of religion. There is a tremendous diversity of religions in Iraq: half of the Muslims are Sunni and half are Shi'ia; various Christian sects and denominations account for 5% of the population, and there is a small Jewish community as well. The country is striving to be a modern, pluralistic society with religion strictly a private matter. If you ask people what their religion is, you'll be regarded as ignorant.

• Also avoid very personal questions, gossip of any kind, and politics (unless you're talking with a relative).

• Realize that men may be more likely to have a conversation with a woman in Iraq than in some other countries. The same subjects are appropriate as in a conversation with a man.

TELEPHONES

• Don't look for public telephones. There aren't any. Go to the post office to make local and long-distance calls if you're not in a home or your hotel.

IN PUBLIC

• Expect to find much less formality in Iraq than in other countries in the Arab world. Flowery expressions and questions regarding your health and your family aren't common in Iraq as they are in other parts of the Arab world.

• Do nothing that would attract the attention of the police. Don't open a map—even a tourist map—in public. Don't photograph anything that could be even remotely connected to the police or the military.

• Never point the soles of your shoes at another person. For example, don't rest one ankle on the other knee.

• When offered food or drink, refuse the first time in order to be polite.

• Look for public bathrooms only in hotels, restaurants, and shopping centers, the only places you'll find public toilets.

• Don't expect to find *hammams* (public baths) in Iraq.

• Feel free to bargain almost everywhere other than fixed-price grocery stores.

DRESS

• Prepare to see men and women of the upper and middle class elegantly dressed in Western style. With their Western-style clothes, some men still wear the red-and-white-checked *kafiyyah* (scarf) on their heads. Only peasant women wear the *abah*—the head-to-ankle covering with only the face exposed.

• For casual wear, jeans are acceptable for both sexes, but not shorts.

• When invited to a meal in a home for the first time, men should wear suits and ties and women a dress or a dressy skirt and blouse.

• To business meetings, men should wear suits and ties and women suits or dresses (a long skirt isn't necessary). Outfits with jackets are appropriate because they look professional and are not revealing.

• In no circumstances should women wear sleeveless tops or low-cut, revealing dresses or blouses.

• If you're visiting Iraq during the winter (December, January, and February), expect to find offices and houses very cold. Dress accordingly.

MEALS

Hours and Foods

Breakfast: Between 7:00 and 8:00 A.M. There will be bread (pita, a circular puffy bread, or one similar to French bread), cheese with *dibis* (a date syrup), butter, boiled or fried eggs, plain tea, or milk.

Lunch: About 1:00 to 2:00 P.M. There will probably be a stew of lamb, vegetables, tomatoes, fresh lemon, and garlic—served with rice. Accompaniments will be salad, bread, and then fruit.

Tea: 5:00 or 6:00 P.M. A snack—bread and cheese or *kulai-*

cha (dough filled with walnuts and sugar or dates and then baked in the oven)—with tea flavored with cardamom. In summer, the snack might be watermelon served with white or yellow cheese.

Dinner: Some time between 8:00 and 10:00 P.M., unless there are guests, in which case dinner will be at 10:30 or 11:00 P.M. in the summer (June through August) and 9:30 or 10:00 in the winter (December through February). A typical meal will begin with *hummus* or tabbouleh or *baba ganouzh* (see "Specialties" for descriptions of these dishes) or *talattouri*—yogurt mixed with cucumbers and olive oil, eaten in individual dishes with a spoon. (Before a special meal, there will also be bowls of olives, chick-peas with olive oil and lemon, potato salad, pistachio nuts, and *hub*—a mixture of several kinds of melon and squash seeds.) Following will be something grilled—kebab (skewers with ground lamb mixed with parsley and onion) or *tika* (like shish kebab but usually with whole pieces of lamb or chicken) or *bourag* or *kubbat haleb* (see "Specialties" for descriptions of these dishes)—and salad.

• Expect rice, either plain (called *timman*), or cooked in chicken stock with saffron, ground lamb, and almonds (*timman z'af-*

faran), to be part of every lunch or dinner.

• Don't expect to be served beef—Iraqis rarely eat it—but there will often be lamb, chicken (grilled, fried, or stewed), or fish.

• Leave room for the fruit that is usually served after a meal—melons in summer (June through August) and bananas and oranges in winter (December through February). For special occasions, there will be a dessert—*baqlawa* (like Greek *baklava*), *zilabiya* (a sweet rosette of pastry soaked in syrup), *mahalaby* (a pudding made of rice, milk, sugar, and rosewater), *zurda halib* (layers of *mahalaby* in a bowl, alternating with date syrup). After the meal there will also be small glasses (called *istakhan*) of sweet tea. You may find tea spilled into the saucer—to signify the generosity of your host.

Beverages: With a meal, water. In the summer, a drink called *leben matrook,* yogurt blended with water and ice. Avoid this drink, and ask for a soda instead.

• Note that the popular alcoholic drink is *arak*, made from dates or grapes and flavored with aniseed. There are also locally produced red and white wines.

• Tea is the most popular hot drink, with coffee second.

• If you're invited to dinner in a home, there will be soft drinks, and, depending on the family, there may be alcoholic beverages.

• Remember that alcohol is usually served only at parties for both sexes. There won't be liquor at an all-female party.

Table Manners

• Remember that alcohol is usually served only at parties for men or for both sexes. There won't be liquor at an all-female party.

• If you're invited to dinner with a group of people, don't be surprised if the table isn't large enough to seat everyone. In that case it's usual for women to be seated and the men to eat standing. Another solution to the seating problem may be a buffet dinner.

• Expect all the dishes to be served at the same time on platters in the center of the table. Each diner has an individual plate with a spoon or with fork and spoon. Only a few dishes are eaten with the hand—such as *tishreeb*, bread soaked in lamb stock and eaten with yogurt and garlic.

• Realize that older people may eat with their hands while the younger generation uses utensils.

• Eat rice with a spoon.

• Start with small servings, because people will push you to eat, and there's no telling how many courses there may be. When you're

finished, state *very firmly* that you have had enough.

• At the end of the meal, expect to adjourn to the living room for Turkish-style coffee and pastries.

• When you leave, don't be surprised if your hostess sprinkles rosewater on your head from a silver decanter. This gesture signifies that you should take the pleasure of the visit away with you.

Eating Out

• Remember that Iraqis rarely go out to eat except on special occasions.

• Don't expect to see Iraqis in restaurants before 10:00 P.M., though the restaurants begin serving dinner earlier.

• Look for both Western and Arabic foods in first-class restaurants and in hotel dining rooms. There are also Chinese and Italian restaurants as well as special steak restaurants.

• Don't look for menus to be posted in restaurant windows.

• Note that people don't join others at a table in a restaurant.

• To call the waiter, say *"Garçon."*

• Don't even try to split the check. The one who invites pays for the group. Invite your host to a meal to reciprocate.

• Women traveling alone should

note that they can eat in restaurants alone and go around freely during the day—but not at night, since women alone at night are considered prostitutes. Have your evening meal in the hotel dining room.

Specialties:

Appetizers: hummus—a paste of crushed chick-peas, lemon juice, garlic, and parsley, served as a dip with bread; *baba ganouzh*—an eggplant and sesame puree with garlic, lemon, olive oil, and parsley, served as a dip with bread; tabbouleh—a salad made of *burghul* (cracked wheat), parsley, spring onions, mint, olive oil, lemon juice, and tomatoes.

Meat Dishes: Kubba burghul —cracked wheat that is mixed with minced meat. The mixture is flattened and stuffed with meat, nuts, raisins, onion, parsley, and spices, rolled into balls and boiled. *Dolma*—stuffed vine leaves, cabbage, onions, squash, or eggplant filled with rice, ground meat, and spices. *Guss*—slices of meat arranged in a cone shape and grilled on a vertical spit. *Batata charp*— potato cakes filled with spicy meat or a tomato and parsley stuffing. *Murag*—meat stew of beef or lamb, onions, tomatoes, and allspice. *Kubbat haleb*—ground meat

and rice mixed together with spices, rolled out flat and stuffed (with more meat, raisins, nuts, and saffron), then rolled up, dipped in egg, and fried. *Bourag* —thin dough filled with meat and fried. *Tika*—cubes of marinated chicken or lamb grilled on skewers.

Lamb Specialties: lahmi b'ajeen —a pizzalike crust topped with tomatoes, ground lamb, and parsley; *hamuth heloo*—lamb with cinnamon, apricots, yellow raisins, onion, soaked and pureed dried dates; *mumbar*—lamb and rice sausage; *tashreeb*—stewed lamb shanks and tripe prepared with dried limes, chick-peas, and tomatoes; stuffed *quzi*—grilled whole lamb stuffed with rice, almonds, raisins, and spices.

Fish: Masgouf—a fish from the Tigris River. It's split down the middle, opened like a fan, and grilled in the open, leaning against a tepeelike structure. It's often served with lime chutney and Indian curries.

Salads: Look for salads to be made with date vinegar and a popular herb called *rashad,* which looks like coarse dill and has a peppery flavor. A popular salad is *jajik*—yogurt, chopped cucumber, garlic, and mint or dill.

Sweets: Zlabiya—a sweet pastry rosette in syrup. *Kolaicha*—sweet cakes made of barley flour, sugar, oil, and cardamom seed. They are made for the *Id* (the breaking of the fast after Ramadan) and are also a common dessert. *Leban*—a thick yogurt, served with dates, sugar, or date syrup. In the summer (June through August), it's eaten for breakfast.

TIPPING

• Give porters 250 *fils* to 1 *dinar* for each person's luggage.

• Tip taxi drivers 150 to 500 *fils*, depending on the length of the journey.

• Leave waiters 2 to 4 *dinars*, depending on the size of the check. There is no specific percentage you're expected to leave.

• Don't tip gas station attendants.

• Give hairdressers 250 *fils* to 1 *dinar*.

• Leave the person who cleans your hotel room 1 *dinar* per day.

• Tip guides 10%.

HOTELS

• Realize that you cannot pay your hotel bill in Iraqi *dinar*. You must use dollars, traveler's checks, or a credit card.

• Note that there are five luxury hotels in Baghdad. Each has 24-hour room service as well as telex facilities.

PRIVATE HOMES

• Feel free to drop in if you're a close friend; otherwise, call in advance. Keep a "drop in" visit short.

• Don't call people at home between 4:00 and 6:00 P.M. because they will be resting during those hours.

• If you're staying with a family, expect schedules to be flexible. Your hosts may accompany you on sightseeing trips, or they may invite friends over to entertain you. You can also go around on your own.

• If you are a family's guest and some people from your country are in the area, feel free to ask if you can invite them over for coffee, but don't ask to extend the hospitality to a full evening or overnight.

• If your visit is for just a few days, expect any offer to help with housework, cooking, or food shopping to be refused.

• Ask your hostess when it is convenient for you to have a bath or shower (showers are more common than baths). In some homes, there will be constant hot water. In others, water must be heated. If there is only one bathroom and the family is large, try to ration yourself to a bath or shower every other day.

• Be aware that many homes have two separate toilets—one Western style and one Turkish style (a hole in the floor). Older Iraqis usually prefer the Turkish-style toilet.

Gifts: When invited to dinner, bring cookies or chocolates.

• From abroad, bring cigarettes and liquor (if you're *sure* that the recipients drink).

• Note that during Muslim holidays (at the end of Ramadan, for example), it's customary to give money or gifts to the children of friends. To young children give the equivalent of $1.00; to older children, give the equivalent of $5.00.

• Don't be offended if your hostess takes your gift and puts it aside without opening it. That is the accepted response.

BUSINESS

Hours

• Remember that the weekly closing is on Friday and that offices and banks close 30 minutes earlier in the summer (June through August).

Banks: Saturday to Wednesday, 7:30 A.M. to 2:00 P.M., and Thursday, 7:30 A.M. to 1:00 P.M.

Businesses: Saturday to Thursday, 9:00 A.M. to 1:00 P.M. and 4:00 to 7:00 P.M.

Government Offices: Saturday to Wednesday, 8:00 A.M. to 3:00 P.M., and Thursday, 8:00 A.M. to 1:00 P.M.

Shops: Saturday to Thursday, 9:00 A.M. to 1:00 P.M. and 4:00 to 8:00 P.M. (Many shops do not close for lunch and remain open until 10:00 P.M.)

Currency

• The monetary unit is the Iraqi *dinar* (abbreviated ID), which is made up of 1,000 *fils*.

• Coins are 5, 10, 25, 50, 100, 250, and 500 *fils* as well as ID 1.

• Bills are ID ¼, ½, 1, 5, 10, and 25.

• Keep in mind that credit cards are accepted in major hotels but not in shops or restaurants.

Business Practices

• Get in touch with the United States-Iraq Business Forum in Washington, D.C. The staff can be very helpful to anyone hoping to do business in Iraq. Other good sources of contacts are the Iraqi Embassy and the U.S. Department of Commerce. They will help you learn about the legal system and find an Iraqi lawyer. The lawyer can help you through the maze of legal steps about acquiring an agent—a local person who will expedite commercial planning.

• Consider having a booth at the Baghdad International Fair, which takes place every year in October or November. It's a good way to make contacts in Iraq.

• Prepare to make several trips to Iraq if you're proposing a major transaction. Iraqis will want to be sure they know the person with whom they are dealing.

• Realize that foreign businesses must deal directly with the Iraqi government. The government purchases 90% of the foreign goods and services sold in Iraq, so you'll be negotiating your deal with the Iraqi government. There are very few business opportunities for foreign contractors in the private sector.

• Keep in mind that you'll find some ministries centralized—with decisions made by a few people at the top—while others are decentralized. Try to begin by dealing with the Director General of any ministry with which you wish to do business.

• Be aware that to open an office in Iraq you must have a contract or business with the Iraqi government. After establishing the business relationship, you will register with the Minister of Planning and be given permission to open your office.

• Don't try to get an appointment confirmed in advance from abroad. Send a telex or letter stating when you plan to be in Iraq, and then call as soon as you arrive. (Responses to letters may take a long time, but if the government is interested, you'll get one eventually.)

• Try to arrange your business in Iraq for the months of November through April. Many busi-

nessmen vacation between June and September.

• Realize that major four-star hotels have fax machines, but most businesses do not. It's best to send messages via telex.

• Be aware that business—especially with government officials —begins as early as 7:00 A.M. People work until 3:00, then return home for lunch, and nap until 6:00 P.M. Some high officials may return to work from 6:00 to 8:00 P.M.

• Expect Iraqi technicians and officials to speak English. Such people are highly educated, and English is widely taught in Iraq.

• Don't feel you have to bring business cards translated into Arabic. Do include on the business cards your telex and fax numbers. However, don't be surprised if your Iraqi counterpart doesn't offer a business card.

• Be on time for appointments. Unlike people in other countries in the area, Iraqis are punctual and expect others to be also.

• Realize that at a business meeting you may be introduced to people by their titles, and you may never find out the names of the people with whom you're doing business.

• At meetings with government officials, be prepared to listen to a speech about the glories of socialism before you begin to discuss business.

• Don't be surprised if you're *not* offered a drink at a government office.

• Keep in mind that Iraqis don't indulge in—and don't tolerate— the elaborate, flowery language and use of hyperbole common in other Arab countries.

• If you're doing business with the government, prepare to cope with constant bureaucratic regulations. However, government officials do work long hours, and they work conscientiously, so problems may be resolved more quickly than in other countries.

• Make no promises that you aren't absolutely certain you can keep. You *must* be able to deliver what you promise and on the *exact* date for which you've promised it.

• Realize that Iraqis are honest and straightforward, and they will not demand additions or changes once an agreement has been reached.

• Be patient. Decisions are made slowly, and there's nothing you can do to speed up the process.

• Never try to bribe anyone. Iraq has very strong anti-corruption policies, and an Iraqi official could be executed for taking a bribe.

• Note that Iraq has had equal rights for women for 20 years. Women are managers, lawyers, government officials, archeologists, professors, architects, and radio and TV personalities. West-ern women should have no problems doing business in Iraq.

• Expect business entertaining to be in a restaurant rather than in an Iraqi's home. Don't anticipate discussing business. Meals with business colleagues are social occasions.

• Remember that when entertaining a foreign businesswoman, Iraqis usually include their wives in the party. A foreign businessman traveling with his wife could ask, "Is it permissible to bring spouses to this function?" This will probably signal the Iraqi to bring his wife. If a foreign businessman is alone, wives won't be included.

• To please Iraqis, invite them to a restaurant at night (as a social occasion). Ask at your hotel about special and popular restaurants.

Gifts: In general, avoid giving business gifts other than books. (Books aren't regarded as gifts that might compromise someone.) Books are especially popular with educated Iraqis because they have not had access to European and American books for a long time. From the U.S., bring books with pictures of your area, books on art, on American folk crafts, or short stories by American authors.

• A foreign businesswoman can give an Iraqi woman silk scarves by American designers, small leather change purses, or any kind of folk craft—such as a quilt. Men should, however, stick to books. A foreign businesswoman who wishes to give a gift to an Iraqi businessman should give a book.

• If an Iraqi *insists* on paying for a gift, take the money. If he doesn't pay for the item, he may be violating laws against accepting bribes.

HOLIDAYS AND SPECIAL OCCASIONS

For observances governed by the Muslim calendar, see "Introduction," pages 1–7.

• Expect to find banks, offices, and shops closed on the following secular holidays: New Year's Day (Jan. 1); Army Day (Jan. 6); Baathist Revolution of 1963 (Feb. 8); Labor Day (May 1); Republic Day (July 14); Peaceful Revolutionary Day, commemorating events of 1968 (July 17).

• Note that July 14 and July 17

are celebrated with fireworks and are not holidays that families celebrate together.

TRANSPORTATION

Public Transportation

• Don't look for subways in Iraq. There are none.

• On buses within cities, buy your ticket when you get on. You don't need exact change. There are no inspectors checking on payment of fares. These buses are not air-conditioned and are often crowded. It's best to avoid these buses if you don't know Arabic, since all signs are in Arabic.

• Get a cab on the street, or you can call one from your hotel. Taxis are red and white. Though many have meters, fares can also be negotiated in advance.

• Consider hiring a car and driver or a taxi at one of the major hotels. Taxis are inexpensive and plentiful, and parking in Baghdad is very difficult. Hiring a car and driver is relatively expensive, but if you have several appointments on the same day, the cost will be worth it.

• Note that trains have two classes, first class and "regular" class. For overnight journeys, the first class has compartments with beds and air-conditioning but no bathrooms in compartments. Reserve your ticket either in person or by phone at the Baghdad International Station.

• Consider using the plane service between Baghdad, Basrah, and Mosul.

Driving

• There are car rental agencies in Baghdad. To drive in Iraq, bring an International Driver's License.

• Remember that Iraqi law requires wearing a seat belt.

• If you drive outside Baghdad, take a generous supply of drinking water with you.

• Note that most gas stations are self-service, and long lines are common.

• Realize that there are on-the-spot fines for violations, but police may be easier on you as a foreigner.

• Don't offer a policeman a bribe.

LEGAL MATTERS, HEALTH, AND SAFETY

• Don't bring in or take out videocassettes. Customs agents may suspect that they contain political material.

• Realize that informal meetings with Iraqis will be extremely difficult since people can get into trouble with authorities.

• To visit a mosque, first obtain permission from the Ministry of Culture.

• Note that liquor is available throughout the country in licensed hotels, restaurants, bars, and "casinos" (outdoor restaurants).

• Drugs (including antibiotics) are readily available at pharmacies without prescription. Nevertheless, it's a good idea to bring an ample supply of any prescription drugs you may be taking. Be sure to bring any contraceptives you think you'll need. It will be very difficult to find them in Iraq, since the country is very "pro-birth" in its desire to replace the vast numbers of men lost in the Iran-Iraq War.

• Women should note that both sanitary napkins and tampons are available in pharmacies.

• Women should travel with another woman or a man. Otherwise you will raise a great deal of curiosity, since there are very few unescorted foreign women traveling in Iraq. If a woman and man who aren't married are traveling together, they should pretend to be married during their stay in Iraq.

• Women should not take taxis at night. Stay in your hotel, and eat your evening meal in your hotel dining room.

• Don't forget that if you plan to stay more than five days, you must have an AIDS test; the fine for arriving without one is $1,600.00. A test performed in the U.S. may or may not be accepted. The cost for a test performed in Iraq is $330.00.

Because of the volatile political situation in the Middle East, be sure to phone the number given in the Introduction under "Legal Matters, Health, and Safety" to learn whether or not if is safe to travel to Iraq, and, if so, what precautions to take.

ISRAEL

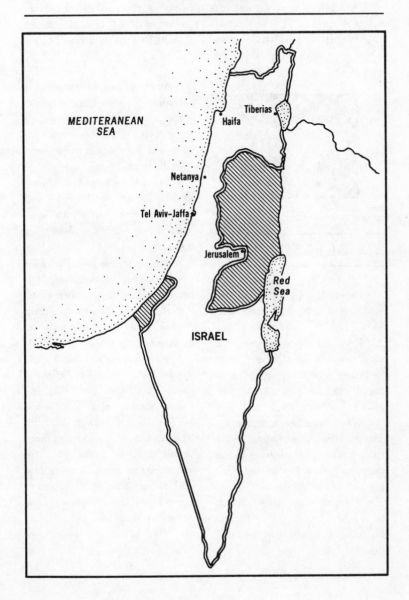

MEDITERANEAN
SEA

Haifa
Tiberias

Netanya

Tel Aviv-Jaffa

Jerusalem

Red
Sea

ISRAEL

If America is the "melting pot" of the Western Hemisphere, Israel is the "melting pot" of the Middle East. Since the country's founding, Jews from all parts of the world have immigrated to the country.

When you meet people native to the country, they will identify themselves as "*sabras*." The term means "prickly pear," a fruit of the cactus. Like the prickly pear, Israelis pride themselves on a tough exterior beyond which is a warm, hospitable interior.

GREETINGS

• Expect Israelis to be very informal and to use first names as soon as you're introduced.

• Keep in mind that Israelis are extremely demonstrative. Both sexes hug and kiss in greeting—members of their own sex as well as the opposite sex.

• When meeting someone for the first time, shake hands, unless the person is very religious and of the opposite sex. In that case, simply say, "How do you do?"

• Women often shake hands with other women. Wait for the Israeli woman to extend her hand first.

• At parties, expect the host to introduce guests to one another. However, *sabras* usually introduce themselves, while non-native Israelis wait for the host to make the introductions.

• Use titles—Mr., Mrs., Miss, Doctor (M.D. or Ph.D.), and Professor—until an Israeli suggests using first names, as most will very quickly.

• Make sure that you treat older people respectfully. (Among Oriental Jews, family members often kiss the hand of the oldest male relative, a custom a foreigner is not expected to observe.)

• Note that *shalom* (shah-lóme), which means "peace," is the Israeli "hello" and "good-bye." The informal Arabic "hello" and "good-bye" is *ahalan sahalan* (ah-hah-laĥn sah-hah-laĥn). Use this form if you know an Arab well. The formal Arabic expression is *salam aleikum* (sah-láhm ah-lay-kóom).

• When leaving a person or a group, shake hands.

CONVERSATION

• Don't be surprised to be asked very personal questions—even by someone whom you've just met—e.g., "What is your salary?" "How much do you pay for rent?" "How much did you pay for your shirt?" Assuming that you don't care to answer such questions, try to change the subject or be evasive. In response to the questions about money, be vague. "Just enough" or "Not very much" may discourage the questioner. On the other side of the coin, Israelis may share confidences and intimate details of their lives shortly after meeting you.

• If you are a foreign Jew, don't bring up how much you may have helped Israel with donations. You may prompt a response such as, "I gave my son."

• Avoid voicing your opinion about the political situation unless you are a very, very close friend. Many people have lost sons in the fighting, and your views may suggest that you think they died in vain. A good general rule is to avoid bringing up politics or religion, though Israelis don't shy from discussing those subjects.

• Be careful about telling jokes until you know people and their background well. Many Israelis don't understand American humor.

• Good topics of conversation: your country of origin, general economics, and soccer (the most popular sport). If you know about music, bring it up. Many Israelis are enthusiastic concertgoers.

TELEPHONES

• Look for public phone booths on the street. You can also ask to use the phone in a shop or cafe and then pay the proprietor.

• Note that instructions for the use of public phones are in both English and Hebrew.

• For public telephones, buy tokens—called *assimonim* (ah-see-mo-néem) at post offices, hostels, hotel desks, newsstands, and central bus stations.

• Keep in mind that local calls last for six minutes. There is no tone signal to warn you that your time is up. You can insert another token and call back, or you can insert several tokens at the beginning of your call to prevent being cut off.

• When you're calling from a phone booth, the accepted practice is to first repeat the number of the phone from which you are calling so that the other party can call you back if your time runs out.

• For distant area codes within Israel, a token may last only 20 seconds. (Israelis usually carry bags of tokens for calling outside the local area—and also because the phone system is so erratic.)

• Dial 14 for telephone number information.

• To make a long-distance call overseas from a booth, call Operator 18, who will place the call for you. You must know the country code and area code. In homes and almost all hotels, you can dial international calls directly. Main post offices have special booths for overseas calls. (You don't need coins for these phones.)

• Note that you can also use a telephone credit card from your country.

IN PUBLIC

• People tend to be more polite and less bureaucratic if you speak English rather than Hebrew.

• If you speak Hebrew, be very careful not to make any derogatory remarks about Arabs. One may be standing near you, and most Arabs in Israel speak and understand Hebrew.

• If you see C.E. after a date— e.g., 1950 C.E.—it means "Common Era," a designation used instead of A.D. The equivalent of B.C. is B.C.E.

• Remember that Israelis are not punctual; it's a surprise if anyone shows up on time. Foreigners are expected to be punctual for business meetings but not for social occasions.

• Always allow extra time for tasks such as asking for information or cashing traveler's checks. You may think that a trip to a bank for a simple transaction will take about 30 minutes, but, because of the long waits, it may take double that time.

• Be aware that there are no queues for anything. People push and shove to get ahead in any line. They aren't polite to tourists or to other Israelis.

• Always give your seat on a bus or train to a pregnant woman or an old person.

• Ask permission to smoke, whether you're in a public place or someone's home. Women should not smoke on the street, but men may smoke anywhere. Smoking in hotel public areas and restaurants is usually not allowed from sundown Friday to sundown Saturday out of respect for religious people.

• Be aware that from sundown Friday to sundown Saturday elevators in hotels stop at every floor.

• Remember that men (of any religion) visiting a synagogue must wear a skullcap called a *keepáh*. They are available when you enter the synagogue.

• Recall that in orthodox synagogues women must sit separately from men.

• Keep in mind the photography is forbidden in most churches, synagogues, and museums. Check your camera at the door. Never try to photograph Chassidic Jews (the ultra-religious) or Arabs. Obey signs at army installations warning that photography is strictly forbidden.

• Don't forget that many Arabs and religious Jews refuse to be photographed. If you are discreet, you might catch them unawares. However, if they suddenly become aware that you're photographing, they may throw stones at you or try to grab your camera.

• A gesture to remember: gathering the fingertips of the right hand together, with the palm facing inward, and moving the hand up and down rapidly means "Wait a minute."

• Look for clean public bathrooms in hotels, business premises, and good restaurants. Try to avoid those at railroad stations, gasoline stations, or inexpensive restaurants. You'll see a few facilities in parks or on the streets. They are mostly for men and aren't recommended.

• Note that rest rooms are labeled 00 or with pictures of men and women. Those labeled 00 are unisex.

Shopping: Remember that most stores have fixed prices, but feel free to bargain in markets, called *shuks* (shooks).

• Remember that V.A.T. of 15%, charged on all goods, is included in the purchase price. Tourists who buy goods exceeding $50.00 in cost are entitled to a discount of at least 5% at stores recommended by the Ministry of Tourism and a refund of the V.A.T. at the port of departure. Look for signs in store windows that say: "Tax V.A.T. Refund +

5% Discount on Purchases Made in Foreign Currencies." This arrangement does not apply to tobacco products, cameras, film, photographic supplies, and electrical appliances.

• To get your refund, obtain a receipt from the shop, stating the amount of V.A.T. paid. This invoice should be attached to the purchase, which is placed in a clear, plastic bag that must remain sealed until you leave the country. Present your purchases to the customs official at your point of departure so that he/she can stamp them. If you leave from Ben-Gurion Airport, you may receive your refund at the Bank Leumi Le-Israel counter in the departure hall. The bank charges a fee of $2.00 for refunds up to $30.00 and $5.00 for refunds above that amount. Tourists leaving from other departure points will receive a check at their home.

• Keep in mind that the town of Eilat is a free-trade area. Many stores there are duty-free, and no V.A.T. is charged.

DRESS

• Remember that Israelis are very fashion conscious and always try to wear what's up-to-date. To fit in, women should dress simply and elegantly.

• Note that jeans are fine for all ages, but only teenagers should wear shorts.

• Feel free to wear sandals for "everyday" wear. They are the accepted everyday footwear for both men and women.

• For business, men should wear a sports jacket, shirt, tie, and pants. Most Israeli businessmen wear slacks and open-collared shirts, but suits and neckties are becoming more common. If it's hot, your Israeli host will probably invite you to remove your jacket. Women should wear a suit or dress or a skirt and blouse.

• When walking in the religious area (*Mea Shearim*) in Jerusalem, visiting the Western Wall or synagogues, women should wear long sleeves and skirts or dresses that cover the knees.

• In churches, women should not wear miniskirts and should be sure that their shoulders are covered. (If necessary, you'll be loaned a shawl at the church.)

• If invited to a meal in a home, women should wear a nice blouse (preferably silk) and dress pants or skirt or a dress. Men should wear a jacket, shirt, and tie. Remove the jacket if others aren't wearing one. On Friday nights people dress up more than on other nights, since the Sabbath begins at sundown on Friday.

• Remember that winters are cold, (December through February) and houses in Israel tend to be cold. Dress warmly.

• Note that Israelis don't usually have occasions for which formal dress is required. The only exception is embassy parties.

MEALS

Hours and Foods

• First a few words about kosher food (you'll find that some homes and many restaurants are kosher): (1) There are separate dishes and utensils for meat dishes and dairy dishes because meat and dairy products can never be combined —e.g., you could not eat meat and potatoes with butter at the same meal or chicken with a cheese sauce. (2) Only meat from a cud-chewing animal with a divided hoof can be eaten (therefore, no pork). (3) Only fish with fins and scales can be eaten (no shellfish). (4) Animals must be slaughtered according to a special ritual.

Breakfast: Some time between 7:00 and 9:00 A.M. For people in a hurry, breakfast will be Nescafe or tea with milk and a roll. A more leisurely breakfast would include cottage cheese, tomatoes, and occasionally eggs. Should you be visiting a kibbutz (a collective settlement), there will be a huge breakfast, consisting of eggs, bread, olives, and salad.

Lunch: Between noon and 2:00 P.M. It's the main meal of the day. The first course is either herring, chopped liver, eggplant salad, or soup (hot in winter, cold in summer). The main course will probably be chicken or turkey, unless you're near the coast, where it's likely to be fish—always served fried. There will also be a potato or rice; a salad of tomatoes, scallions, and radishes; and then a dessert of Jell-O or pudding. Beverages served with the meal will be water, lemonade, or soda. Coffee and tea may or may not be offered.

Tea: 4:00 or 5:00 P.M. Expect coffee, tea, little sandwiches, fruit, and pastries.

Dinner: Between 7:00 and 10:00 P.M. It's usually an informal, light meal consisting of herring or salami, cheeses, and eggs.

• If you're invited to a home for a meal, it will probably be the midday meal. There may be appetizers before the meal; if so, they may be cheese; *hummus* (a paste of chick-peas, lemon, oil, and garlic, which you scoop up with pita, an Arabic bread); *tchina* (a paste of ground sesame seeds, lemon, oil, garlic, and parsley, which you scoop up with pita).

• Don't expect to be offered alcoholic drinks before dinner, though some Israelis drink beer. Most Israelis prefer soft drinks, fruit juices, cider, water, soda water, coffee, or tea. Very little liquor is consumed.

• Expect both tea and coffee to be offered in many variations: Tea might be brewed strong with mint or lemon; it might be served with milk or as iced tea. Coffee might be Turkish, espresso, instant, dripolater, or iced.

• Note that fruits and vegetables make up the bulk of the Israeli diet, with milk products such as yogurt and cheese eaten at least once a day. However, don't expect fruit to be served as a dessert.

• For the Sabbath, Yemenites prepare a yeast bread, served with eggs that are roasted overnight in the oven and turn brown. Don't be alarmed by the color. The eggs are good.

• Expect olives to be served with almost every meal.

Table Manners

• If you're guest of honor at a dinner, expect to be seated to the right or left of the host.

• To eat as the Israelis do, keep the knife in your right hand and the fork in your left. The knife isn't put down. The food is eaten from the fork in your left hand.

• Expect a great deal of conversation during a meal.

• Don't be embarrassed to leave some food on your plate, unless you're dining at the home of Oriental Jews, who may take offense.

• Stay about an hour after dinner, unless you're at the home of close friends, with whom it's fine to stay longer. Leave before 11:00 during the week; weekend dinner parties will probably last longer.

Eating Out

• Look for many different national cuisines at Israel's restaurants, since Israelis come from more than 60 different countries. Some examples of the cuisines available in restaurants: Yemenite, German, French, Chinese, seafood, Middle Eastern, vegetarian, Viennese (cafes), Indian, Italian, Rumanian, Hungarian, Argentinean. There are also dairy restaurants.

• Expect several foods to be available from street vendors: roasted sweet corn; pizza; falafel—deep-fried chick-pea balls in pita pockets with tomatoes, onions, and *tchina* sauce (sesame seed paste); and ice cream. Usually, the food sold on the street is safe. Take note of the cleanliness of the food and the utensils. If you want to be safe and also want to try falafel (which is to Israel what the hot dog is to the United States), ask your guide or someone at your hotel what would be the cleanest and best place for it.

• Check the restaurant's window before going in, as some restaurants post their menus. A restaurant will also post a sign in the window if it's kosher. You won't be able to get pork or shellfish there, nor will you be served dairy products and meat at the same time.

• If you have a yen for shellfish, seek out an Arab restaurant.

• Keep in mind that most restaurants and cafes in Jerusalem close at midnight, while many in Tel Aviv remain open later. Kosher restaurants close early on Friday afternoon and on the eve of Jewish holidays. They remain closed on Saturday until sundown.

• Expect non-kosher foods to be indicated on the menu.

• When ordering liquor, specify a brand—e.g., Johnnie Walker—to prevent being served a drink of inferior quality.

• If you ask for soda, expect to be served soda water.

• If you want ice in your drink, ask for *lots* of ice; otherwise, you'll get a single cube.

• Should you simply order "coffee," expect Turkish coffee. To get American-style coffee, ask for *"nes"* or *"neskafeh"* (instant coffee).

• Note that the same item may be spelled many different ways on Israeli menus. Check "Key Words and Phrases" (page 237) for phonetic pronunciation, which is more important to know than the spelling. Often, the attempts to put words or phrases on menus yield hilarious results. One traveler found a menu in which "cheese balls" were rendered as "chef's balls."

• Avoid ordering beef in Israel. It's imported, frozen, often tough, and always extremely expensive.

• Note that pork is now available in Israel. It's called steak *lavan* (lah-váhn), which means "white steak."

• Summon the waiter by raising your hand and catching his eye.

• Ask for separate checks or one check for the group. Credit cards are popular, especially among business people. If you're going to a medium-priced restaurant, check ahead to find out if they accept credit cards and, if so, which ones.

Specialties

• Since Israel has drawn its citizens from all over the world, the specialties range from the foods of the Eastern Mediterranean to those of Russia. In general, the food of the Oriental Jews is spicier, while that of the Western Jews is blander.

• As noted above, the dish most identified with Israel is falafel—ground chick-pea balls, fried and served in pita bread with lettuce, tomato, and *tchina* sauce.

• Other specialties: *hummus*, a dip made of chick-peas, lemon juice, garlic, and parsley; tahini, a dip made of crushed sesame seed with garlic, lemon, oil, and parsley; blintzes, similar to crepes, they are rolled up with cottage cheese and pan fried; *salat Turki*, hot and spicy tomato and pepper salad; knishes, meat turnovers; *bo-*rekas, phyllo dough turnovers filled with potato, cheese, or spinach; kebab, spiced and grilled hamburger (small, oval-shaped hamburger balls cooked with four to five on a skewer); *shishlik*, grilled skewers of beef or turkey; *shwarma*, slices of lamb grilled on a vertical spit; schnitzel, breaded fried cutlets of chicken or turkey; roast chicken; pita, flat round bread.

• Yemenite food is spicier than other Israeli foods. It uses many different spices: coriander, red chilis, garlic, cumin, cinnamon, cloves, ginger, fresh mint, and saffron. A major specialty is *chamin* (ha-méen), a soup with beans, meat, and herbs. Yemenites make five different types of pita, the flat Arab bread. They don't serve desserts, but after a meal offer a mixture of nuts, raisins, and chickpeas. Other Yemenite specialties: *bamia*, okra in a thick tomato sauce; *leben*, like sour cream, but thinner; *shamenet*, like sour cream, but thicker.

• Sweet specialties: *ugat dvash*, honey cake; *shtrudel peyrot yivehshim*, dried fruit strudel; *kugel gezzer*, carrot pudding; *listan tapuzim*, orange pudding; *mandlebrodt*, an almond cookie.

HOTELS

• Note that Israel's busiest periods are July, August, Passover, Easter, Rosh Hashanah (Jewish New Year), Yom Kippur (Day of Atonement), Chanukah, and Christmas. In general, November to February is low season, except in Eilat, where it is warm in the winter.

• Realize that a five-star hotel will not be up to the standard of the five-star hotels in other countries—e.g., the food may be mediocre.

• Note that some hotels have refrigerators in the rooms.

• When you're turning on the tap in the bathroom, use the one with the red dot for hot and the one with blue for cold.

• Keep in mind that if you pay for everything in the hotel with a credit card, you won't be charged the V.A.T.

• Consider alternative accommodations: (1) People of any age can stay at youth hostels. Some are air-conditioned, and all provide meals. Some have family rooms and cooking facilities. (2) Many *kibbutzim* have guest houses, which should be booked in advance through a travel agent. They are immaculate, air-conditioned, with phones, TV-radio, and private baths. Many have swimming pools. They don't have room service, but there is a special dining room for guests with two choices for every course. The only disadvantage is that you can be isolated with no transportation.

• If your stay will be a long one, investigate a service that enables you to rent an apartment or private home. The agency is called Homtel and has offices in New York City and Tel Aviv.

• Look for bed-and-breakfast pensions.

• Remember that in Eilat, Nahariya, and other beach resorts, people rent private rooms. Before taking the room, ask to see it. Check out the bathroom and kitchen facilities, and agree on a price in advance.

• If you'll be staying at a small hotel and plan to use a credit card, make sure that the hotel accepts credit cards before you check in.

• Most hotels provide a large breakfast at no extra charge. Often it's a buffet with cereals, breads, cheeses, fruits and vegetables, eggs, fish, and a selection of juices, coffee, and tea.

• Be assured that a major hotel

will have a good doctor available should you fall ill while you're staying there.

• Avoid making overseas calls from your hotel room. There is an enormous surcharge on such calls. Even if you call collect, there will be a huge charge for placing the call. If you can't arrange for people from overseas to call you, try to make your calls from the public phone in the hotel.

TIPPING

• Check your restaurant bill. If it states, "Service Not Included," leave 10 to 15%. Don't be surprised if waiters ask for the tip in cash. Otherwise they have to pay income tax on it.

• Give taxi drivers 15%. (Drivers don't expect tips from natives, but they do from foreigners.)

• Tip porters the equivalent of $1.00 per bag.

• Leave the hotel maid the equivalent of 50 cents to $1.00 per day.

• Give hairdressers 10%.

• If you hire a guide for the day, tip 10 to 15%.

PRIVATE HOMES

• Note that most visiting is done on Friday evening or Saturday (if people are not religious), since most people work during the day. Call beforehand to make arrangements. Religious people will not travel or willingly receive visitors on Saturday—until sundown.

• Don't expect to be invited to a meal in a home. Houses and apartments tend to be small and don't have the most up-to-date kitchen supplies. You may be invited to come around 8:00 P.M. for coffee, tea, and pastries. To make sure that the 8:00 invitation is *not* for dinner, say to your host, "That's great. We'll come over after dinner."

• Should you be invited to a party in a home, expect it to be more integrated in terms of age than in many other countries. There will probably be a tremendous range in age—from young children to very old people.

• When staying with a family, adapt to their schedule. Ask what you can do to help while people are at work. Discuss your daily plans with your hosts. Since so many people work, you may be expected to sightsee on your own. Your hosts will probably suggest interesting places to go. If they are free and have a car, they may offer to take you around.

• Expect to be treated as a member of the family, so don't give the impression that you're sitting around waiting to be entertained. Pitch in by helping with dishes, etc. (Your offer of help may, however, be turned down.) Take the whole family to a restaurant one evening to reciprocate for their hospitality.

• Be sure to make your bed and leave your room and the bathroom tidy.

• Note that people bathe daily and often twice during the summer.

• If you're staying in an older home, water for the bath may have to be heated in advance. Ask your hostess when it is convenient for you to bathe.

• Never make comparisons about how much larger the refrigerators are in your country or how many more kitchen gadgets people have.

• If you stay in a very religious (i.e., Orthodox) home during the

Sabbath (sundown Friday to sundown Saturday), be aware that you will not be allowed to turn on the stove, turn on the lights, light a match, smoke, handle money, or do work of any kind. It is a day of complete rest.

• In a religious home, if you help with setting the table or washing the dishes, be sure to ask *which* set of dishes and silverware you should use and exactly *where* they should be put after being washed. If the sets are mixed up, they have to be thrown out.

• Realize that houses can be very cold inside during the winter months (December through February). They are built to keep out the heat during the hot summer months. If you'll be in a private home during the winter, dress warmly.

• Note that many people hire women to come in and clean a few times a week. At the end of your visit, tip her the equivalent of $5.00. If you've met her on another trip, give her a small gift such as instant coffee.

Gifts: When invited to a meal, bring flowers, candy, Israeli wine, or nuts, or send flowers or a plant ahead of time. Don't, however, send calla lilies, because they are associated with funerals.

• If you know people well, bring from abroad plastic food wrap and aluminum foil. Both are very expensive in Israel. Another item you might not think of as a gift but that is expensive in Israel and therefore welcome is instant decaffeinated coffee.

• From abroad, for a new baby bring a "Busy Box," a good brand of baby oil, or a fine picture frame for snapshots.

• For small children, bring toys (for example, Legos), since all foreign toys are extremely expensive in Israel. Children also enjoy sugarless gum and M&Ms.

• Give teenagers the "latest of the latest" cassettes or a beach mattress with a built-in pump.

• Adults appreciate a wide variety of gifts from abroad: a Plexiglas tray or napkin holder with attractive, thick paper napkins (Israeli napkins are very thin and not absorbent); liquor (always name brands—e.g., Johnnie Walker scotch); drip-dry tablecloths; household gadgets; automatic cameras and film, photo albums; battery-operated digital watches; Reebok shoes; good quality stationery; books (in English).

• Women enjoy perfume, fine body lotions, and skin creams.

• Don't bring American videos; they won't work in Israeli video recorders.

• Unless you know that people smoke, don't bring a tobacco product. (It is not now popular to smoke in Israel, and smoking is forbidden in many places.)

BUSINESS

Hours

Banks: Usually Sunday, Tuesday, and Thursday, 8:30 A.M. to 12:30 P.M. and 4:00 to 6:00 P.M. Monday and Wednesday, 8:30 A.M. to 12:30 P.M. Friday and holiday eves, 8:30 A.M. to noon.

Government Offices: Sunday through Thursday, 9:00 A.M. to 1:00 P.M.

Businesses: Sunday through Thursday, 9:00 A.M. to 1:00 P.M. and 4:00 to 7:00 P.M. On Friday, most offices close early in preparation for the Sabbath.

Shops: 8:00 A.M. to 1:00 P.M. and 4:00 to 7:00 P.M. Department stores are usually open from 8:30 A.M. to 7:00 P.M. Shops in hotels are often open until midnight. Both shops and department stores close at 1:00 P.M. on Friday.

• Businesses, stores, and restaurants run by Arabs usually close on Friday but are open on Saturday

Currency

• The monetary unit is the *new shekel*, abbreviated in English as NIS. Coins: 1 *agora*, 5 *agorot*, 10 *agorot*, ½ *new shekel*, 1 *new shekel*.

• Bills are 5, 10, and 50 *new shekelim*. Remember that 1 *new shekel* is equal to 1,000 *old shekelim*.

• When you receive change, make sure that it is *new shekelim*. You may be given *old shekelim*, which aren't used any more.

• To avoid the Value Added Tax of 15%, pay with foreign currency, credit cards, or traveler's checks for restaurant meals, hotels, rental cars, and airplane tickets.

Business Practices

• Plan on more than one trip to conclude your business. People will want to know you well before doing business with you. It is impossible to predict the speed of your negotiations. They may take only a few days or they may drag on for months, depending on the people with whom you're dealing and the complexity of the business at hand.

• Remember also that Israel is a nation of immigrants from all parts of the world, and each national group has its own style—doing business with someone from

South Africa will be different from doing business with someone from Iran. Adapt your style and speed of negotiations to those of your counterpart. If you've done business in other Middle Eastern countries, you will probably find the pace faster in Israel than elsewhere in the region.

• Arrange for appointments—by phone, telex, or fax—two to three weeks in advance. Make appointments from 8:00 A.M. to 3:00 P.M., Sunday through Thursday, and on Friday from 8:00 A.M. to noon.

• Create a positive image, but one which is relaxed and normal, not overdone. You need not stay at *the* best hotel, and don't feel you'll improve your image by giving expensive gifts.

• At all major hotels, expect full secretarial services—typing, photocopying, telex, and fax.

• Don't encumber your luggage with photocopies of your presentation. Copy machines are easily available.

• Don't plan to use an interpreter; Israeli businessmen are fluent in English. In the rare case when you may want one, call a secretarial agency.

• Be punctual, even if your Israeli counterparts are not.

• For first business conversations, discuss the general business climate and the structure of business in Israel. If an Israeli brings up politics, listen, but try to avoid giving your opinion. Don't discuss either religion or sex unless a *very* close relationship has been established.

• Have your fax number printed on your business card.

• Feel free to make your first presentation in English, but any brochures you use should be translated into Hebrew.

• Use charts and visuals if you wish, but don't go overboard with them—too many, too complex, etc.

• Even though Israelis form close-knit clans, as an American, expect to be received with great hospitality and warmth. However, you may be promised more than can be delivered, so it is important to have a local contact able to evaluate the situation for you. If you don't have one, get in touch with the Commercial Attache at the Israeli embassy or consulate in your area or the manager of an Israeli bank. Israelis—more than the people of any country in the area—will be helpful in introducing you to their social, business, and army contacts. People will then see you soon, without a lengthy wait.

• Know your competitors and what they have to offer.

• When you're talking of time schedules, be aware that Israelis may promise an earlier delivery than they are able to make. To say what they think you want to hear, they may gloss over unexpected problems. For example, a key person may be called up to the army for a month or so, or there may be political developments (a change in government or ministerial policy), which have a bearing on your dealings. You will probably encounter this discrepancy between what is promised and what can be produced more with Oriental Israelis than with other Israelis.

• Expect very aggressive bargaining before you arrive at a written contract (and be sure to have a written contract before you leave). There may be attempts to change the agreement before it is signed, but after the signing the contract will be observed.

• Keep in mind that final decisions in government corporations involve numbers of people, while private owners make their own decisions.

• If you're a businesswoman, expect to be taken seriously in Israel. You can lead your company's delegation, but you probably won't encounter many Israeli women at the upper echelons of companies. You can have business lunches alone with an Israeli businessman and pay. For a dinner, invite the businessman's wife.

Business Gifts: Cross pens; Walkman for cassettes; Ray-Ban sunglasses.

Entertaining: Include all negotiators. Ask the head negotiator who should be invited.

• Note that business lunches are more popular than business dinners.

• If you wish to entertain an Israeli business colleague in a restaurant for dinner, ask at your hotel for the most "in" restaurant. Tastes change very quickly, and people like to be taken to the most popular, "trendy" restaurant of the moment.

• To please Israelis, take them to restaurants that serve Middle Eastern, Yemenite, Chinese, or continental food. They also enjoy restaurants offering steak or fish.

• Ask if the people you're entertaining are kosher. If they are, ask at your hotel for a recommendation for a really good kosher restaurant.

• Expect wives of both foreigners and Israelis to be included in dinner invitations. If the Israeli has met the foreign wife, he will usually ask her to join the group. A visitor should invite the Israeli wife.

HOLIDAYS AND SPECIAL OCCASIONS

Because most holidays are based on the lunar months of 28 days, dates vary from year to year. In some cases, businesses, banks, and restaurants close; in other cases, they remain open. We've indicated after each holiday whether you will find places open or closed. When the holiday indicates "closed," businesses, banks, etc., usually close during the early afternoon before the holiday. You may find a few restaurants open on days noted as "closed." Check with your travel agent to find out if your trip to Israel will coincide with any holidays.

• Note that there are three fixed holidays: Independence Day (May 10), and Bank Holidays (January 1 and August 10).

• Don't forget that *Shabbat* (from sundown Friday to sundown Saturday) is a day of rest. Religious Jews do not ride, light fires, or use the telephone, and they spend part of the day at the synagogue or in studying religious books. Secular people go to the beach, work in the garden, etc. Muslims celebrate the Sabbath on Friday; Christians celebrate it on Sunday.

• Other holidays in Israel:

1. Rosh Hashanah (New Year), a family holiday, which usually falls in September. It's a custom to eat apples dipped in honey or honeycakes to symbolize a forthcoming sweet year. Send cards to families you know. *Closed for two days.*

2. Yom Kippur (Day of Atonement). It occurs ten days after Rosh Hashanah. Many people fast for 24 hours, from sundown on the eve to sundown the following day, and many attend synagogue. Since the Holocaust, even many Jews who consider themselves secular participate in the fast. *Closed.*

3. Succot (Feast of the Booths) falls four days after Yom Kippur. It commemorates the bringing of the first fruits to the Temple in Jerusalem. Each family builds a small shelter (in remembrance of the temporary shelters in which people slept) in their backyard and hangs fruits in it. The traditional dish is rolled cabbage, since it would keep warm while being transferred from house to booth. *Closed one day.*

4. Chanukah (Feast of Lights) usually occurs in December. It celebrates the finding of oil to relight the candelabra in the Temple that was destroyed. There was enough oil for only one day, but, miraculously, it burned for eight days. Children receive gifts of money. People eat food fried in oil; some eat potato pancakes called *latkes,* and others have doughnuts. *Open.*

5. Tu B'Shvat (New Year of the Trees) usually falls in early spring. People plant trees along roadsides and in forests. *Open.*

6. Pesach (Passover) is an eight-day spring festival in March or April commemorating the exodus of the Jews from Egypt. In Israel, on the first day people hold a *seder* (a great feast). The meal consists of a number of symbolic foods: bitter herbs and hard-boiled eggs dipped in salt water to symbolize the tears people shed while they were slaves in Egypt; *matzoh,* an unleavened bread people baked en route because they had no time to bake bread before fleeing (nothing made with yeast can be eaten throughout Passover). A special book called *The Haggadah,* telling the story of the Jews' escape from Egypt, is read throughout the meal. *Closed first and last days. Some businesses open during intermediary days, and some do not.*

7. Purim, occurring in March or April, celebrates the rescuing of the Jews of Persia by Queen Esther. People eat *oznei Haman* (Haman's ears)—cookies filled with poppy seed or prunes, and they bring plates with treats to neighbors and family. *Open.*

8. Lag B'Omer (the 33rd day of the counting of the Omer—a period of mourning, when people aren't allowed to marry), falling in the spring, is celebrated with bonfires. Children go out into the forest with bows and arrows as their ancestors did when they pretended to hunt while actually studying religious subjects. The food associated with the feast is roast potatoes. *Open.*

9. Shavu'ot (literally "weeks") signifies the end of Omer and comes seven weeks after Passover. It commemorates Moses' giving of the Ten Commandments. The foods are cheese products. *Closed.*

10. Tisha B'Av (the 9th day of the Hebrew month of Av) is a midsummer feast day recalling the fall of the Temple in Jerusalem. Now that the Wailing Wall (also called the Western Wall) is in Israeli territory, many people make a pilgrimage to pray there. *Open.*

TRANSPORTATION

Public Transportation

• On intracity buses, get on at the rear and pay the conductor.

• If you're lucky enough to get on a newer intercity bus, expect air-conditioning. Older buses aren't air-conditioned.

• Buy a ticket in advance at the bus station if you're taking a long-distance bus, or buy a ticket from the driver or the conductor at a bus stop for an intercity bus.

• If you don't know the fare on an intercity bus—it's based on zones and the length of the trip—have small change on hand (though you don't need exact change). An inspector may get on the bus, so keep your ticket until the end of the journey. Be prepared for a great deal of pushing and shoving as you board. You'll have to be assertive.

• Be aware that bus service begins at 5:30 A.M. and ends at midnight. Except in a few places (such as Haifa), buses stop running one hour before the Sabbath begins on Friday evening and start again one half hour after sundown on Saturday. Cities with large Arab populations have independent buses that run all week.

• If you're traveling by bus on Sunday, remember that from early Sunday morning until about 8:30 P.M., buses are crowded with soldiers returning to their bases.

• Hail a taxi in the street, or call from a home or hotel. Taxis in the cities are metered.

• Note that there are private taxis called *sheruts*, which travel on a specific route, picking up passengers along the way and letting them off as they request. If a *sherut* is honking, that means there's available space, and you can hail it. The fares are similar to bus fares, but *sheruts* are more comfortable because people aren't pushing and shoving to get on and off. They operate when buses aren't running (Saturdays and late at night). At those times they charge an additional 20%. *Sheruts* run within cities as well as between cities. For trips between cities, individual seats are sold at fixed prices, which are only slightly higher than bus fares.

• Though Israel has no subways, look for overhead cable cars at some tourist sites. Buy your ticket at the site.

• Be aware that train service is very limited, both in terms of times of service and destinations. You'll find a few trains in the morning and a few in the evening. The routes are Tel Aviv–Jerusalem; Tel Aviv–Haifa, on to Nahariya; Tel Aviv–Beersheva. If there's train service to your destination, you'll find it the most economical way to travel. There's only one class, but there are individual cars with reserved seats. There are no sleepers or dining cars, but vendors come through with sandwiches and drinks. Buy tickets in advance at the train station.

• Don't hitchhike. It can be *very* dangerous.

• Realize that for security reasons, you can't reserve a seat on El Al (the Israeli airline). You must obtain your seat assignment when you arrive at the airport for your flight.

Driving

• If at all possible, don't drive in Israel. The country has more cars per kilometer than any other country in the world, and it is also the leader in number of automobile accidents. Hiring a car and driver is only slightly more expensive than renting to drive yourself. Should you decide to rent a car, there are some things you should know:

1. Driving is on the right.

2. Passengers in the front seat must wear seat belts. Young children must sit in the back and must wear seat belts.

3. Don't drive during rush hours (6:00 to 8:00 A.M. and 5:00 to 7:00 P.M.

4. Road signs and street names are in Hebrew, Arabic, and English. Signs are frequent and clear, but the roads are not in good condition.

5. There are strict laws about drinking and driving.

6. When a yellow light flashes, don't go. It's a signal that the green is about to come on.

7. You may be assessed an on-the-spot fine. *Never* try to bribe an Israeli policeman.

8. You cannot take a car rented in Israel into any of its neighboring countries.

9. Gas prices are astronomical (at least three times the cost of gas in the U.S.)

10. On Saturdays and Jewish holidays, it's almost impossible to have any repairs done on a car, even getting a flat tire changed. Some gas stations are closed on Saturday.

11. If you arrange a car rental from abroad, be sure to specify if you want an automatic shift. Otherwise, you'll be given a stick shift.

LEGAL MATTERS, HEALTH, AND SAFETY

• Be aware that if you are planning to travel to Jordan or another Arab country, your passport cannot show any evidence that you've been to Israel. When you arrive in Israel, ask to have your entry visa stamped on a separate piece of paper. You can throw the paper away after you leave Israel. (Some diplomats and business people have two passports—one for Israel and one for Arab countries.) Countries that do not admit travelers with Israeli-stamped passports will also refuse travelers with Egyptian-Israeli border entry stamps.

• Don't bring in to Israel plants, seeds, fresh fruits, or vegetables.

• If you want to bring a video camera into the country, be aware that there's a huge deposit (hundreds of dollars) required.

• Be prepared to have your bags inspected before entering any public building and to undergo a body search before entering the Knesset (Israel's Parliament).

• When dealing with the police, tell the truth, and don't try to excuse yourself if you've broken a law.

• If you need help in Jerusalem, seek out one of the special tourist police. They speak many languages and can help in such tasks as filling out insurance forms. Approach any policeman; he'll find one of the tourist police for you if he himself doesn't speak your language.

• Remember that it's forbidden to export antiquities (man-made objects made before 1700) without an export permit from the Department of Antiquities and Museums in Jerusalem. You'll pay an export fee of 10% of the purchase price.

• Be aware that the tap water in Israel is perfectly safe.

• If you go off the beaten path, be sure to take a thermos of liquid. You'll need it during the warm months (June through August). (Water is probably the best choice, since most soft drinks don't quench—and often increase —your thirst.)

• Note that a woman can travel alone without fear. Feel free to take taxis after dark. Ask someone what the route is and how long it should take to avoid being overcharged.

• Women should be aware that they will have no problem having dinner alone. Some men may try to flirt, but they are probably harmless. Women will be bothered less by men than in most other Middle Eastern countries.

JORDAN

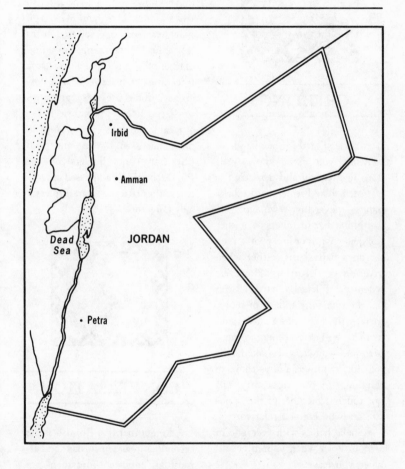

In Jordan, you can visit the lowest point on earth—the Dead Sea—but your Middle East journey will also reach a high point in that country, one of the cleanest and safest in the world. Everywhere you will find reminders of the ancient world and the Roman Empire. You can even bathe in the same thermal waters that soothed Herod the Great's aches and pains 2,000 years ago.

GREETINGS

- Always shake the hand of someone you don't know well, both in greeting and departing.
- Men should remember to shake hands—never kiss—women.
- Note that members of neither sex shake hands or kiss people they see on a daily basis, either when greeting or departing. However, when good friends haven't seen one another for a month or more, men will kiss other men and women will kiss other women. Men and women will shake hands with one another, unless they are religious; in that case, they will not touch a member of the opposite sex who is not a relative.
- Shake hands with everyone in a room both when you enter and when you leave.
- If you are seated at a party when a new guest arrives, stand and greet her/him.
- Offer your hand, unless you know that the other person is religious. People who are religious may say, "I'm sorry; I don't shake hands." Your gesture won't have offended them.
- Upon greeting people you don't know well, use the English titles of Mr., Mrs., and Miss. You may hear someone referred to as *Abu* plus a first name (meaning "father of") or *Um* and a first name (meaning "mother of"). As a foreigner, don't use these greetings until you know a person well.
- Education is important to one's status in Jordan, and both physicians and holders of the Ph.D. should be addressed as Doctor. Other titles used are Professor and Director.

CONVERSATION

- Remember that English is the second language in Jordan, and almost all educated Jordanians are bilingual in English and Arabic.
- Realize that many people who speak English are Palestinian. Very soon after meeting you, they will want to know your views on the Israeli-Palestinian situation. Be *very* diplomatic. You might say

something such as, "I don't think we have the full picture in my country." Avoid giving a direct opinion.

• Show concern for the person with whom you're talking. People appreciate compliments, e.g., "I like your country. Your people are hospitable, generous, and warm."

• To indicate even more interest in the country, ask advice about places to see, restaurants, and good shops.

• Ask questions regarding people's children. They will appreciate your interest. Good questions: "How old are they?" "What are they doing?" "Where do they go to school?"

• Mention the beauty of the Queen (who is American). Americans might say, "She ties our countries together."

• Avoid any negative comments on the royal family.

• Don't discuss sex or make sexual jokes.

• Don't ask questions about a man's wife.

• Be prepared for frankness. Example: "You've gained weight." (To a Jordanian, that means that you look healthy.)

TELEPHONES

• Expect to find telephone booths on the street, at newsstands, or in grocery stores. Deposit three *piastres* for three minutes. When you hear a beep, deposit more.

• Ask to use the phone at shops and hotels. It will be easier than using public phones on the noisy public streets.

• Go to the post office for overseas calls. However, you cannot call overseas from all towns, even at the post office.

• Note that telephone directories are in Arabic and English.

• Realize that there is no telephone service between Jordan and Israel.

IN PUBLIC

• Be conscious that Jordan is much less conservative than other countries in the Arab world. For example, men and women often visit restaurants together. However, Jordanians frown on affectionate behavior in public. A foreign woman would make a *major* blunder by kissing a Jordanian male friend in public. In fact, a woman should not even make eye contact with men. One woman traveler said, "I tried to act a bit like a nun in public."

• Women who are blonde may want to cover their hair with a scarf to avoid being touched. Brunettes will have less of a problem.

• Women should not smoke on the street, though it's acceptable for them to smoke in homes and restaurants. Men may smoke anywhere.

• Learn some important landmarks if you plan to go walking in Amman, since the city has very few street signs. However, since the city is built on seven hills, walking is difficult.

• To beckon a person, wave all the fingers of your hand inward. Don't just extend the forefinger and move it back and forth, since that's the way to summon an animal.

• Recognize that a click of the tongue with the chin point up means "No," while a slight shaking of the head from side to side means one of three things: "What's the matter?" "What's wrong?" or "Sorry, I didn't hear you."

• Ask permission before photographing people or their possessions. Many people don't like to have their pictures taken. Don't photograph people who are praying.

• Be aware that photographing in military zones is forbidden. So is photographing bridges. Some people have had trouble with the police when taking pictures in downtown Amman, because photos of crumbling buildings create a bad image for the country.

• Be cautious if you're on the Syrian border or in the West Bank area. In some places photography isn't allowed. You may also find that your passport will be checked frequently.

• Realize that there is bargaining in *all* markets and shops. The merchant will name a price. Offer 50% and bargain from there. If you're satisfied with the final price offered, accept it. If not, leave. Sometimes if you walk away after the merchant has offered the "final price," he will call you back and accept *your* final price.

DRESS

• For casual wear in the resort area of Petra, and in a tour group, women can wear jeans or Bermuda shorts but never tight or see-through pants. In the same circumstances, a sleeveless jersey is okay. Don't wear shorts. A woman traveling alone should dress conservatively. Men can wear a shirt and long pants, but not shorts. Men should wear shorts only in private sports clubs. Even teenagers should not wear shorts on the street.

• When invited to a dinner in a home, women should wear a longish full skirt, since you'll be eating on the floor. To an outdoor meal, wear a long skirt or pants for eating on the ground. To dinner in a home, men should wear suit and tie.

• For business, men should wear suit and tie, and women should wear a plain suit or dress.

• Expect to see young women from both upper-class families and from villages wearing Western-style clothing. Older women wear black or long, white, embroidered dresses. Long white veils cover the hair but not the face. Jordanian women don't wear face veils.

• Note that formal dress is required only for diplomatic functions. To them, men should wear a tuxedo and women cocktail-length dresses.

MEALS

Hours and Foods

Breakfast: Some time between 7:00 and 9:00 A.M. The usual meal is cheese (usually white sheep's cheese), *hummus* (a paste made of ground chick-peas, lemon juice, oil, parsley, and garlic), tabbouleh (a salad made of *burghul*—a grain—parsley, scallions, mint, lemon juice, tomatoes, and olive oil), omelettes, pita bread, with tea or coffee.

Lunch: Between noon and 2:00 P.M. Usually there will be a dish featuring chicken, beef, or lamb, accompanied by rice, bread, yogurt, fresh vegetables, and fruit. Tea or water will be served with the meal, and mint tea after the meal. (See "Specialties" for some of the typical entree dishes.)

Dinner: A light meal, served between 7:00 and 11:00 P.M. It usually consists of eggs, cheese, *hummus*, cucumber salad, and fruits.

• Expect fresh fruit to be served for dessert. Jordanians don't serve the sweet, syrupy desserts common in other Middle Eastern countries. Pastries are served on special occasions—for example, during religious festivals, at weddings, and when people break the fast during Ramadan.

• Note that before the meal there will be many small dishes of appetizers—*hummus*, tabbouleh, *baba ganouzh* (eggplant dip), pickles, and olives. This spread is called *mezze* (meh-zeh).

• Consider trying the national drink, *arak* (an anise-flavored liquor).

• With meals, expect bottled water or soda or tea. (An excellent bottled water available in restaurants and grocery stores is *Kawthar*.) When people stop by for a visit, the usual beverage is tea with a great deal of sugar and mint, or

Turkish coffee. It's thick, so let it settle before you drink it. Don't swallow the last mouthful, or you'll have a mouthful of coffee grounds.

• *Never* offer a Muslim an alcoholic beverage unless you are very close friends and are sure that he drinks.

• For special occasions such as a wedding, a feast day, or a meal for important guests, expect *mensaf* (a meal of freshly slaughtered lamb, yogurt, rice with cinnamon, pine nuts, and almonds, accompanied by bread). This traditional Bedouin feast is also available at restaurants. As each guest finishes, he licks his fingers, leaves to wash his hands, and returns for fruit and coffee. At the end of the meal, guests say *"Daimah"* ("May you always have plenty") and the host responds *"Sahtain"* ("I hope you enjoyed the meal").

Table Manners

• Remember that people sometimes eat on the floor, seated on low mattresses placed against the wall, and sometimes at a table.

• Expect people to eat with their right hand from platters in the center of the table.

• Note that men and women often eat together; however, sometimes the hostess doesn't eat with the guests because she is busy serving. Usually men and women will eat separately if there are more than five or six guests, if the home is a very religious one, or if the occasion is a traditional dinner or wedding. (In fact, men and women may be separated for the entire evening.)

• Before meals people say *"Sahtayn"* ("To health"), as the French say "Bon appétit." On a ceremonial or feast day, the phrase before dinner is *"Bismillah"* ("In the name of God"). When you've finished eating, say *"Amar"* (Ahmahr), which means "I've had enough." When the meal is over, say *"Daimah"* (roughly translated, "May you always have plenty at your table").

• Recall that it's polite to leave some food on your plate.

Eating Out

• Don't expect to find a great number of restaurants in Amman. The typical Jordanian restaurant mainly offers Arabic food, with some basic European dishes. You'll find some Italian, Chinese, Korean, and Japanese restaurants.

• Realize that cafes in general are just for men. They serve tea and coffee, and some have water pipes, called *nargila*, for smoking.

• Recall that food stands selling *shwarma* (Arab bread filled with sliced lamb that has been cooked on a vertical spit) and falafel are usually very clean—so it's safe to eat food sold there.

• Plan for restaurant lunch between 1:00 and 3:00 P.M. and dinner after 8:00 P.M.

• Expect to be able to buy alcoholic beverages in most restaurants.

• To call the waiter, say *"Garçon."*

• Note that the person who issues an invitation usually pays. If you go out with a group of Jordanians, offer to pay your share. Should a Jordanian pay, be sure to invite the same people and pay next time.

Specialties

• An appetizer you may be offered is *fatteh*: *hummus* decorated with whole chick-peas, cumin, parsley, and olive oil.

• Some popular entrees: *daud pasha*—a stew of onions, tomatoes, pine nuts, and meat balls, served with rice; *kidreh bil-furn*—meat, rice, chick-peas, and spices baked in an earthenware jar; *kubbeh*—cracked wheat, ground meat, and spices, shaped into croquettes, stuffed with meat and onions, and then deep-fried; *mahshi*—baked stuffed eggplant; *maqlouba*—a stew of meat with either eggplant or cauliflower, which is served on rice topped with yogurt; *Musakhan*—chicken in olive oil and onions, roasted on Arabic bread.

• A frequently served side dish is *fattush*—a salad of purslane, parsley, mint, onion, garlic, cucumbers, tomatoes, lemon juice, and olive oil. Another salad is *salata bi-tahini*—tossed salad with sesame seed paste.

• At every meal, you'll find *khubiz*, a pitalike bread.

HOTELS

• Realize that there are simple, quiet hotels at which Jordanians stay. (They are usually rated two-star.) There will be a private bathroom with constant hot water. There won't be air-conditioning, but there will be ceiling fans.

• Expect continental breakfast to be the morning meal available in a hotel. Lunch in a hotel dining room will be served from 1:00 to 3:00 P.M. and dinner after 8:00 P.M.

• Note that some hotels provide bottled water in their guest rooms.

If your hotel doesn't, buy some and use it for drinking and for brushing your teeth.

• Recognize that liquor is very expensive in better hotels and in nightclubs. If you want to serve liquor in your room, buy it at a retail store. If you want to have a drink while socializing in a hotel bar, you'll have to pay the price.

• Look for nightclubs in larger hotels; usually only couples are admitted.

• Consider staying at government resthouses near historic sites. They provide meals and accommodations at reasonable prices in out-of-the-way places. Since some fairly large cities (e.g., Jerash and Madaba) have no hotels, you'll have to use government resthouses there.

• There are no youth hostels, so young travelers must stay in hotels. Since the inexpensive places (especially in Amman) are usually in noisy places, request a room at the back.

TIPPING

• At restaurants, leave 10%.
• Give porters 500 *fils* at the airport. At hotels give 200 *fils* per bag.
• Note that taxi drivers don't expect a tip.
• Leave 200 *fils* per day for hotel chambermaids.

PRIVATE HOMES

• Note that the best time for visiting is between 3:00 and 5:00 P.M.
• Check all invitations—dinners, receptions, weddings—because some are for men only.
• If you smoke, accept your host's cigarettes, though it's not a problem if you prefer your own.
• Expect to have coffee just before you leave. If you prepare to leave and coffee appears, stay to drink it.
• If you're visiting Bedouins, expect coffee to be served in a pot. The cups look like small egg cups. Sip slowly. The coffee is usually bitter and flavored with cardamom seeds. To indicate that you've had enough, move the cup by shaking your wrist back and forth.
• If you're staying with a family that isn't wealthy, don't be a burden to them. The family will probably not allow you to buy groceries, but be sure to buy special treats, such as chocolates or pastries.
• Always wear shoes or slippers. Never walk around a home in bare feet.
• Women should never become too familiar with the males in a family with which they are staying.
• Make your compliments about a home general ("What a lovely room this is"); if you compliment a specific object, your host may feel obliged to give it to you. Be sure to reciprocate with a gift if your host gives you an object from his home.

Gifts: Don't give expensive gifts, as people will feel obliged to buy an expensive gift for you.

• When invited to a meal, bring flowers, candy, fruits (bananas, apples, or oranges), cookies, or toffees packaged in fancy containers.

• Note that gifts from abroad are welcome, since Western goods are very expensive. Some good choices: electronic wristwatches; a Walkman; battery-operated clocks; cassettes of American music; T-shirts. If you know a man has children, bring a gift for them. Calculators, cassettes, and T-shirts are especially popular with the young.

• Don't tip the maid if you've been staying with a family. However, if you bring the family gifts, give her one as well—material for a dress, hand lotion, etc.

• If you are invited to a wedding, bring a blouse, a sweater, or jewelry for the bride—even if you've never met her.

• Should you be invited to visit a couple who have a new baby, hold the baby and tuck three *dinars* into the folds of the baby's clothing.

BUSINESS

Hours

Banks: Saturday through Thursday, 8:30 A.M. to 12:30 P.M. (Some banks are open in the afternoon.)

Government Offices: Saturday to Thursday, 8:00 A.M. to 2:00 P.M.

Businesses: Saturday to Thursday, 9:00 A.M. to 1:00 P.M. and 3:00 to 7:00 P.M.

Shops: Saturday to Thursday, 9:00 A.M. to 1:30 P.M. and 3:00 or 3:30 P.M. to 6:00 or 7:00 P.M.

• Remember that Friday is the weekly day off. Saturdays and Sundays are normal working days, but some companies close on Sunday.

• Keep in mind that during Ramadan, government offices are usually open from Saturday to Thursday, 9:00 A.M. to 1:30 P.M., while most businesses are open Saturday to Thursday, 9:00 A.M. to 4:00 P.M.

• Note that *souks* (markets and street stalls) are open every day, including Friday.

Currency

• The Jordanian *dinar* (JD) is divided into 1,000 *fils*. Ten *fils* are also called a *piaster* (pt.).

• Bills: JD 50, 20, 10, 5, 1, and ½ (500 *fils*).

• Silver coins: 250 *fils* (25 *piasters*), 100 *fils* (10 pt.), 50 *fils* (5 pt.), 25 *fils* (2.5 pt.), and 20 *fils* (2 pt.).

• Copper coins: 10 *fils* and 5 *fils*.

• Always carry small change, as it is in short supply. Be prepared to be given an item from a shop in place of small change.

• Recall that major credit cards are accepted by well-known restaurants, hotels, car rental firms, and some boutiques.

Business Practices

• Plan business trips November through April, when the weather is coolest. Jordanian businessmen vacation in July and August. Avoid the two weeks before and after Christmas, the Easter period, and the month of Ramadan.

• Keep in mind that Friday is the weekly holiday for Muslims. Though some businesses and embassies observe Sunday as a holiday instead, don't plan meetings or make appointments for Friday.

• If you're going to be dealing with a government official, telex for an appointment a month in advance.

• Make business appointments in the morning. The best times are between 9:00 A.M. and noon. It's especially important to observe these times for government officials, since they finish their work day at 2:00 P.M.

• Approach the Amman Chamber of Commerce for lists of manufacturing and trade firms that give information about foreign trade and domestic industry. The Chamber also sponsors overseas and local trade missions, exhibitions, and other joint ventures.

• If your company doesn't have an office or a branch in Jordan, seek out an agent in the country. Send representatives to find someone to act as agent and distributor. Most Jordanian importers act as agents and deal with a wide variety of products.

• Expect Jordanians to conduct business in a more straightforward manner than in most other countries in the area. There is a free enterprise system and less bureaucracy than in other countries. Most business is with the private sector (rather than the government).

• Be aware that appointments with people in the public sector— especially with senior officials—

can be erratic. (They may be very late for appointments or change an appointment at the last minute.) People in the private sector are both more prompt and more accessible.

• Realize that younger businessmen are aware of Western services and goods, as well as business and social practices. Decision makers in both the public and private sectors are receptive to Western techniques and ideas. The more educated and sophisticated the people you're dealing with, the more quickly business will proceed.

• Don't forget that people will want to know you well before getting on with business. There will be numerous preliminary conversations, so that Jordanians will be convinced that you are a person of honesty and integrity, before they discuss your business credentials.

• In business conversation, avoid discussing the large amount of foreign aid that Jordan receives.

• Be punctual to make a good impression, but do not expect Jordanians to be on time.

• Feel free to use business cards in English.

• Always accept a few cups of Turkish coffee. If you have several appointments, you'll have to drink several cups.

• Suggest discussing business in a coffee house in order to avoid the constant interruptions and group-style business interviews that occur in offices.

• If your deal involves land, remember that it is measured in *dunums*. One *dunum* equals 1,000 square meters or two-thirds of an acre.

• Negotiate to have new or used machinery imported duty free.

• Be sure to fulfill deliveries on the date you've agreed on. Otherwise you may lose subsequent orders.

• Expect to find fax service in all major Amman post offices and in large hotels.

• Realize that it will take time for Jordanian men to take foreign businesswomen seriously. If a woman handles herself in a professional manner and if the Jordanians *have* to do business with the company she represents, she will be given honorary male status. People will be surprised if a woman is sent to do business, but there shouldn't be any major problems.

• Note that business entertaining is usually done in a home. Mealtimes are traditionally a time for the whole extended family to get together. In the past, people pitied those who ate in restaurants because it meant that they had no family.

• Realize that lunches and dinners are social occasions and not for discussing business.

• If you are a male invited to the

home of a Jordanian businessman, it will probably be an all-male evening. Don't ask if you can bring your wife. If you want to bring a gift, bring it for the *man*, not for his wife. (See "Gifts" above.)

• Entertain Jordanians in the restaurants of the best hotels. Ask a businessman if he wants to bring his wife. If he gives an excuse (e.g., "She is busy with the children"), don't insist.

• If a woman must meet clients outside the office, the best situation is a luncheon meeting at a business restaurant.

HOLIDAYS AND SPECIAL OCCASIONS

• Check with Jordan's tourist office for religious holidays, since they are moveable. The following are secular holidays observed on fixed dates: Tree Day (Jan. 15); Arab League Day (March 22); Labor Day (May 1); Independence Day (May 25); King Hussein's Accession (Aug. 11); King Hussein's Birthday (Nov. 14).

TRANSPORTATION

Public Transportation

• Keep in mind that in Amman buses' destinations and numbers are written in Arabic.

• When you take buses in cities, pay when you get on. The fare is based on the distance traveled. Buses tend to be *extremely* crowded. Get off at the back.

• Hail taxis on the street or phone for one. In major cities, you can hire taxis for an extended period. These "regular" taxis have a yellow square on the front door and a yellow light on the roof. "*Servees*" are taxis that operate like buses—on fixed routes within cities. They are five-passenger cars and run along a set route in town and to outlying areas. They have a white square on the front door and a white light on the roof.

• When taking a taxi, have someone at your hotel write your

destination in relation to a familiar landmark, so that the taxi driver will be able to find it.

• Make *sure* that the driver turns on the meter. If he doesn't, get out of the taxi.

• Don't look for passenger trains or subways. There aren't any.

• Be aware that some long-distance buses (run by JET) have TVs, VCRs, toilets, air-conditioning, and hostesses. You can reserve in advance. (The longest—in distance—bus ride in Jordan is a three-hour trip.)

Driving

• Drive on the right side of the road, as in North America.

• Realize that road signs will be in Arabic and English.

• Use seat belts. They are required for those in the front seat of a car.

• Never try to bribe police.

• Try not to drive in towns, because there are no street numbers and few street names. Destinations are described in relation to landmarks.

• Remember that Jordan has excellent roads, and you can drive anywhere in the country. However, on some roads you may encounter checkpoints where you will have to produce identification (e.g., a passport).

• If you want to drive in remote desert areas, check first with Desert Police Patrol to arrange for an escort. You can recognize these police by their dress—khaki uniforms with red trim and red-and-white-checked head scarves. Never travel alone in the desert. Your car could sink into desert tracks when it rains. Be alert for police posts stationed in the desert. (See advice on "Desert Driving" in "Customs and Manners in the Arab World.")

• Keep your eye on the gas gauge. Gas stations are scarce between main towns.

LEGAL MATTERS, HEALTH, AND SAFETY

• Look for tourist police in areas frequented by tourists. You can recognize them because they wear arm bands. Go to them with any problem. They speak several languages.

• Realize that sale of liquor is forbidden during Ramadan, although at other times it is readily available in grocery stores.

• Don't try to visit a mosque. Such visits are forbidden to tourists.

• Bring in or take out as much Jordanian currency as you wish. There are no limits.

• Don't drink tap water. Don't eat raw fruits and vegetables that cannot be peeled. Don't eat pastries and desserts sold by vendors on the street.

• Expect to find birth control readily available in pharmacies.

• Women alone should not take taxis at night and should not go out after 7:00 P.M.

THE MAGHREB

Algeria, Morocco, Tunisia

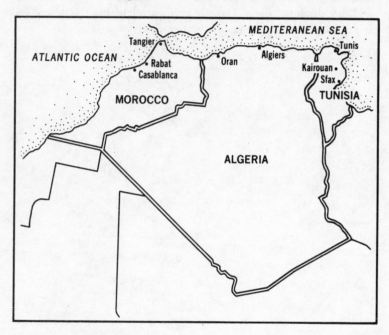

Travelers are drawn to the *Maghreb* by the chance to explore the mysteries of the Sahara and the magic of the imperial cities of Morocco.

There are countless other reasons to visit the area. The history buff will find sites and lore from the Romans and the Berbers. Outdoor types will find beaches and skiing. Businessmen will find markets for their products and their expertise.

Algeria

Algeria, the largest of the three countries in the *Maghreb*, is also the most conservative. The country's population is almost entirely Muslim, and, outside Algiers, many women still wear the veil.

Algeria's three main languages are Arabic (the official language), French (the language of the administrative and intellectual elite), and Berber. Listening can often be confusing, because people will mix French with Arabic or Berber with Arabic.

GREETINGS

• Shake hands when introduced. Remember, however, that religious men never shake hands with a woman.

• Note that very good friends of the same sex kiss one another in greeting.

• When you're introduced to someone, use the last name with Mr., Miss, etc. (See "Key Words and Phrases," page 227 for titles in Arabic.)

• Remember that titles—Doctor, Lawyer, and Professor—are important. (See "Key Words and Phrases" for the Arabic translation of the titles.)

• If you wish, use French forms of address, even if you're speaking Arabic: *Monsieur, Madame, Mademoiselle, Professeur, Docteur, Avocat* (attorney).

• When using Arabic titles, use the title plus the first name. When using titles in French or English, use the title plus the last name.

CONVERSATION

• Don't discuss a person's family at a first meeting.

• Try to learn something about soccer. People are intensely fond of the sport, and it's a good "ice-breaking" subject for conversation.

• To please Algerian acquaintances, remark on the beauties of the country and the quality of the food.

• Have some anecdotes ready about life in your country. You'll almost surely be asked.

• Don't bring up anything relating to France, since most Algerians are sensitive about their colonial past.

• Avoid mentioning religion or the Mideast situation.

TELEPHONES

• Expect to find very few public telephones and to see *long* lines of people waiting to use them.

• For a local call, deposit a one-*dinar* coin for three minutes. At the tone, add more money to continue the call.

• Make long-distance calls at the post office in the countryside. In Algiers, use the international telephone office, which is open 24 hours a day. Calls to Europe can be dialed directly from Algiers.

• If you're calling from outside Algiers, realize that international calls have to be routed by an operator through Algiers, and it can

take a long time to get through to Algiers.

IN PUBLIC

• Don't fear being accosted by young men who want to be your guide (as you will be in Morocco). Tourism is not a major source of revenue.

• Note that men and women are separated at both public and private gatherings.

• If you go to the beach, don't look for the amenities you're accustomed to find at many beaches —drink stands, umbrellas, bathrooms, etc.

• A woman should never go to the beach alone.

• Keep in mind that Algerian women rarely attend sports events, so a Western woman should never attend one without a man. Even with an escort, she may feel conspicuous.

• Women should note that young men often harass Algerian women verbally. As a foreigner, deal with the similar harassment by saying *"Sib-nee fi-hah-lee,"* which means "Leave me alone."

Away from the main tourist route, women are less likely to encounter harassment. However, the farther from tourist areas they go, the more likely they are to be treated as inferior.

• Look for public bathrooms in hotels, restaurants, and cafes.

• Bargain everywhere (except in grocery stores). Sometimes you may be able to barter—to trade a camera, jeans, or running shoes for the item you want.

• Remember that women usually don't like to have their pictures taken, so be very discreet if you try to photograph them. In the south of Algeria, both sexes of the Touareg people may object. Ask before you take photos.

• Obey the international signs (a camera with a red line through it) in various areas—e.g., defense zones—that forbid photography.

• If you wish to use a public bathroom, find one in a hotel, where it will be Western style. In other places (restaurants-cafes), the toilet may be a hole in the floor, and the bathroom may not be clean.

DRESS

• For casual dress in public, women should not wear jeans, shorts, or slacks. Wear skirts and tops with sleeves. Men should not wear shorts.

• Business attire for men is a suit and tie. Women should wear a simple but elegant suit and comfortable shoes—not high heels.

• For a meal at a home or a party, men should wear suits and ties and women should wear dinner or cocktail dresses that come below the knee. Women shouldn't wear anything revealing.

MEALS

Hours and Foods

Breakfast: Between 7:00 and 8:00 A.M. There will be baguettes, *galettes* (a thick Syrian bread), croissants, or brioches, with butter and homemade marmalade or jam. The usual drink is café au lait, made with strong Turkish coffee and boiled milk.

Lunch: The main meal, served between noon and 2:00 P.M. Often there is a soup, *salade Niçoise* (served as a first course if there is no soup), *couscous*, fruit, and coffee (like espresso). On special occasions, the dessert will be pastry. With the meal, people drink soda, water, or soft drinks.

Dinner: About 7:00 P.M. in the winter (December–February) and 8:00 or 8:30 P.M. in the summer (June–August). A light meal, a typical dinner might be couscous with various sauces, *makatafa* (a soup made of lamb, tomatoes, and herbs), or *torta* (phyllo turnovers filled with ground lamb, cheese, and parsley).

• Note that oranges are a very popular fruit, and in summer people enjoy melons of all kinds and grapes.

• Expect the typical bread to be the baguette (a long French loaf).

Beverages: People usually drink water, milk, or a kind of buttermilk called *l'ben*. If you want Algerian bottled spring water, ask for *saida* (sye-dah). Algerian beer, which comes in an unmarked bottle, is weak and watery.

Table Manners

• Don't expect appetizers or drinks before a meal.

• Remember that in religious families men and women eat separately, except when immediate family members dine. When guests are present, the sexes always part.

• Even if you're the guest of honor at a dinner, don't expect a special seat.

• Prepare to encounter different styles of eating: some people sit on low couches with a big table in the middle; others sit on special mats on the floor around a low table; still others sit on chairs around a standard dining table.

• Note that some people eat with silverware and others with the right hand. Couscous is always eaten with a large spoon. The use of eating utensils often depends upon the dish: Steak is eaten with knife and fork, while stew is eaten with a fork and the sauce is scooped up with bread.

• Don't feel that you're insulting your hosts if you don't finish everything on your plate. Do try to taste everything.

• Feel free to stay up to two hours after dinner. People don't jump up and leave at meal's end as they do in some other countries.

Eating Out

• Try one of the several restaurants that serve French and Algerian cuisine. The country also has Thai, Chinese, and Vietnamese restaurants.

• Be aware that service can vary considerably in quality, since the state owns most restaurants.

• Women should note that in Algiers there are French-style cafes to which they can go alone or with friends. In other towns, women should not go to cafes.

• Check outside to see if the restaurant has posted the menu in the window. Many do.

• To call the waiter, say *"Garçon."*

• Realize that the person who issues the invitation pays for everyone.

• If you're in Algeria during Ramadan, don't worry that you won't be able to find food. Many restaurants stay open for non-Muslims, even though Muslims are fasting.

Specialties:

Appetizer: Bourek—a flaky turnover of phyllo dough stuffed with mushrooms, spinach, shrimp, or eggplant.

The Staple: Couscous—steamed semolina served with eggplant, chicken, fish, lamb, or mixed vegetables. It can also be made with sweets and served as a dessert.

Soups and Stews: Chorba beida—chicken soup with chicken, onions, cinnamon, parsley, peppers, chick-peas, and vermicelli (there are other types of *chorba*—white beans or meatballs and rice, or lamb and potatoes or lentils); *sferia*—a chicken *tajine* (stew), cooked in a clay pot called a *tajine*, and flavored with onions and cinnamon and served with chick-peas and cheese-flavored croquettes; *chicken thikha*—a stew of chicken with a sauce of tomatoes, onions, garlic, and potatoes.

Entrees: *Dolma*—vegetables such as cabbage, green peppers, artichokes, or zucchini stuffed with chopped lamb, onions, chick-peas, parsley, cinnamon, and rice; *makouda*—a sauteed mixture of eggs, potatoes, and parsley; *merguez*—a fried sausage made of lamb or beef; *dess b'l-besla*—lentils cooked with garlic, cumin, cinnamon, olive oil, chili pepper, and bay leaves.

HOTELS

• Be aware that Algeria does not have enough hotels. You'll find hotels in main towns and along the coast fully booked. (Reserve *well* in advance if you want a room during the summer (June through August.) Service is usually not very good.

• To stay at one of the oasis hotels, where rooms are difficult to obtain (especially in winter—December through February) and which are generally excellent, sign up for a tour with O.N.A.T., the state tourist agency. The organization's only offices are in Algeria.

• The government travel organization, ALTOUR, operates lodgings at recreational sites and mineral springs. The quality varies greatly; some may not be properly cleaned, heated, or well lit. Always bring bottled water if you're staying at one. Most of these lodgings have restaurants, but, again, the quality of the food and service varies considerably.

• Bring food for any road trip. The restaurants along roadsides are not usually acceptable.

• In every town, expect to find at least one hotel with decent accommodations, though possibly indifferent service. Since these hotels are run by the government, your currency forms may be checked.

• Stay at one of the middle-to-lower-range hotels and you'll find yourself back in Algeria's colonial days. There will be "antique" beds and sinks, bidets, and window shutters. (These accommodations may sound romantic, but the places are usually fairly run down.) Breakfast sometimes costs extra, but you *must* pay for breakfast or you won't get a room. Many newer hotels don't force you to pay for breakfast whether or not you want it.

• When you register, check to find out during what hours the hotel has water. Some have water for only a few hours a day.

• Keep in mind that you can't pay for hotel bills with a credit card. You must use traveler's checks or cash.

TIPPING

• At restaurants, a 15% service charge will be included in the bill. Any extra tip is optional.

• At the airport, the official charge for porters is 5 DA per suitcase.

• Don't tip taxi drivers or gas station attendants.

• At hotels, give 10 to 20 dinars for carrying your luggage.

• Give a guide you have hired for the day the equivalent of $5.00.

• Tip a hairdresser the equivalent of $2.00.

PRIVATE HOMES

• Unless you're a close family friend or a relative, call before visiting. Women are usually available for visits at any time, while the traditional time for males to visit one another is between 6:00 and 7:00 P.M.

• If you develop a relationship with an Algerian, don't be surprised if you're invited to stay with the family.

• Realize that homes in Algiers will have constant hot water—when water is running. However, there are frequent water shortages, which lead to water being cut off in Algiers and throughout the country. Some people fill buckets with water when it's available. Ask your hostess when it is convenient for you to bathe.

• Offer to help with household chores. Your offer will be appreciated, but it will probably be refused.

• If you're a foreign woman, expect people to be very protective. For example, you probably won't be able to shop or sightsee on your own.

• At the end of a visit with a family, give the maid a gift—e.g., perfume.

Gifts: If you're invited to dinner by members of the older generation, bring pastries such as napoleons or *millefeuilles*. If the invitation is from a young couple, bring flowers. Good choices are pink or red roses or tulips. Don't give violets, since they are associated with sadness.

• Consider bringing one of the following, valued because the government has a tight control on imports: cameras, instant coffee, jeans, good-quality sunglasses, T-shirts, running shoes, or good-quality chocolates.

• Welcome gifts from abroad for children—T-shirts, sneakers, jeans, toys (there's not much of a toy selection in Algeria); for women—material for making dresses, make-up; for men—whiskey (if you know that the person drinks), American cigarettes (if you know that the person smokes).

• If you're stopping in Europe, where the current is the same as it is in Algeria, bring small electric appliances—coffee makers, blenders, toasters.

BUSINESS

Hours

Banks: Sunday to Wednesday, 8:00 A.M. to noon and 3:00 to 5:00 P.M. Thursday, 8:00 A.M. to 2:00 P.M.

Government Offices: Saturday to Wednesday, 8:00 A.M. to 5:00 P.M. Thursday, 8:00 A.M. to noon.

Business Offices: During the winter, Saturday to Thursday, 8:00 A.M. to noon and 2:00 to 5:30 P.M. During the summer, 8:00 A.M. to noon and 3:00 to 5:30 P.M. During Ramadan, 8:30 A.M. to 4:00 P.M.

Shops: Saturday to Thursday 9:00 A.M. to noon and 2:00 to 7:00 P.M. During Ramadan, 9:00 A.M. to 4:00 P.M., Thursday included.

Currency

• The abbreviation used for Algerian currency is AD (Algerian *dinar*). One *dinar* equals 100 *centimes*.

• Coins: 5, 10, 20, and 50 *centimes* and 1, 2, 5, and 10 *dinars*.

• Bills: 20, 50, 100, and 500 *dinars*.

• Remember that the AD 500-note has been taken out of circulation. Never accept one, because it won't be worth anything.

• Don't be surprised if you are given prices in French—e.g., *deux milles* (2,000 *centimes*) instead of AD 20. If you don't want to juggle three currencies in your mind, ask to have the price translated into *dinars*.

• Keep your credit cards in your wallet. You won't be able to use them. Prepare to pay for everything in traveler's checks.

• If you want to change money and the banks in Algiers are closed, try one of the better hotels.

Business Practices

• Be prepared to make several trips to Algeria to accomplish your goal. Since almost all business dealings are with an Algerian government organization, you will probably be dealing with one, and it's likely to be very bureaucratic. In fact, a Ministry may agree to negotiations only if they *really* want the project and if the contract is large. After your negotiations are complete, you'll have to deal with another government agency, since both the State Planning Secretariat and the Ministry of Finance must approve all contracts with foreign companies.

• Don't make overtures to an Algerian company or to the government if your company is 100% owned by foreigners. You must have some Algerian investment.

• For contacts to pave your way in Algeria, get in touch with the Commercial Section of the Algerian embassy in your country, the National U.S.-Arab Chamber of Commerce (you'll find a Chamber of Commerce in major towns in Algeria), and the Algerian Mission at the United Nations.

• Try to make appointments one to two months in advance, though

Muslims may resist making a commitment so far in advance. If your business is in Algiers, note that there are frequent flights to and from Europe. However, if you're working in the south of Algeria, there may be only two flights each *week*.

• Realize that businesses use telexes, not fax machines. The best hotels, however, will have fax machines.

• If possible, arrange appointments between 9:00 A.M. and noon.

• Be punctual—especially when dealing with top-level businesspeople—even though Algerians tend to be late.

• Have your business cards translated into either French or Arabic. Have any materials you plan to use in your presentation translated into French.

• Be aware that correspondence, bids, and contracts must be in French with metric measurements.

• If you aren't fluent in French and your Algerian counterparts aren't fluent in English, hire an interpreter. To find one, call on the Commercial Section of your country's embassy in Algiers.

• Don't move immediately to the business you want to accomplish. Express interest in the Algerian company, since the Algerians will want to know about yours. Be prepared to talk about your company—what projects it has completed, its achievements, and the benefits for Algeria of working with it.

• Expect Algerian contracts to have deadline dates, performance requirements, and other obligations written in. A contract may require foreign companies to fulfill certain obligations and to pay a penalty if they don't. They will be subject to this penalty even if Algerians have not fulfilled their obligations. Example: If a foreign company agrees to have a building constructed by a certain date, and the Algerians don't provide the materials that were in the agreement, the foreign company will *still* have to pay a penalty. To protect yourself, allow twice as much time for a project as you would in the U.S. or Europe.

• Be sure that all terms of agreement are *written* into your contract.

• Before making a final commitment, find out if your Algerian customer has an import license (A.G.I.—Autorisations Globales d'Importation) so that he can import equipment. Otherwise, you'll experience long delays in customs and have to pay warehousing costs.

• Businesswomen should expect to be accepted in Algiers. You will be treated with respect.

• Don't be surprised if you're asked to stay with the family of your Algerian counterpart *after*

your contract is signed. He won't issue such an invitation before negotiations are complete, because business in Algeria is very competitive, and he would be showing you favoritism during the negotiating process.

• If you're at a restaurant with an Algerian with whom you're negotiating, and you're not sure if the person drinks alcohol, don't order an alcoholic beverage—you could lose the deal.

• To entertain a businessman, take him to the restaurant in one of the best hotels or to a seafood restaurant near the beach.

• Note that business dinners are more popular than lunches because of the intense heat in the middle of the day.

• If you're traveling with your wife, feel free to ask an Algerian businessman if he would like his wife to join you for dinner. If he is conservative, he will probably refuse, but he won't be offended that you asked.

HOLIDAYS AND SPECIAL OCCASIONS

• For religious holidays, celebrated according to the Muslim calendar, see "Customs and Manners in the Arab World." On the following secular holidays, celebrated according to the Gregorian calendar, expect to find banks, businesses, government offices, and many shops and restaurants closed: New Year's Day (Jan. 1); Labor Day (May 1); Commemoration Day (June 19); Independence Day of the F.L.N. (National Liberation Front) (July 5); Day of Revolution (Nov. 1).

TRANSPORTATION

Public Transportation

• Note that the bus system in Algiers provides route maps at all main stops and signs in Arabic and French. However, the public buses in Algiers are extremely overcrowded and run on erratic schedules. Outside Algiers, the numbers of the buses are written in Arabic only. Pay when you get on the bus. In general, it's wiser to take a taxi than the bus. Taxis are safer and more secure.

• Be aware that both local and long-distance taxis are yellow. Negotiate the fare in advance. Use Algiers' radio-taxi service to phone for a taxi. Be prepared for a 15- to 30-minute wait during the three rush hours—8:00 A.M., noon, and 5:00 P.M.

• Consider taking one of the large, shared taxis, called *louages* (loo-azh). They operate only between cities in the north of Algeria. They don't run on a set schedule but leave when they are full. They are worth the extra cost over bus travel, but you may wait a long time until the *louage* has a full complement of passengers.

• If you're taking a long-distance bus trip from Algiers, you can buy your ticket 24 hours in advance at the main bus station.

• Realize that trains connect all major cities. They have first (reserved seats with four to a compartment) and second (no reserved seats) classes. Both classes are crowded and not very clean, and trains are often late. You'll find snack bars serving sandwiches and soft drinks. On long-distance trains (e.g., Algiers–Tunisia) making overnight journeys, there will be *wagons-lits*, individual compartments with a bed.

• For the cleanest and most comfortable transportation between cities, fly. There is a domestic air service connecting all cities.

Driving

• Realize that most rental cars are unsafe by Western standards.

• If you decide to drive, have an International Driver's License or a French driver's license.

• Be wary of driving in Algiers, where the narrow, hilly streets make driving difficult and where parking is time-consuming.

• Be conscious that in many towns, street signs are in Arabic only.

• When planning a drive on a weekend, recall that a 30-mile trip can take up to six hours because of the heavy traffic.

• Be extra alert when driving, and drive defensively at all times. Algeria's highway fatality rate is higher per capita than that in the entire developed world combined.

• If you plan to drive in the Sahara, pay special attention to the section on "Desert Driving" in "Customs and Manners in the Arab World."

LEGAL MATTERS, HEALTH, AND SAFETY

• If you're visiting Algeria from the U.S. or Canada, realize that you'll need a visa.

• Declare all currency on the Currency Declaration Form you'll receive at your port of entry. This special form must be filled out in duplicate. In addition to currency, declare anything of value you're bringing in—cameras, jewelry, a Walkman, etc. Keep this form, and record on it every change of money. When you leave the country, you will turn in the form.

• Realize that it is forbidden to bring in or take out Algerian currency.

• Don't bring marijuana into the country or use it while you're in Algeria. It's illegal, and you could be jailed.

• As a non-Muslim, feel free to visit mosques—but not during prayer time and not during Ramadan.

• Be aware that alcohol, including Algerian wine, is available only in international hotels.

• Don't eat raw fruits or vegetables that cannot be peeled. Drink only bottled water, never tap water, and don't use ice cubes.

• Don't eat raw shellfish.

• Don't swim in rivers or streams because of the risk of the parasitic disease bilharzia.

• Avoid swimming off the beaches near Algiers, since the waters are polluted.

Morocco

Who can forget Bing Crosby and Bob Hope's departure line, "Like Webster's Dictionary, we're Morocco bound." Travelers in increasing numbers follow the pair to the delights of Morocco, where they can ski in the Atlas mountains, swim off the beaches of Agadir, or shop in the *souks* of Fez and Marrakesh. Since tourism is important to Morocco's economy, you'll find the country prepared to cater to both your needs and whims.

GREETINGS

• Men shake hands with both men and women when introduced. If you're introduced to someone of the lower class, be prepared for a woman to greet another woman by kissing her on one cheek for a long time and then on the other cheek, also for a long time.

• If a woman is shyly standing behind her husband and doesn't offer her hand, just nod.

• Always extend the right hand, *never* the left.

• Expect good friends of both sexes to kiss on both cheeks—the right side first—when greeting and saying good-bye.

• Note that there are two important titles: *Haj* (masculine, pronounced *hahj*) and *Haja* (feminine, pronounced *hahjah*) that signify that the person has been to Mecca. As a Westerner, don't use this title. Do greet doctors (M.D. or Ph.D.) and professors by the title plus the last name.

• Whether in greeting or conversation, women should never make eye contact with men who

are strangers. They would see it as an invitation.

• At a party or group gathering, expect to be introduced individually. Be sure to shake hands with each person.

• Note that older people will shake hands and then place their right hand over their heart.

CONVERSATION

• Realize that most Moroccans are bilingual in Arabic and French, and many who have studied abroad also speak English. In the North, many people speak Spanish. (Expect to see signs in Arabic and French.)

• For initial conversations, ask about families—but *not* about wives. Other good subjects are sports, such as soccer, track (Morocco has had two Olympic track stars), and golf.

• Before you leave, learn a little Moroccan history so that you can ask intelligent questions about the country's culture and architecture.

• Avoid talking about Israel or sex, and do not make negative comments about either Islam or the King.

• Don't be surprised if people ask you your view of Islam. It's easiest to say that it has some very beautiful customs but that you are of another religion.

TELEPHONES

• Expect people of the professional class to have phones in their homes.

• Look for public telephones in cafes and public places such as bus and train stations, or ask at a small shop if you can use theirs—only for local calls, of course.

• Note that public telephones accept 10, 20, and 50 *centimes* or 1 *dirham* coins. For a local call, deposit 1 *dirham* for three minutes. A signal will tell you to deposit more money.

• Remember that most people in the countryside don't have telephones. Go to the post office, place your call, and pay when you finish.

• Use telephones at the post office for long-distance calls. To call overseas, you may have to wait several hours. Bring reading material.

IN PUBLIC

• If you want to use a gesture to say "Come here," use the Western good-bye wave. In Morocco, it's a beckoning signal.

• Don't attempt to visit a mosque. Foreigners aren't allowed in them.

• Don't be surprised to see men and men or women and women holding hands. The gesture has no sexual implications.

• Realize that official guides are authorized. You can arrange for one through your hotel. However, whenever you go out, you will be pursued by hordes of "unofficial guides" who want to turn a quick profit. You won't get rid of them by ignoring them or getting angry; they will continue to follow you. Saying "No, thank you" in Arabic will probably work. However, despite the fact that many barely speak English or French, you might want to agree to let one serve as your guide. First, they will fend off all the other unofficial guides. Second, in a city like Fez it's almost impossible *not* to get totally lost, trying to wind your way through the labyrinth of cobblestone alleys, where you'll have to lean against walls to let donkeys go past. The unofficial guides charge only the equivalent of $1.00 for a few hours' service. (You won't be bothered by "unofficial guides" if you're with an official guide.)

• A woman traveling without a man should be sure to arrive at her destination while it's still day. Morocco is very conservative, and a woman alone at night is regarded as a prostitute and will be harassed.

• A woman alone will be asked frequently if she is married—and if not, why not. You might want to wear a wedding ring, and, when asked where your husband is, say that he'll be joining you in a few days.

• Women with long hair should wear it up. Moroccans consider long hair very sensual.

• If you're taking photographs in Marrakesh in the area of Djema-el-Fna, expect performers and watersellers to demand money if you want to take their picture. Give them 3 DH.

• Never go shopping with a guide. He will take you only to shops from which he will get a commission, and you'll end up paying more. In newer parts of cities, shops are easy to find by yourself. In the *medinas* (the original Arab sections of cities), you'll be

totally lost without a guide, since there are many places where you can't even see the sun to find directions from it. Use a guide in the old sections, but be sure that *you* choose the places at which you want to shop.

• If you're interested in rugs, realize that vendors will pull down hundreds of rugs from piles up to the ceiling to show you. Don't feel intimidated or obligated to buy just because they have gone to a great deal of trouble. That's their job.

• Bargain everywhere except in restaurants. Never show special interest immediately in what you really want to buy. Browse around. Then ask the price of what you want. Offer half the asking price, and continue until the dealer reaches a figure with which you are comfortable. Consider agreeing to buy when you've reached a discount of about 33%.

• Never bargain for something that you have no intention of buying. You'll create bad feeling.

• Whether in bus or trains stations or restaurants, expect to find a "squat" toilet—a hole in the floor. The local method of cleaning after using the toilet is to use your *left* hand with a bucket of water or water that runs from a tap near the hole. If you don't feel that you can adapt to this practice, bring along tissues, put them in a plastic bag after use, and dispose of them when you find a wastebasket.

• Note that public bathrooms in hotels and better restaurants are Western style.

• Don't go into a community *hammam* (public bath) alone or with other Westerners. (See "Private Homes" for more on using a *hammam*.)

DRESS

• For casual dress, women should be sure that their shoulders are covered, that their sleeves are at least three-quarter length, and that their skirt is mid-calf or longer. Men should wear a shirt and pants; they should not wear shorts.

• Women should never wear valuable or ostentatious jewelry.

• For business, men should wear suits, and women should wear a skirt and blouse (with three-quarter or long sleeves) and a jacket in cool weather, or a dress with sleeves, or a dress and jacket.

• For going to dinner in a home, men should wear a jacket, shirt, and tie; women should wear a dress

with long sleeves or a blouse with long sleeves and skirt (be sure that a dress or skirt comes below the knees) or a caftan with long sleeves.

• Don't expect formal events for which a tuxedo or formal evening dress is needed. For dressy occasions, men should wear a dark suit, and women a cocktail dress with long sleeves.

• If you're going to be visiting *medinas* (old sections of towns), wear good walking shoes with rubber soles for walking on slippery cobblestones.

• For a winter visit (December through February) to the northern part of Morocco's Atlantic Coast, bring warm clothing.

MEALS

Hours and Foods

Breakfast: 7:00 or 8:00 A.M. Strong French-style coffee or mint tea, served very sweet, along with bread, honey, and jam.

Lunch: The day's main meal, served about 2:00 P.M. Expect *ta-*

jine (see below), bread, and salad or couscous (see below).

On Friday, there will always be couscous. After the main courses will come fruit (e.g., orange slices with cinnamon) and then mint tea after the meal. There probably won't be a beverage with the meal, as people believe that couscous would swell in the stomach.

• Note that food cooked in a *tajine,* a terra-cotta pot with a cone-shaped cover, is called *tajine,* which means a stew. (See "Specialties" for the various kinds of *tajines*). Couscous, made of semolina flour, salt, and water, is usually heaped on a tray. A hollow made in the middle is filled with a stew of chicken or lamb and then garnished with raisins, chick-peas, onions, and sometimes almonds and pieces of pickled lemon. The usual accompaniments to couscous are a side dish of broth with boiled vegetables and a bowl of hot pepper sauce.

Dinner: Some time between 8:00 and 11:00 P.M. It's a light meal, often consisting of bread and cheese, or soup and spaghetti.

• If you're invited to a home for the first time, anticipate the offer of several courses: salad, *tajine,* couscous, fruit, and mint tea. If there is an appetizer—as there may be in an upper-class home—it will be served when people are seated at the table.

• If an appetizer is served, look for a Moroccan salad: very small dishes of olives, diced liver, pureed eggplant, grated carrots with orange juice, sweetbreads, brains, and mint.

• At a formal meal, expect a fairly elaborate feast—for example: *harira* (soup); *bstila* (layers of pastry with pigeon; *tajine;* lemon chicken; *mechoui* (roast mutton); couscous with chicken and mutton. After the meal, there will usually be mint tea and pastries.

• Expect the bread to be round, unleavened Arab bread (pita).

Beverages: Coca-Cola, orange soda, and lemonade are served before and after meals. In the unlikely event that there is a beverage with the meal (more likely in an urban than a rural home), it will be fruit juice or tea. After meals, mint tea is the most usual offering. Other beverages: *halib luz* (a drink made of almonds and milk—very expensive); *Judor* (lemonade-like but not so sweet); two varieties of bottled water—*Oulmes* (carbonated); *Sidi Harazem* (non-carbonated). *Halib luz* is not safe to drink; *Judor*—a bottled drink —is.

• Note that there's a ceremony that goes with the serving of tea. The pot is filled with boiling water and then emptied. Green tea and sugar are put into the pot with boiled water. That mixture is

THE MAGHREB
161

boiled; when it's ready, more water, sugar, and mint are added. Then it's poured into a glass and back into the pot. When serving tea, women raise the pot into the air and pour it so that a ring of bubbles—called a *fez*—forms around the inside rim of the glass. The tea hasn't been poured properly if there is no *fez*.

Table Manners

• Don't be surprised if men and women eat separately. Usually men eat first, and women have the leftovers. If the family's father is at home, the father and boys will very likely eat together. If the father isn't at home, the women and children eat together.

• Before—and sometimes after —the meal, expect a servant to bring a pitcher and bowl. He'll hold the bowl under your hands and pour water over them. It's very important to wash your hands in front of everyone. Don't say something such as, "I just washed up in the bathroom."

• Never put your left hand on the table. Keep it in your lap.

• Note that the guest of honor is seated next to the host, so that the host can push the best parts of the meat to the guest.

• Check to see how many table-cloths there are to determine how many courses will be served. Ta-

bles are often set with a number of cloths, with one being removed after every course. If you determine the number of courses, you can pace your eating so that you can sample some of every course and not fill up on the first one.

• Don't be shocked if the table is covered with plastic, and if people throw bones and other inedible food onto it. At the end of the meal, the plastic sheet and bones are thrown out.

• Seating is generally on low couches with pillows around a low round table. There will be one communal dish. Eat from the section of that dish directly in front of you, progressing at the pace of your host. Start by breaking off a piece of bread and dipping it into the sauce. Don't touch the meat until your host moves it directly in front of you and urges you to eat. Never reach beyond your space of the communal dish.

• Don't be surprised if, as a foreigner, you're offered a spoon for eating couscous. If you are not offered a spoon, take a tablespoon of couscous in your right hand, roll it around to form a ball, and pop it into your mouth. Try not to touch your mouth with your hand because you're going to put your hand back into the communal plate. (As you can imagine, this technique isn't easy and is perfected only with practice. Do your best!)

• Wipe your fingers on a piece of bread between bites. *Lick* your hand only when you've finished completely. Licking symbolizes that you've had enough.

• If you take a bone, suck the marrow. If you don't, people will think that you're wasting the bone.

• Feel honored if you're offered chicken, especially the neck. Chicken is a delicacy and the neck is considered the best part.

• If you don't want to eat something, say that you have a health problem or are allergic.

• Be aware that you might find one communal glass for water. If you don't want to share a glass with everyone in the group, ask for a soft drink. You will then usually be given your own glass, from which no one else will drink. If no soft drink is available, you could say that you aren't thirsty.

• Don't finish everything or it will look as though your host didn't serve enough food.

• Expect people to push you to eat more and more. (One traveler said, "You practically have to fall over dead before they take a refusal of more food seriously.") Try saying *"Sah-fee,"* which means "That's enough."

• A gesture to indicate that you're full: Take the back of your hand, raise it to your chin, and tap the underside of your chin.

• If you are the senior guest, don't be surprised if you are asked to prepare the tea. If you don't feel confident of your ability to create a *fez* (see above), you might want to decline graciously.

Eating Out

• In urban areas, try one of the many excellent French restaurants. In the North, Spanish restaurants are common.

• For breakfast, consider one of the French-inspired cafes. Help yourself to croissants at the bar, and then tell the waiter how many you've had. Women should know that most cafes are frequented only by men. Don't go in unless you see other women inside. In large cities, you will probably find cafes with students and some foreign women. Feel free to stop in at such places.

• Women alone should eat only in hotel restaurants or fine restaurants. Otherwise, expect to be harassed by men.

• In any restaurant—even those at the best hotels—ask what the day's specialty is. It probably won't be on the menu, and it may be exceptionally good.

• Don't order fish unless you're on the coast. It may not be fresh.

• In small towns, eat only in hotel or kebab restaurants. Other places may not be hygienic.

Specialties

• Should you be in Morocco during Ramadan, note that *harira*—a chicken soup thickened with flour and eggs and flavored with pepper, cinnamon, lemon juice, and saffron—is served every night to break the fast. It's served at other times as well, sometimes accompanied by dates or figs.

• Expect to encounter *tajines* frequently. There are many types of this stew (named for the terracotta pot in which it is cooked), the most popular being one of chicken, olives, and brine-preserved lemons. Other popular *tajines*: chicken with grapes, raisins, or almonds; lamb with prunes; quail with apricots; beef with apples; duck with figs. You may also find *tajines* made with mutton, pigeon, fish, turkey, or camel meat. All are cooked with honey, nutmeg, cinnamon, ginger, and cardamom. They may also include lemon slices, green olives, mint, grilled hot peppers, garlic, and tomatoes.

• Some pastry-based specialties are: *briouats*—thin deep-fried pastry filled with chopped meat, rice, and almonds (filled with honey and almonds, *briouats* are a dessert); *rghaifs*—stuffed, fried pancakes; *grionches*—twisted strips of pastry with honey and sesame seeds, served as a snack or dessert; *kaabel ghzal* (which means "gazelle's horns")—pastry in a horn shape filled with almond paste and orange flower water and served as dessert; *bstila*—a huge, stuffed flaky pastry filled with pigeon, cinnamon, eggs, sugar, almonds, onions, ginger, saffron, and coriander.

• Other main course specialties: *mechoui*—a whole roasted sheep; *djaja mahamara*—chicken stuffed with almonds, semolina, and raisins; *merguez*—spiced lamb sausage.

• Remember that the container that you think contains pepper probably contains cumin, the main spice used in Morocco. Other flavorings are fresh coriander, ginger, garlic, and onions.

• At dessert, look for *seffa*—couscous sprinkled with confectioners' sugar.

HOTELS

• Book ahead for peak periods in the main cities and resorts: August, Christmas, and Easter.

• Realize that Morocco has hotels of almost unimaginable luxury—including one in Marrakesh to which Winston Churchill used to go in the winter to paint.

• Expect the best hotels, and even two- and three-star hotels, to have Western-style bathrooms.

• Prepare to pay extra for the continental breakfast of juice, croissants or rolls, and coffee. Prices for the standard tourist breakfast are set by the government and depend on the class of hotel.

• Before you check into one of the less expensive hotels, check the room. Make sure that the room is clean, that the ceiling fans work, and—most important—that the locks work.

• If you're staying at a hotel in the countryside, prepare to do without water during the day. Water is often cut off from late morning to early evening. When you arrive, ask during what hours water is available.

• In small hotels outside major cities, check to make sure that the sheets are changed.

• Foreign women traveling alone should be aware that you are considered fair game. If you stay in a small hotel, make sure that there is a working lock on the door and that the room has a private bath. (If the bathroom is down the hall, men may harass you as you go from your room to the bathroom.) Never open the door if someone simply knocks. Insist on identification.

• Note that hotels have formal complaint books in which guests can register any dissatisfactions. Government inspectors check the books periodically.

TIPPING

• At restaurants, if the service is not included, leave 10%.

• Give cafe waiters from 50 *centimes* up, depending on the size of the bill.

• Tip porters 5 to 8 dirhams per bag.

• Don't tip taxi drivers.

• Give official guides 10 to 20 dirhams for a few hours' service.

• Tip ushers at cinemas 50 *centimes*.

• Give hairdressers 2 dirhams.

• Leave maids in hotels 5 to 10 dirhams per week.

PRIVATE HOMES

• Visit between 3:00 and 6:00 P.M. It's all right to drop in on people because most don't have telephones.

• Always enter a home with your right foot first.

• Don't be upset if people appear to be screaming at one another and sound angry. That's the normal tone of voice.

• Don't admire someone's possessions, or they may feel obliged to give them to you. Don't feel obligated to give any of your possessions that someone else admires.

• If you stay with a family, remember that women will usually be allowed to help with chores (kitchen, etc.) but male guests never will.

• Should you stay with a family, realize that you are guaranteed protection as well as exceptionally warm hospitality. Don't expect to tour on your own. The family will feel that you are their responsibility, and they will be concerned with their reputation as hosts. The women of the house may hover around you, supervising your every move. You won't be able to avoid this protectiveness, unless you are going out with someone the family knows.

• Don't be surprised if your host family changes or abandons the day's agenda without telling you. Example: Plans were made to go shopping at 10:00. The time arrives and no one—except you—is prepared to leave. You ask when people will be leaving, and someone says "In a little while." People may change or cancel plans without saying anything to you. You don't have much choice but to "go with the flow."

• Treat maids with respect. They are considered part of the family. Don't tip them. If you wish, ask your hostess if you could buy the maid a gift, and, if so, what to buy.

• If you have a gas heater in your room, don't leave it on at night. Left on, it could be dangerous.

• Be aware that people don't use toilet paper. They wash themselves (with the left hand) instead. Putting toilet paper into a toilet that's Turkish style—i.e., a hole in the floor—can damage the toilet. Options: (1) Use your own tissues. put them in a plastic bag, and dispose of them in a wastebasket, (2) Adapt to the local custom. Use your left hand and wash yourself with water that's in a bucket or that flows from a tap near the hole.

• Expect Western-style toilets in the homes of wealthier people.

• Also look for showers and baths in the homes of the wealthy, where taking a daily bath is customary. Don't take a very long shower, because you'll use up the hot water supply.

• If there is no private bath, anticipate a trip to the *hammam* (public bath), which is both a place to bathe and a place where men socialize with other men and women with other women. A foreign woman should go with a Moroccan. Foreigners are usually not allowed in *hammams* built next to mosques. Hours for women are usually 9:00 A.M. to 7:00 P.M. and for men 7:00 P.M. to 1:00 A.M. and sometimes 5:00 to 9:00 A.M.

It's important that your bottom be covered, even while bathing, so men wear underpants or swimming trunks and women wear pants. For sanitary reasons, everyone should wear thongs on their feet. Bring a bag, go to the changing room if you're a woman, or undress facing the wall if you're a man. Put your clothes into the bag, and give it to an attendant. You can put your clothes on a hanger in your cubicle, but they will almost certainly get wet. Don't bring any valuables with you.

Bring with you a bucket, soap,

and black gloves (which feel like a loofah). Pay as you enter and get soap and towels. Go to the central bathing area. There you will find individual cement cubicles with a shower and a wooden bench. An attendant will come around, pour water over you, wash you, and put henna in a woman's hair, if she wants. Friends scrub one another —often very hard to slough off dead skin. Don't be surprised if you're asked to scrub someone's back. That person will then scrub yours. Don't stand behind anyone and slosh your dirty water at them. Floors are washed after each person finishes.

• Never take photographs in a *hammam*.

Gifts: When invited to a meal by a family living in a city, bring nuts, figs, dates, candy, pastries, flowers, or cassettes. A typical gift in the countryside is sugar, which comes in a cone shape. (People break off pieces to put in mint tea.) A gift of sugar is a sign of friendship.

• Don't bring alcohol unless you know that the family drinks.

• Good gifts from abroad: solar calculators; high-intensity flashlights; Ray-Ban sunglasses; cassettes of American popular music; children's clothing. Children also like Frisbees and teenagers enjoy getting T-shirts with the insignia of a city or a university.

• Don't expect people to thank you profusely when you give them a gift. They will say "Thank you" and put the gift aside. They don't want to appear materialistic.

BUSINESS

Hours

Banks: Monday to Friday, 8:30 to 11:30 A.M. and 3:00 to 5:30 P.M. During Ramadan, 8:00 A.M. to 2:30 P.M.

Government Offices: Monday to Friday, 8:30 A.M. to noon and 2:00 to 6:00 P.M.

Businesses: In Tangier, Monday to Friday, 9:00 A.M. to noon and 4:00 to 8:00 P.M. In the rest of the country, 9:00 A.M. to noon and 3:00 to 6:00 P.M.

Shops: Monday to Saturday, 8:30 A.M. to noon and 2:30 to 6:00 or 7:00 P.M. Most shops close on Sunday, but a few close on Friday.

Currency

• The currency is the *dirham* (abbreviated DH). 1 *dirham* equals 100 *centimes*.
• Coins: 5, 10, 20, and 50 *centimes* and 1 and 5 *dirhams*.
• Bills: 5, 10, 50, and 100 *dirhams*.

Business Practices

• Note that the Moroccan government wants to stimulate foreign business because it creates jobs. In the past, everything was owned by the government, but in recent years, there has been a trend toward privatization and the creation of competition.
• Enlist a representative in Morocco to take care of paperwork and to obtain all the official stamps and permits.
• Realize that you will need a letter of credit to conduct business. Most foreign companies are encouraged by their own governments and have ties with their embassies in Morocco.
• Look for contacts through international banks, most of which have branches in Morocco.
• Make personal contacts through your embassy in Morocco. These relationships will be important when doing business with the private sector.

• Plan to make several trips to Morocco before you will be able to accomplish your business goals.

• Note that large businesses and top-class hotels have fax machines.

• Don't bother trying to contact people by telephone when you're in Morocco. It can take up to an hour for a call to go from place to place within the same city. Go to an office in person. Note, however, that a call from overseas may take as little as ten minutes. After you've established a relationship with the company, you can request appointments by telex or fax.

• Try to make arrangements and appointments as far in advance as possible—even two months before you plan to go to Morocco—but don't be surprised if someone who is a Muslim is unwilling to make a commitment that far in advance.

• Be punctual, but don't be surprised if a Moroccan businessman is late. The concept of time is influenced by the religious idea of *insha'allah*—"God willing."

• Bring business cards that are printed in both English and Arabic.

• Expect the Moroccans to be very formal, much as the French were 30 to 40 years ago. French culture is regarded as the ideal, and anything French is considered superior to its American counterpart.

• Be aware that you will find business organizational structures rigid. The pattern is the French bureaucratic system. Find out who will be making the decision about your project. Deal with that person and try to establish a relationship with her/him.

• Take time to develop relationships with your Moroccan counterparts before doing business. Otherwise you will be considered cold and inhuman.

• Avoid political discussions, since you could put your Moroccan counterparts in an uncomfortable position.

• Hire an interpreter if you don't speak French. Most educated Moroccans studied in France and are sophisticated about Western culture. You can find an interpreter through one of the better hotels, through the Tourist Bureau, or through the American Language Centers in some cities (the centers are a division of the United States Information Service).

• Prepare to participate in the customary drinking of tea, without which business is never done.

• Be aware that business discussions may occur in hotels and restaurants, but final deals are always made in an office.

• When a deal becomes final, shake hands with the Moroccan with whom you've made it. This gesture indicates that you have both made a moral contract to carry out your word. You must have a written contract, but a person's word is considered more binding than any written contract, no matter how long or detailed it is.

• Note that a foreign businesswoman can be successful if she is part of a team. Moroccans will treat businesswomen as they do men if they need or want something from her. It's best, however, not to send a woman to do business on her own.

• Expect lunches with business colleagues to be informal social occasions. No business will be discussed.

• Be discreet if you're with a Moroccan with whom you had an alcoholic drink—perhaps the day before—and they refuse one when there are other people with you. Don't comment on the fact that they have drunk alcohol with you—for example, don't say, "You don't like gin and tonic any more?"

• Realize that Moroccans frequently invite foreign businesspeople to their homes for a meal. Don't refuse, or they will be insulted. At the meal, the men will eat together. You won't see any women.

HOLIDAYS AND SPECIAL OCCASIONS

• For holidays observed according to the Muslim calendar, see the "Introduction." On the following secular holidays, expect to find banks, government offices, businesses, and many restaurants and shops closed: New Year's Day (Jan. 1); Feast of the Throne (March 3); Labor Day (May 1); Green March, commemorating the day on which the Moroccans took the Sahara back from the Spanish (Nov. 6); Independence Day (Nov. 18).

• Remember that Ramadan is strictly observed by Moroccans, but tourists in vacation resorts will not be inconvenienced since hotels and restaurants in those areas are geared toward tourists.

TRANSPORTATION

Public Transportation

• Taking an intracity bus, pay when you get on. You don't need exact change. The buses are not air-conditioned and are very crowded. There is also the danger of pickpockets. *Petits taxis* are much better than buses.

• Always keep your passport with you. On certain bus routes, police stop the bus and check each passenger's identification.

• Note that there are two types of taxis: *Petits taxis* are small blue and red cars with rooftop luggage racks. They have meters and are inexpensive. They are allowed to travel only within cities and to airports. *Grands taxis* are larger and a bit more expensive, but they are allowed to travel anywhere. They also have meters. In both types of taxis, drivers rarely—if ever—use the meters, so be sure to arrange the price of your fare before you get in.

• If you take a taxi after 8:00 P.M., be aware that there is a 50% surcharge. Ask at your hotel what the fare for your journey should be.

• Remember that long-distance buses are usually crowded and are air-conditioned only on certain routes.

• Note that there are three classes of trains: third class—seats are just wooden planks; second class—seats with wooden slats, *extremely* cramped with many people standing; first class—air-conditioned, clean, uncrowded, with upholstered seats, and affordable for most Westerners. For a long train trip, bring your own food and beverages.

• Be sure to be at the train station well ahead of departure time. Trains have been known to leave early.

• A woman alone going on a long train trip should try to attach herself to a family.

Driving

• Hire a driver or take other means of transportation rather than rent a car. People drive under the influence of hashish, and most cars don't have seat belts.

• Feel free to bargain if you rent a car from a local agency. It's safer, however, to use one of the international car rental agencies.

• If you're leaving a city to drive into the countryside, make sure that you have a full tank of gas, since gas stations are concentrated in major cities.

• In reading a map, note that the letter "P" indicates a main road and "S" a secondary road. Moroccan roads have an identification number, which is marked on kilometer stones and on signs at major intersections.

• Recall that Morocco has an extensive road system with some of the most rigorously maintained roads in North Africa. However, in the countryside there are many unsurfaced roads as well as mountain and desert tracks called *pistes*. These roads may be impassable during the rainy season—from November to the end of April. In mountainous areas, there may be heavy snowfalls between December and May.

• Don't be surprised if you're stopped at a checkpoint on a major highway and police ask to see your license, insurance certificate, and car registration. Such inspections are routine.

• Always be prepared to stop in the countryside. People crossing the road may not be used to the speed of an oncoming car and may not cross rapidly enough to get out of your way.

• Never drive at night. There may be vehicles, animals, or people on the roads, and there are no lights.

• Note that street signs are in Arabic and French. Sometimes *rue* is replaced by *zankat* and *avenue* by *charia*.

LEGAL MATTERS, HEALTH, AND SAFETY

• Realize that citizens of the United States, the United Kingdom, and most other countries do not need a visa to enter Morocco.

• Be aware that while hashish (also called *kif*) and marijuana are smoked openly, they are *not* legal. A tourist caught smoking one of them could receive a jail term. (Police officers sometimes pose as drug dealers.)

• Remember that you aren't allowed to bring alcohol into the country. Some customs officials may ignore just one bottle, while others will confiscate it.

• Remember that you are not allowed to import or export *dirhams*. Save your receipts for money changes.

• If you're bringing a piece of electronic equipment into the country as a gift, take it out of its original box, and customs officials will probably not impose a duty.

• Drink bottled water *only*. Be sure that the bottle is completely sealed before it's opened for your drink. If you're in a home and someone offers you a glass of water, say "Thank you" and put it down, but don't drink it. Avoid ice cubes since you don't know the source of the water from which they were made.

• Don't eat fresh, uncooked vegetables and fruit that can't be peeled. Don't eat food bought from street vendors.

• Don't swim in rivers or streams because of the risk of the parasitic disease bilharzia, caused by a freshwater snail that is infested with a parasitic flatworm. These parasites can enter your bloodstream and do permanent damage to internal organs. The cure involves highly toxic medicines that may not work.

• Bring with you all prescription medicines that you may need. American and English brands of medicine are rare, but French brands are available.

• Women should never be out on a street after dark unless escorted by a man.

• Women should note that tampons are available in general stores in towns, *not* in pharmacies. They aren't available in country areas.

• Keep in mind that there are two types of police—the *gendarmerie* and the *sûreté*. The former run security and are at checkpoints in the Rif and in the South. The latter are found other places and are preferable if you need to report a crime. Should you be the victim of a crime, report it first at your hotel or to the family with whom you are staying. They will know correct procedures.

• Never try to bribe a policeman. It would be considered a grave insult. However, it is acceptable to tip a maitre d' or a doorman in advance to ensure good service.

Tunisia

Remember "Ancient History" or "Latin II"? Queen Dido of Carthage and her paramour Aeneas? The Punic Wars? Cato's ringing warning to the Romans, "Carthage must be destroyed"? And where was/is Carthage? It was—and still is—in Tunisia, the country jutting into the Mediterranean right next to Algeria.

Writer Terry Palmer calls Tunisia "a compact country on the sunnier side of the Mediterranean with its backyard extending into the vast emptiness of the mystic Sahara."

Of the three countries in the *Maghreb*, you'll find Tunisia the one most influenced by French culture, manners, and cuisine.

GREETINGS

• Remember that, when introduced, men shake hands with both men and women. Women may shake hands with other women or kiss on both cheeks.

• Note that men and women who are good friends shake hands, but women and women kiss on both cheeks; in rural areas women hold each other's right hand and kiss the other's hand. Men and men shake hands, unless they hav-en't seen one another for a long time—then they hug one another and kiss on both cheeks.

• Expect traditional people to shake hands with the right hand and then briefly put their right hand over their heart.

• When meeting anyone for the first time, use French titles—*Monsieur, Madame, Mademoiselle*. Use the professional titles *Docteur* for an M.D. or Ph.D. and *Professeur*.

• When greeting senior company officials, use *Monsieur* or *Monsieur* and surname.

• Address government ministers as *Monsieur le Ministre*.

• When addressing someone in Arabic, use Mr., Mrs., Miss, etc. (See "Key Words and Phrases", page 227 for translations.)

CONVERSATION

- Note that most educated Tunisians are bilingual in French and Arabic. In Tunis and resort areas, some people speak English.
- Ask about Islam. People will be flattered by your interest. Don't, however, discuss Western religions in a way that suggests that they are preferable.
- Inquire about places to visit, where traditional food and crafts can be found, Tunisian foods and where to find them.
- Don't withdraw from discussing politics *if* a Tunisian raises the subject. Tunisia has a more democratic society than other countries in North Africa.
- Avoid defending American policies on the Palestinian issue or voicing support of Israel.

TELEPHONES

- Look for call boxes in post offices, in many cafes, and in some hotels.
- To make a call with a public phone, deposit 100 *millimes* for three minutes. When there's a beep, deposit more money to continue the call.
- To save the hefty surcharge hotels make on long-distance and overseas calls, go to the post office (PTT) to make long-distance and international calls. You'll be assigned a booth; make your call, and then pay. In the summer, make your calls between 2:00 and 5:00 P.M. There won't be crowds at that time, so you won't have to wait for a booth.

IN PUBLIC

• If you don't read French or Arabic, bring a French phrase book, since signs, menus, and official notices are printed in French and Arabic.

• To beckon someone, hold your hand with palm downward and fingers waving up and down.

• Joining the thumb and fingertips with the palm held upwards means "Wait. Be patient." In conversation, the same gesture signifies authority—i.e., "I know what I'm talking about."

• Keep in mind that the head tossed back accompanied by the clicking of the tongue means "No."

• The Western "O.K." gesture (thumb and index finger forming a circle) indicates "I'm going to get you."

• Be aware that it is customary for men to wear jasmine on a stick behind their ears in the evening. The adornment has nothing to do with sexual preference. Women wear necklaces of fresh jasmine.

• Don't be surprised to find men holding hands. The gesture has no

sexual meaning. Don't pull away if you're a man and a Tunisian man takes your hand.

• Men should remember not to show affection to a woman, *especially* in villages.

• While women alone may be subject to harassment, men alone will have no problems, other than being approached by beggars or solicited by homosexuals.

• Be aware that Tunisia passed a law banning non-Muslims from entering the prayer chamber of a mosque. The only exceptions are a few mosques in Kairwan and Sousse, which tourists may enter. You will need an escort to enter even the outer halls of other mosques.

• Should you fall in love during your stay in Tunisia, keep this in mind: A Christian man must convert to marry a Muslim woman, but a Christian or Jewish woman does not have to convert to marry a Muslim man.

• Try not to let the two calendars confuse you. The Gregorian calendar is used widely, but the Muslim calendar is used in official documents and for moveable public holidays and festivals. The Muslim calendar is based on lunar months with 354 days in a year and 355 for leap year.

• If you would like to visit a *hammam* (public bath), ask someone at your hotel to direct you to one, since they are usually well hidden. (For women travelers, visiting a *hammam* is a good way to meet Tunisian women, since the baths serve as social centers. Women's bathing hours are usually in the afternoon.) Most *hammam* have lockers for valuables. Wear a bathing suit or underwear, since total nudity isn't acceptable. Go to the steam room, bathe, and sit around and relax. A masseur for men or a masseuse for women will give you a massage and then use abrasive gloves to scrub off dead skin.

• Expect to find public bathrooms only in train stations, bus stations, hotels, and restaurants. Use those in bus and train stations only in an emergency, because they aren't usually clean. The public bathrooms at the airport are spotless. If you have a cup of coffee in a restaurant, you may use the bathroom. In some public bathrooms, there will be an attendant. Tip a few *millimes*. Keep a supply of tissues for use in public bathrooms.

• For shopping, become familiar with the going prices of crafts by checking the fixed-price Artisanat shops, which are state run. When you shop in the *souks*, you'll be able to bargain better. Try for a price about 25% less than you would pay at an Artisanat shop.

• Don't try to bargain in a *magasin-général*, which is much like a small department store with a supermarket section.

• Don't photograph women.

• Be sure to ask first if you want to photograph an old, decrepit house. People are often ashamed of them and don't want pictures taken.

• While Tunisia is more Westernized and liberal than most countries in North Africa, women alone are still regarded as "available." Especially in the South, travel with another woman or a group. Traveling with a boyfriend —as opposed to a husband—will not earn respect.

DRESS

• For casual dress, men should wear shirt and pants, and women should wear pants, skirt, or dress. No miniskirts for women.

• Women need not wear a head scarf.

• To a meal in a home in a city, men should wear a suit and women a dress or skirt and blouse.

• For business, men should wear a suit and tie, and women a dress or blouse and skirt. Sleeves should be at least three-quarter length.

• Should you be invited to a formal occasion (e.g., a wedding), men should wear a dark suit and women a cocktail dress with sleeves.

• Expect most Tunisian women to wear Western dress, but older women wear an outer cloak with which they partially cover their faces in public.

MEALS

Hours and Foods

Breakfast: 7:30 or 8:00 A.M. Baguettes and butter or croissants and Turkish coffee.

Lunch: 12:30 or 1:00 P.M. A lighter meal than the noon meal in some other countries, it usually consists of an omelette and *brik* (see "Specialties").

Dinner: The main meal, it's not served until about 10:00 P.M. There will be couscous with fish or meat, a *tajine* (see "Specialties"), a salad, and finally coffee.

A European-oriented family will serve wine with the meal. Other families will provide soft drinks and water. However, some Tunisians may not drink at all with the meal, since they believe that the liquid would cause couscous to swell in the stomach.

• Remember that Tunisian food is *very* highly spiced. *Harissa*—a mixture of crushed, dried, hot red peppers, ground cumin, and salt —is added to almost every dish except dessert.

• Expect a baguette (long French loaf) to be the main bread.

Beverages: Try Tunisia's wines. They have won international competitions. Tunisian beer, *Celita*, a light lager, is rather watery.

• Try *Thibarine*, an orange liqueur similar to Cointreau, or *bukha*, a dry brandy made from figs.

• Consider one of the refreshing mineral waters. The most widely available brands are Safia and Melliti.

• Wine and other alcoholic beverages are available in hotels, bars, and in some supermarkets. However, on Friday, alcohol is not drunk outside hotels nor is it sold in stores.

• Mint tea is extremely popular. To make it, a teapot is filled with boiling water, emptied, and then refilled with green tea, sugar, and cold water; the mixture is then boiled. When the tea is ready, more sugar, water, and mint are added, after which it's poured into glasses, back into the pot, and then back into glasses. When everyone has finished, more water is added to the pot. Usually, children and elderly people are served the third round, when the tea is weaker.

Table Manners

• In wealthier, more educated families men and women may eat together, while in traditional families, the two sexes eat separately. Custom dictates that on formal occasions such as weddings, men and women eat separately.

• Be prepared for parties in homes to be informal buffet-style lunches or dinners.

• If you're not dining in an upper-class home, where people tend to sit at standard dining tables, don't be surprised if the hostess sets up a table for you, as a foreigner, while the rest of the family eats at a low table while seated on the floor. Even if you're with the group on the floor, you may be offered a fork or spoon. Tunisians usually sit on the floor and eat with their hands.

• Be aware that it's important to wash your hands in front of everyone. Usually a pitcher of water and a basin will be passed around to each person.

• Don't put your left hand on the table.

• As a guest, expect to be served first.

• When couscous is served, each person uses a spoon and eats from her/his section of a central platter in the middle of the table. There are no individual plates.

• Assume that there will be only one cup of water, which is passed to everyone to share. Don't drink water. Ask if you could have a soft drink instead.

Eating Out

• Most restaurants are either Tunisian or French.

• Cafes outside tourist areas are usually for men. Women alone will feel uncomfortable in these cafes and shouldn't go into one unless accompanied by a man.

• To summon the waiter, say *"Monsieur"* (Me-syeuh).

• If you order *bukha* (a brandy distilled from figs) in a cafe, assume that you'll also receive marinated raw vegetables—e.g., carrots, celery, zucchini, cauliflower. You can eat the carrots, if they have been peeled. Avoid the other vegetables.

• Note that no pork is served, except in tourist restaurants.

Specialties

• First courses: *mechouia*—grilled tomatoes, peppers, and onions, with olive oil, tuna fish, sliced hard-boiled egg, lemon juice, and capers; *slatit blanquit*—a mixture of cheese, olives, tuna, capers, oil, vinegar, and *harissa* (hot red pepper paste), spread on slices of bread; *felfel mihchi*—peppers stuffed with meat, onions, parsley, bread crumbs, eggs, and olive oil, all then fried in oil; *kemia*—assorted hors d'oeuvres such as pistachios, *boutargue* (dried and salted mullet eggs), black or green olives, and tuna fish.

• One appetizer with which you may have a bit of difficulty is *brik à l'oeuf*, two layers of phyllo dough filled with an egg and spinach and deep fried. Be careful when you eat it because the yolk is runny and drips out—and you eat the *brik* with your hands. Other *brik* appetizers that are easier to handle are *brik* with meat and *brik* with tuna.

• Main courses: couscous—the national dish (semolina) is available in some 50 varieties, some examples being chicken, lamb, beef, chick-peas, and vegetables; *mechoui*—lamb cooked on a spit; *musli*—lamb or beef stew with olive oil, potatoes, and saffron; *guenaoia*—meat stew with onions, coriander, *harissa* (hot red pepper paste), tomatoes, and okra; *odija*—brains.

• Another popular main course is *tajine*, a stew that takes its name from the earthenware dish in which it is cooked. There are a number of varieties. One is spinach *tajine*, made with beans, beef, onions, tomato puree, pepper, spinach, and egg, and then baked in the oven. A few other varieties of *tajine*: chicken *tajine* with pickled lemons; chicken *tajine* with prunes and honey; lamb *tajine* with artichokes; lamb *tajine* with tomatoes and string beans; lamb *tajine* with prunes.

• An interesting cheese is *numidia*—ewe's milk cheese resembling Roquefort. It's safe to eat.

HOTELS

• Keep in mind that the Tunisian tourist office is much stricter in regulating the quality of hotels than the tourist offices in Morocco and Algeria. A sign showing the number of stars (the highest number is four) is displayed at the entrance to all hotels.

• Remember that prices change

three times a year, according to the season. High season goes from July 1 to mid-September; mid-season covers mid-September to the end of October plus April, May, and June; low season is the rest of the year, November 1 to March 31.

• To avoid an unpleasant surprise when you get your bill, check whether the price for your room is per person or per room. Most hotels charge per person.

• Prepare to fill out a questionnaire when you register at a hotel.

• Even three-star hotels are clean and have air-conditioning and Western-style toilets.

• Realize that there is no age limit on youth hostels (called *auberges de jeunesse*). Bring a membership card from your country's youth hostel association.

TIPPING

• Give a porter 100 M (*millimes*) per bag.

• Tip a doorman 100 M for a service such as getting a taxi for you.

• For a week's stay at a hotel, leave 2 to 3 DT (*dinar*) for the maid.

• For a taxi driver, round the fare off to the nearest *dinar*.

• Tip an official guide 5 to 7% of the fee. An unofficial guide should get 100 to 200 M.

• Give a cinema usher 50 to 100 M.

• Tip a lavatory attendant 50 to 100 M.

PRIVATE HOMES

• Don't visit between 1:00 and 5:00 P.M., when people are eating and resting. Drop in if you're in the countryside, but not if your friends live in a city.

• Don't be surprised if men and women are entertained in separate rooms. Usually if you're staying with a family for a while, everyone will be together.

• Couples should remember that it's rude to show affection in front of family members.

• Both men and women should avoid wearing shorts in the house, and women should be careful not to wear anything provocative or revealing.

• Keep in mind that Tunisians have a very different sense of privacy from Westerners. A woman's problem will be that she will not be allowed to be alone. Be prepared to spend a great deal of time with the family *at home*. A woman traveling with her husband may find that the host takes out her husband, and she is expected to stay at home with the women. A woman traveling alone won't be allowed to go out alone, while a single man will have no such problem. These attitudes prevail except in households of the elite upper class.

• Anticipate several bathrooms in the homes of upper-class families, most of whom live in cities. Middle-class homes usually have Turkish-style toilets (i.e., a hole in the floor).

• Note that in urban areas people bathe regularly. In rural areas, there will be a room off to the side of the house with a bucket of warm water for bathing. Some homes have electric water heaters that are left on to provide a constant supply of hot water.

• If there is a gas heater in the bathroom, *be sure* to ask your hostess how it works. The heaters can be extremely dangerous, because gas can leak and asphyxiate anyone in the room. Leave the bathroom window open a bit. If you smell gas, get out of the bathroom.

• Never leave a gas heater on in your bedroom when you go to sleep.

Gifts: When invited to a meal, bring fruit (people in the countryside appreciate watermelon) or cakes.

• Don't bring "souvenir"-type gifts (ashtrays, pens, plates with the name of a city). Tunisians don't like them. If you want to give an expensive gift, give gold. Tunisians value gold tremendously.

• From abroad, bring kitchen gadgets, quality pots, casserole dishes, or coffee-table books with photos of your area. If you know a family well, bring clothing (e.g., jeans, T-shirts with insignias) for children.

BUSINESS

Hours

Banks: Between October 1 and July 1, Monday through Friday, 8:00 to 11:00 A.M. and 2:00 to 4:00 P.M. During the rest of the year, 7:30 or 8:00 A.M. to 11:00 A.M. or noon. During Ramadan, 8:00 to 11:00 A.M. and 1:00 to 2:30 P.M.

Government Offices: Monday through Friday, 9:00 A.M. to 1:00 P.M., and 3:00 to 5:30 P.M. Saturday, 8:00 A.M. to 1:30 P.M.

Business Offices: Monday to Friday, 8:30 A.M. to 12:30 P.M. and 2:00 to 6:00 P.M. Saturday, 8:30 A.M. to 1:00 P.M. During Ramadan, business is restricted to the morning.

Shops: During the winter, 8:30 A.M. to noon and 3:00 to 6:00 P.M. During the summer, 8:00 A.M. to noon and 4:00 to 7:00 P.M. In cities, shops close on Sundays, while in beach resorts they close on Mondays.

Currency

• The unit of currency is the Tunisian *dinar* (DT), which consists of 1,000 *millimes* (M).
• Coins: 2, 5, 10, 20, 50, 100, and 500 M; 1 DT.
• Bills: 1, 5, 10, and 20 DT.
• Note that small amounts are sometimes stated in *millimes*—e.g., 2,500 M = 2 DT, 500 *millimes*.
• Remember that small change is scarce.
• Large hotels and travel agencies can change money (though ho-

tels are often reluctant to do so), but the rate is not so good as that at banks.
• Keep in mind that banks in the provinces don't change money on Monday mornings.
• Be sure to keep your exchange receipts, since they may be checked when you leave the country.
• Assume that you can use major credit cards in large hotels and better restaurants. You can also use them in exchange banks for buying *dinars*, but you may have to wait as much as 30 minutes while a phone call is made to Tunis for an authorization. You won't be charged for the call. Few shops will accept credit cards, but many traders in the *souks* will.

Business Practices

• Make initial contacts through the Commercial Office of your country's embassy in Tunis.
• Expect to make several trips to Tunisia to complete your business; the process will, however, be shorter than it would be in Morocco.
• Hire an agent in Tunisia. There are no laws about having a local agent as there are in other countries. However, a good agent is vital to doing business—especially when complicated equipment will require service after the

sale has been made. There is no American-Tunisian Chamber of Commerce in Tunis, so go to the Commercial Section of your country's embassy in Tunis, or visit the Commercial Section of Tunisia's embassy in your country.

• Make appointments during the months of October through May, but avoid the weeks around Christmas and Easter.

• Try for appointments between 8:00 A.M. and noon or between 3:00 and 6:30 P.M.

• Make appointments from abroad, but don't expect them to be confirmed until you are actually in the country—unless you are dealing with government officials at a high level.

• Note that major hotels and most large businesses have fax machines.

• If you don't speak French, arrange for an interpreter, since French is the language for both business and technical matters. (Most educated Tunisians go to France for their higher education.) You can hire an interpreter through your hotel, through the Tourist Office in Tunis, or with the Tunisian embassy in your country before you leave for your trip. Unless you are fluent in spoken and written French, you will need someone to handle translations, since bids, documentation, brochures, and instructional materials should be in French. Also

be sure to have translated into French any materials you plan to use in your presentation or that you are distributing to members of the company.

• Expect punctuality *only* from people at the highest levels of the government. However, a Western businessperson is expected to be on time.

• Learn at least a few phrases of Arabic, especially words of greeting. You will make a good impression by showing a sensitivity to the fact that Arabic is the country's main language.

• Always give your business card to the highest ranking person at the meeting first and then to the others present.

• Keep in mind that Tunisian businesspeople will be interested in your background and education. If you have a Ph.D., let it be known, since Tunisians will likely be impressed.

• Don't discuss business when tea is served—as it surely will be.

• Don't bring up or make inquiries about a businessman's wife, since family privacy is very important. Also avoid discussing male-female relationships.

• Defer to the highest-ranking person in the organization, because those at the top make decisions. However, be sure to give copies of any material to everyone involved in your project.

• Enhance your presentation

with charts and visuals to impress Tunisian businesspeople.

• Be aware that Tunisians can be unreliable about deadlines to which they have agreed. Don't get impatient, or the work will be further delayed.

• Don't be surprised to be invited to someone's home before being invited to a restaurant. Families are very important in Tunisia.

• Remember that, except among the elite and well-educated, women stay at home. If you're unsure whether to include a businessman's wife in an invitation to dinner—traditional and modern Tunisians differ in their attitudes —you might ask, "Would it be proper to invite your wife to come too?"

• Entertain business colleagues at French restaurants, since Tunisians hold French culture in high esteem.

• For a good business gift, bring a coffee-table book with pictures of your area. It's acceptable to bring a business gift to your first meeting.

HOLIDAYS AND SPECIAL OCCASIONS

• Religious holidays are celebrated according to the Muslim calendar. On the following holidays, expect to find business and government offices, banks, and most restaurants and shops closed.

• Secular holidays: New Year's Day (Jan. 1); Revolution Day (Jan. 18); Independence Day (March 20); Martyr's Day (April 9); Labor Day (May 1); Victory Day and Youth Day (June 1 and 2); Republic Day (July 25); President Bourguiba's Birthday (Aug. 3); Women's Day (Aug. 13); Memorial Day (Sept. 3); Evacuation Day, commemorating the evacuation of Bizerta (Oct. 15).

• Note that Sunday is the weekly holiday, but in the countryside Friday (the Muslim Sabbath) is vaguely observed.

• If you're going to be dealing with Jewish businesspeople or friends, remembers that Jews in Tunisia celebrate their holidays according to the Jewish calendar.

• Keep in mind that Ramadan is strictly observed in Tunisia. However, you won't have any difficulties in resort areas since the hotels and restaurants there are prepared to serve tourists.

TRANSPORTATION

Public Transportation

On intracity buses, get on at the back, and get off at the front. You won't need exact change. City buses are very crowded, and taxis are inexpensive, so they are a good alternative to the bus.

• In Tunis, be aware that the taxis are metered and take up to four passengers within the city and its suburbs. There is a charge of 100 *millimes* per suitcase and a 5% surcharge on fares at night.

• Expect to find two types of taxis: (1) Large cars called *grands taxis* or *voitures de tourisme*. They can take passengers anywhere in the country, but not all have meters. Ask at your hotel what the fare should be, and then negotiate with the driver. (2) Small cars with number signs on top called *taxis*

bébé or *taxis*. They have meters, which the drivers honor, and take up to three passengers within a city and to airports. They are much less expensive than the larger taxis.

• Realize that there are long-distance buses that connect Tunis and every main town. Problem: There are several bus companies and no integration of schedules, etc. When you arrive at a bus station in a small town, you must ask people from several different bus companies for the time of the next bus to your destination. Most companies don't post timetables. Buses have signs stating their destination in the front window, but in the south of Tunisia the signs are in Arabic. Some buses are hot and overcrowded; others are luxury air-conditioned coaches.

• Consider taking *louages*, shared taxis that run between cities. They are inexpensive and more reliable than intercity buses. *Louages* are supposed to take no more than five passengers, but they sometime squeeze in more. They don't leave until they have five passengers. Ask at your hotel for the departure point. Sometimes you can telephone a garage and make a reservation. *Louages* are faster than buses and only slightly more expensive.

• For longer trips between cities, consider taking a train, but be sure to take first class, since second class is very crowded and people often have to stand. There will be a supplement for a seat in the *voiture grand confort* (luxury-class car), but tickets aren't expensive, and some cars are even air-conditioned. Buy your ticket at the train station; if you get on a train without a ticket, you'll have to pay double the regular fare.

• Remember that there are no dining cars, but resist the temptation to eat local foods sold in train stations. The food isn't hygienic.

• To go the short distance from Tunis to Carthage, take the electric train marked *Sidi Bou Said* and *La Marsa*. Again, take first class because second class can be very crowded.

Driving

• Prepare to find street signs in Arabic and French and to find that maps issued by the Tourist Office aren't available because they're out of print. Before you go to Tunisia, buy one of Michelin's excellent maps of the country.

• Be aware that some streets in Tunis require parking on alternate sides of the street on different days. Ask at your hotel (or ask the friends with whom you're staying) if your car needs to be moved.

• Don't forget that no parking tickets are issued. Illegally parked

cars are simply towed away. If this happens to you, have a taxi take you to the car pound.

• Note that the speed limit is 50 km per hour (about 30 mph) in town and 100 km per hour (about 60 mph) on highways, unless otherwise indicated.

• Expect to find offices for the large car rental agencies. Book well ahead for a car during the tourist season. These agencies also offer cars with drivers.

• In towns, look for *gardiens*, because they will help you find a place to park. They wear badges. You may also encounter self-appointed *gardiens*, who will expect a fee of 100 to 200 M to find a parking place.

• Most gas stations are open on Sunday. You'll find plenty of stations in towns, but there are miles of secondary roads without service stations.

• If you're driving in the countryside and see a policeman, pull over to the side of the road. Traffic checks are common, and they are usually cursory, but sometimes the police will ask for proof of identity of each passenger. Be polite and cooperative.

• Don't even consider driving into the Sahara without notifying the *Garde Nationale* post at Medenine or the Saharan Center at Gabès of your itinerary and destination. You must travel in a Land Rover equipped with food, drinking water, tent, gas, oil, spare parts, and repair equipment. (See additional advice in the section on "Desert Driving" in "Customs and Manners in the Arab World.")

• Expect to see *Garde Nationale* car or motorcycle patrols on major highways. Check with them about road conditions, especially if you're on your way to the desert.

• Anticipate finding well-maintained asphalt highways. The unpaved roads, called *pistes*, are manageable except when they are flooded during heavy rains. Before driving on dirt roads, inquire about road conditions, and have a road map with you.

• If you see someone crossing the road in the countryside, drive *very* slowly. People in rural areas aren't used to judging the speed of an oncoming car.

LEGAL MATTERS, SAFETY, AND HEALTH

• Remember that you can't bring *into* the country Tunisian *di-*

nars, weapons other than hunting arms, and immoral or obscene publications. You cannot take *out* of the country Tunisian *dinars*. Exporting antiquities requires authorization from the Ministry of Cultural Affairs.

• Be aware that if your passport shows that you have been to Israel or South Africa, you won't be allowed into Tunisia.

• Save receipts for any money you changed while in Tunisia. When you leave the country you can convert back into your own currency only 30% of the sum you converted while in the country. The maximum you can convert back is 100 *dinars*. To make the exchange, be sure to arrive at the airport early, because you'll have to show all your receipts in order to have your money changed.

• Realize that if you're found to have illegal drugs, the penalties are very stiff. There is no tradition of drug use in Tunisia.

• Use only licensed guides; they carry identity cards issued by the National Tourist Office (ONTT). Many boys or men will ask to be your guide, but they probably will not be so reliable as official guides.

• Be conscious that you will encounter three different types of police: regular police wear blue-gray uniforms with leather belts and gray-and-white caps; traffic police have white cuffs and caps; the gendarmerie (whose principal concern is state security) wear khaki uniforms and white caps. Ask help of any of the three types whenever you need it. Most police are very friendly.

• Note that police tend to give men a harder time than they do women for traffic violations.

• Drink only bottled water. Don't use ice cubes. Don't eat fresh fruits or vegetables that cannot be peeled.

• Keep in mind that one pharmacy in each town stays open all night. (It's not the same pharmacy every night.) All pharmacies will have signs indicating which one is open.

• Recall that most French brands of medicine are available but not English and American brands. Bring with you an ample supply of the prescription drugs you may need.

• Look for condoms and some brands of birth control pills in pharmacies in larger towns. Tampons are available everywhere except in extremely remote towns.

• *Never* swim in rivers or streams because of the risk of bilharzia, a very debilitating disease caused by a freshwater snail that is infested with a parasite flatworm.

SAUDI ARABIA

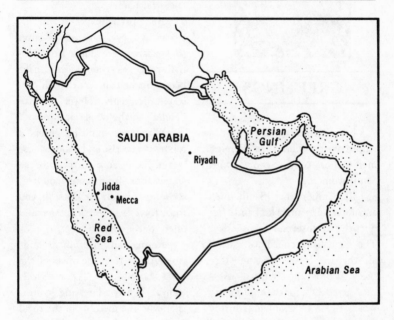

Since tourism doesn't exist in Saudi Arabia, travelers to that country will be businessmen or Muslim pilgrims from abroad. The two holiest cities of Islam are in the country: Mecca, to which millions make pilgrimages each year, and Medina, where the prophet Mohammed is buried.

Women should realize that they will have to accept the role assigned to them by a very strict Muslim society. In order for her to visit certain places and be in the company of men, Queen Elizabeth II had to be declared an honorary man.

GREETINGS

• Expect to be greeted with a handshake by Saudi men. Foreign men will not come in contact with Saudi women.

• Remember that Saudi men and foreign men shake hands frequently, even several times a day. The handshake continues during all the words of greeting. (See "Key Words and Phrases—Arabic," page 227, for the appropriate words.) Don't shake hands firmly or pump your whole hand up and down. Shake limply. During the greeting, there will be many inquiries about the well-being of each one's friends and his family. *Never* inquire or refer directly to someone's wife—e.g., "How is your wife doing?"

• Note that men who are good friends kiss twice in greeting, once on each cheek.

• When you are first introduced to someone, use Mr. and last name, Mrs. and last name, Dr. and last name (for both M.D. and Ph.D.) or *Sheik* (pronounced Shake)—if you know that someone is a *Sheik*—and last name.

• Some people use *ibn* (son of) or *bint* (daughter of) between their ancestral names.

• At a party, expect to be introduced to everyone individually. (If you aren't introduced individually, act as though you have been.) Shake hands with each person individually. Never just say "Hello" to the whole group.

• Whenever someone enters a room, always rise and shake hands.

• If you're at a party with the ambassador from your country, *never* leave before he does. If you must leave, ask his permission and offer your apologies.

• Address all government ministers (other than members of the royal family) as "Your Excellency." When addressing a minister who is a member of the royal family (there are thousands, and you'll have to ask to find out which ministers are royals), call him "Your Royal Highness."

• When meeting the king, men bow and women curtsy. Refer to him as "Your Royal Majesty." Never speak to him directly; always speak through his interpreter.

• When someone leaves your home or office, say *"Fi aman allah"* (Fee ah-man ahl-lah), which means "Go in the care of God."

CONVERSATION

• Remember that Arabic is the country's only language and that European languages are not so widely used as in other Middle Eastern countries.

• Keep in mind that people are more reserved and soft-spoken than in other Middle Eastern countries.

• Offer compliments about the country, its soccer teams, or anything you can admire, but don't praise a specific object (e.g., a painting or some decorative item) because the Saudi will feel obligated to offer it to you.

• As a conversation opener with a man, ask if he's married and, if so, how many children he has. But remember never to inquire about his wife or other adult female relatives. It's appropriate to ask about sons and daughters. (If you know the daughters to be older than 12, don't ask about them.) Saudis will be interested in your family and children, but never discuss personal family matters with a Saudi (for example, "My wife just had surgery.")

• If you know that a Saudi has studied abroad and you are acquainted with the area in which he studied, ask him about his experiences.

• Women should note that children—especially sons—are the most important topic in women's discussions. Don't be surprised if the discussion becomes personal. For example, an American woman who was very slim said that she had three children. Saudi women didn't believe that she could be so trim after three births, so they began feeling her stomach and pelvic area.

• Other good topics for opening conversations with women are cooking and fashion. In fact, a woman who can't talk about clothes may find herself at a loss.

• Avoid any topics detrimental to Islam, Arabs, Saudi Arabia, and the royal family as well as any topics with sexual content. In general, avoid any discussion of politics. And remember never to mention a man's wife or his female relatives.

• When mentioning the body of water usually called the Persian Gulf, always refer to it as the Arabian Gulf.

• Expect Saudis to ask what your salary is. Avoid giving a direct answer. Say something such as "Just enough for a home, food, a car, and support for my children." They won't persist.

• Be prepared for Saudis to ask constantly (as often as 20 to 25 times in a few hours), "How are you?" What they really mean is, "Is everything all right?" "May I get you something?" "Do you want a drink?"

• *Never* swear or use obscenities. Such actions may be unforgivable insults.

• *Never* criticize anyone (Saudi or non-Saudi) publicly. Saudis find such behavior intolerable because it causes a loss of dignity and respect. If, as a foreigner, you scream at another foreigner, Saudis will lose respect for you.

• Remember that Saudis regard women as mindless, so women can ask questions that would arouse suspicion if asked by a man. A woman journalist might elicit more information than a man simply because the Saudis would not take her questions seriously.

TELEPHONES

• Note that the telephone system is excellent. A three-minute local call costs 10 *halalah*, but there are slots for 25 *halalah* and 1 *riyal*. Deposit more money if you wish to talk longer. There will be a signal at the end of three minutes. Deposit more money to continue the call. You can call long-distance within the country from a pay phone. There are special pay phones from which you can make international long-distance calls. In cities, you can make international calls at the telephone office.

IN PUBLIC

• Remember that Saudis touch each other often to heighten communication.

• Be sure to make eye contact. It's very important.

• Expect people to stand very close when talking to you and to look you directly in the eye. They are showing you respect and courtesy.

• When handing an object to someone, always use the right hand.

• Never put your feet up on furniture—a desk, stool, train seat, etc. To show the soles of your feet (with or without shoes) is shocking and offensive. If you're sitting on the floor at a dinner, never stretch your legs so that the soles of your feet face someone.

• Don't use gestures that are obscene in the West. Saudis are familiar with their meanings.

• Never smoke in the presence of any member of the royal family, on the streets of Riyadh (the capital), or anywhere during Ramadan. In any case, never smoke unless your host or the senior guest smokes first. Women should not smoke on the street.

• Remember that foreigners may not enter mosques.

• Try to control your surprise if a Saudi recognizes a female relative in a large group of women, all in the same black garb. An American traveler was once walking with a Saudi friend. Across the street were some 25 women, all of whom looked the same to the American. The Saudi said, "I see my mother and my aunts over there, and I must go talk to them."

• Be aware that Saudis pray five times a day: at dawn (4:30–5:00 A.M.), around noon, in the afternoon some time between 2:00 and 4:00 P.M., at sunset, and one hour after sunset (never later than 9:00 P.M.). Prayer times vary according to the time of the year and the part of the country that you're in. At prayer times, everything stops. If you're in a shop, you'll have to go outside and wait in the heat on the sidewalk for 10 to 15 minutes. To avoid such inconvenience, plan your shopping or errands around the prayer schedule. Shop between 8:00 and 11:30 A.M., 4:00–6:00 P.M., and 6:30–7:30 P.M.

• Don't refuse the offer of a cup of coffee. It's like a slap in the face to a Saudi. If you can't or don't drink coffee, say that you're allergic and ask for tea.

• Plan to bargain everywhere except in supermarkets. If you're going to be in the country for some time, you may want to stretch out your bargaining for a single item over a period of weeks. Keep returning to the merchant every few days.

• About photography: Remember that the Koran prohibits the depiction of the human form by the creation of graven images. A photograph is an image. Always ask if you want to photograph a person, and respect his wishes if he refuses. Since Saudi Arabia is the strictest Muslim country, never photograph women or religious processions. If you're with a Saudi and want to photograph a building or scene without people, it will probably be all right. However, it's better not to take photos in the city. Police may confiscate your film, and you may find yourself in the middle of an unpleasant incident.

• Remember that the Saudis are proud of their efforts to build a modern state, and they don't want to appear "backward." Don't photograph scenes or people that could lead to an impression of "backwardness."

• Don't take photos near airports, planes, or military installations.

• Look for public bathrooms in shopping malls, hotels, restaurants, and other public buildings in the cities. Facilities vary considerably. They may be Western style or Turkish style—i.e., a hole in the floor. It's a good idea to keep a supply of tissues with you in case the bathroom has none. In small towns, look for bathrooms in restaurants. They are likely to be Turkish style. There are no bathrooms in the desert.

DRESS

• Note that Saudi women wear a black dress and head covering called an *abbayah*. In rural areas the veil covers all but the eyes; in urban areas the heavy gauze veils completely cover the face. Western women should wear long sleeves, long skirts—they should cover the ankles—and should completely cover their hair. (Hair is considered highly erotic.) Never wear a low-cut dress.

• Saudi men wear a *thobe*—a long white gown—and on the head a skullcap with a *gutra* (a triangular folded white or red checked scarf) over it. The *gutra* is held in place with an *agal*—a black double-corded ringlet.

• Keep in mind that it gets cold at night in Riyadh during January and February, and it can be damp during the day at the coast. Even though homes and offices have heaters, it may still be chilly indoors, so dress warmly.

• Casual dress for Western men is long trousers, a shirt with long sleeves, which you can roll up if you're hot, and sandals or loafers.

• For women, both casual and dressy occasions call for long skirts and covered arms. If you wear a skirt exposing your knees, your legs will be whipped by the religious police who are in charge of enforcing morals.

• Women should not wear pant suits on the streets.

• Neither men nor women should ever wear shorts, except at a private beach or when playing tennis on a private court. Don't wear bathing suits except at private beaches.

• Wear rubber-soled shoes or sneakers when swimming in the Red Sea, so that your feet won't get cut on the coral.

• For business, men should wear a lightweight suit; in Jeddah, after the first meeting when suits and ties are essential, wear a long-sleeved white shirt and tie. Men should be sure to wear white shirts, especially when dealing with government officials.

• Men should wear jackets and ties at social functions.

• To a dinner in a home, women should wear long, very dressy cocktail dresses. (Some Saudi women wear Dior gowns under their *abbayah*.)

• If invited to an embassy function, and if the invitation reads "casual," men should wear a sports jacket, socks, and shoes (not sandals). If the invitation says "informal," men should wear suit and tie. In either of these cases, women should wear a knee-length or longer dress with high neckline and long sleeves. If the invitation reads "formal," men should wear a dinner jacket or dark suit and women should wear a long gown.

• Sandals are acceptable anywhere in the daytime *except* in offices.

• Remove your shoes when going into a house. Men will find this custom easier if they wear loafers. Sometimes people also remove their shoes before going into an office. If you see a pile of shoes at the door, remove yours. If not, keep your shoes on.

MEALS

Hours and Foods

Breakfast: 7:00–9:00 A.M. Usually there will be tea, fruit, olives, feta cheese, and pita bread (usually warm). You may be asked if you would like an egg. If you would, ask for it boiled, since it will probably be very greasy if it's fried or scrambled.

Lunch: In Riyadh and eastern provinces, noon–2:00 P.M.; in Jeddah, 1:00–3:00 P.M.; in both cases after the noon prayer. Lunch is usually the large meal of the day; however, if guests are invited to dinner, it will also be a large meal.

Dinner: Between evening prayer and night prayer—i.e., in Riyadh, 7:30; in Jeddah, 9:00.
• At either lunch or dinner, there will be fruit, salads, rice, chicken, or—on the coast—fish. On the coast you may be served a fish stew similar to bouillabaisse. If there are guests, then mutton, sheep, or lamb is often served because chicken and fish are not considered festive enough.

Beverages: With meals, the usual drinks are water and fruit juices. Beverages are not drunk with the meal but usually afterward: tea, coffee, goat and camel's milk.

Dessert: It may be set out on the mat with the main course or it may be served with tea at the end of the meal. Typical desserts are apples, sweet dates, bananas, oranges, and pastry covered with honey.
• If you're invited to a meal for a large group, the main dish may be camel, sheep, or goat that has been boiled or roasted. It's served with rice and side dishes of sweets, pastries, fruits, vegetables, and chicken.
• A formal banquet will include *khouzi*—stuffed mutton garnished with almonds and eggs.
• A lavish meal might include soup, fried shrimp, *kabsah* (kebabs of lamb with vegetables), meat, and rice with almonds; ragout of okra; fruits, and cake.

Table Manners

• Remember that alcohol is illegal in Saudi Arabia, but some people have it. Don't expect to be offered an alcoholic drink before a meal, but in more Westernized homes alcoholic drinks may be served. More often, tea will be served before dinner, either by itself or with nuts.

• If you're invited to a meal, expect first to go to a sitting room where you will be offered tea and then invited to another room for the meal. After lunch, tea or coffee will be served. Next a servant with a towel on his arm will bring a basin of water for you to wash your hands, or you will be escorted to the bathroom to clean up there. Afterward your host or a servant will bring a container of incense and hold it in front of each person. Take your hands and pull the smoke toward you. This little ceremony signaling that the party is over is a polite way of asking people to leave. An evening party usually doesn't include this ritual, though it may be done before the meal. It is not, however, a signal to leave. Leave a dinner party after the group has had coffee or tea.

• If you're invited to dinner at 8:00, have a snack before going, because you probably won't be served until midnight. Before the meal, people may play card games (15-minute card games are popular) or listen to music.

• Note that the more formal the party, the shorter the conversation before dinner and the earlier the departure.

• Be aware that men and women always eat separately. However, up to the age of 12, girls can mix with males.

• At meals in homes, people traditionally sit in a circle on the floor in front of a large mat on which platters of food have already been placed. There is always considerably more food than the group can eat.

• To entertain Western guests, Saudis sometimes set the meal on a table. If so, eat in the usual Western style. If the meal is on the floor, either sit cross-legged or kneel on one knee. Don't let your feet touch the mat that the food is on, and be sure that the soles of your feet aren't pointed at anyone else.

• When eating a meal on the floor, put your left hand behind you. People eat with the right hand, as the left hand is for cleaning yourself after going to the bathroom. Always pass anything with your right hand.

• Be aware that there are no individual plates. Saudis pick food from the platters and eat it. If you're the guest, choice morsels will be pointed out for you to eat—e.g., liver or sheep's eyes. Don't feel that you have to eat them. People will understand your distaste, since Saudis have had so much contact with foreigners during the past 15 years.

• Don't expect "assigned" seating, unless there's a party with royalty, when the eldest royal guest of honor will sit down first.

• Don't be surprised if the host doesn't eat with his guests. He may hover around to make sure that everyone is all right.

• As a foreign guest you may be offered a plate or bowl with fork and spoon. Saudis want their foreign guests to feel comfortable.

• Expect Saudis to eat a great deal. If you feel uncomfortable because you're full while Saudis are still eating, nibble on some of the fruit on the mat (be sure that it's been peeled before you eat it). Don't feel obliged to try to keep up with the Saudis. People will encourage you to try things, but they won't be insistent.

• Before drinking coffee, "inhale" it to appreciate the fragrance produced by the cardamom flavor.

• At the end of the meal, emulate Saudis and say *"Bismillah"* (Bees-mahl-lah), which means "Thanks to God," or simply "Thank you," a sentiment acceptable from a Westerner.

• Should you be living in Saudi Arabia and invite Saudis to your home, expect only the men to come. Greet older and distinguished guests at the door of their car and accompany them to the street or their car when they leave.

• Don't suggest that your guests remove their headdresses, since Saudis wear theirs indoors.

• Before the meal, serve coffee, tea, or fruit juice. Conversation and coffee always precede dinner.

• Never serve rare meat. Saudis can't abide it.

• Offer extra helpings several times. Arabs usually wait to be asked more than once before accepting a second serving.

Eating Out

• Note that there are no bars serving alcohol, but there are snack bars serving fresh fruit juices and kebab sandwiches. Snack bars are generally clean and safe because they're inspected by the Ministry of Health once a month. You'll also find pastry shops and cafes. A health note: Fruit juices are okay if ice and water are not added. Kebab sandwiches are fine. Don't eat salads or pastries whose filling is custard or cream.

• Don't expect to find traditional Saudi restaurants. There are places offering chicken and rice or fish and rice, but the dishes won't be at all like those Saudis cook at home.

• Try the Chinese, Korean, Indian, Pakistani, or Ethiopian restaurants. Saudis are especially fond of Chinese food, probably because it's based on rice.

• Don't expect to find menus posted outside restaurants.

• Feel free to join others at a table at an informal restaurant.

• Expect the waiters to be more attentive in less elegant restaurants than they are in hotel restaurants.

• To summon the waiter, say *"Garçon."* Don't snap your fingers.

• If someone invites you to a restaurant, don't argue when the bill arrives and he pays. If you do, you will insult your host. Reciprocating is not expected, but it is appreciated.

• Women should not go to restaurants alone or with another female unless accompanied by a couple or a male relative.

Specialties

• The national dish is *kabsah*—rice and either seafood or meat.

• Meat and dairy products from sheep, goats, and camels are staples of Saudi cooking. Lamb is the most popular meat. Chicken—introduced in the 1960s—is also popular.

• Other staples are rice and bread.

HOTELS

• If you know someone in Saudi Arabia, have him reconfirm your reservation every few days, up until the time you arrive. Also have him give a substantial deposit and obtain a receipt. If you don't take these steps, the hotel may be overbooked and not have a room for you when you arrive.

• Expect many top-class hotels with such amenities as swimming pools and coffee shops. Many of the three-star hotels throughout the country are clean and comfortable, but unless you speak Arabic it's difficult to stay in one.

• Realize that hotels have two dining rooms—one for men and one for families. Foreign women should always eat in the one for families.

TIPPING

- Don't tip taxi drivers.
- Give porters the equivalent of $1.50 for two bags.
- Tip waiters 15%. Check the bill, since the service is sometimes included.
- Don't tip gas station attendants.

PRIVATE HOMES

- If you're moving to Saudi Arabia to work with a foreign firm, expect to be given a furnished apartment. If you need to buy furniture or appliances, always go shopping with a Saudi. He will be able to bargain better than you can.

- Note that most visiting takes place in the late afternoon or after dinner. You need not call in advance, because Saudis will always say, "Please come over." Never visit a Saudi home between 2:00 and 4:00 P.M.

- If you're living in Saudi Arabia, feel free to ask Saudis to telephone before coming over. Otherwise, they'll turn up uninvited since that's the way they're used to visiting. If you invite Saudis to your home, don't be surprised if they come very late, not at all, or several days later. If it's possible, entertain them for a while. Otherwise you risk losing their friendship.

- Be aware that Saudis are unlike other Middle Easterners in that women do not socialize outside the family group. Men who are not related rarely socialize—except for occasional visits to coffee houses. Outsiders will find it almost impossible to be good friends with a Saudi—either male or female—since Saudis themselves don't often have close friendships outside their family group.

- Remember that women are guarded and secluded because the honor of male relatives is tied to women's sexual behavior. If a woman is promiscuous, she can ruin the family's honor forever.

- Men should never speak with other men about Arab women to

whom they have not been introduced.

• If a Saudi man invites a Western man to his home, he is not also
inviting his wife. Some Westernized Saudis may include the wife
in an invitation.

• Remove your shoes at the door
of a Saudi's house. You won't be
given slippers. If you're wearing
sandals, it's okay to go barefoot in
the house. If you're wearing shoes
and socks, keep your socks on,
since most homes are air-conditioned, and you may feel cold.

• Realize that it is unusual for
a Western couple to be invited to
a Saudi home. If you are invited
to a Westernized family whom you
know well or to the home of a high
government official, both sexes
may be in the same room. However, if you are at a large gathering, the men will probably go into
one room and the women into another. It's possible that a woman
may be included at the meal with
the men without the Saudi wife
present. The strong likelihood is
that you will go to the women's
part of the house where women
will ask *very* personal questions
and make very frank comments
about you. Example: If you don't
have children, the women will
keep asking "Why?" Rather than
explaining that you've chosen to
remain childless, simply deflect
the question by saying, "We hope
to have one soon." Women may

sit for hours drinking tea and
sometimes smoking a water pipe
called a *nargila*. One woman may
swing an incense burner at each
woman. The women lift their
skirts to let the incense flow
through their clothing. Late in the
evening food will be served. Leave
as soon as you've finished eating.

• Up to the age of 12, girls can
go around the house freely and
play with boys or be seen with
men.

• If you are invited to visit, expect to have your own room with
a private bathroom.

• Feel free to bathe daily. Saudis
do. Oddly the cold water, which
is stored in a tank on the roof, may
be hotter than the hot water,
which is stored in a tank inside the
house.

• Never connect or disconnect
an appliance—e.g., a hair dryer
—with wet hands or while standing on a wet floor or touching a
faucet. Electricity lines are not always grounded.

• Don't offer to help with the
dishes or other chores since most
people have servants. You are a
guest and will not be allowed to
assume any responsible role within
the family.

• Realize that Saudis treat servants with respect because in the
eyes of Allah everyone shares the
same status. As a guest, be sure to
do the same.

• Don't try to sightsee on your

own. Most families will have a car and driver to take you around, or the host or his son may do so.

• Don't pay for local calls made from a home, but do leave money for international calls (or go to the telephone office to make such calls).

Gifts: When invited to a home, bring toys for the children but nothing for the wife, who is never seen.

• When invited to a meal, bring pastries or a box of imported European candy (readily available in Saudi Arabia).

• If you want to give a memorable gift to someone, give something extremely expensive or very meaningful. An American wanted to give a special gift to a high official whose family had been extremely kind to her over a period of time. She did calligraphy of a section of the Koran and had it framed. The official had tears in his eyes when he received it.

BUSINESS

Hours

Banks: Saturday to Wednesday, 8:30 A.M. to noon and 5:00 to 7:00 P.M., and Thursday, 8:30 A.M. to noon.

Businesses: Saturday to Wednesday, 8:30 A.M. to 1:00 or 2:00 P.M., and 4:30 to 8:00 P.M. (During Ramadan, hours will be shorter.)

Government Offices: 8:00 A.M. to 2:00 P.M. (Before 10:00 A.M., you'll probably find no one but sweepers cleaning up, and after 11:00 A.M., you may find no one but those cleaning the tea cups.)

Shops: There are no set hours. Generally, shops open some time between 7:00 and 9:00 A.M. and stay open until noon, and then reopen about 4:30 P.M. and stay open until 8:00 P.M.

• Note that Thursday and Friday are the weekend. When a holiday occurs on Friday, Saturday is also a holiday.

• All shops and businesses close for the noon prayer and reopen after the afternoon prayer. Between those times, the downtown area of any city is totally shut down.

Currency

• The unit of currency is the *riyal*, abbreviated SR (Saudi *riyal*). A *riyal* is made up of 100 *halabah*.
• Coins: 1, 5, 10, 25, and 50 *halabah* and 1 *riyal*.
• Bills: 1, 5, 10, 50, 100, and 500 *riyal*.

Business Practices

• Don't try to go to Saudi Arabia without a contact in the country. You won't be able to get a visa —a long, time-consuming process —unless a business or a company vouches for you and requests that the government grant you a visa.
• Look for contacts in your country at banks that have representatives in Saudi Arabia. Other sources are the Commercial Section of your embassy in Saudi Arabia or the Commercial Section of the Saudi Arabian embassy in your country.
• Long before going to Saudi Arabia, obtain a copy of the Saudi labor laws, available from the U.S.

Department of Commerce (or its equivalent in other countries). These laws will have major effects on your operations in Saudi Arabia.
• Study the market carefully, and form a partnership with a competent Saudi firm.
• Remember that you must be willing to make a long-term commitment, involving many personal visits to Saudi Arabia.
• Don't try to make appointments during the fifth or sixth months of the Islamic calendar. Those are budget times for government officials, and they won't have time to see you. Avoid the twelfth month of the Islamic calendar, since that is the period of the pilgrimage to Mecca.
• Keep in mind that many Saudi businessmen travel to cooler climates during the summer (June through August) and aren't available.
• Try to make arrangements for meetings beforehand. You can attempt to make appointments from abroad or—better still—have your contact in Saudi Arabia make them for you. All meetings with government officials will be in Riyadh. However, you will have a better chance of getting appointments if you are actually in the country. As devout Muslims, Saudis like to deal with the present and don't want to make plans too far into the future.
• Don't be surprised if someone

suggests an appointment between 8:00 P.M. and midnight. Many people like to work during those hours because it's cooler.

• Don't send a woman to do business, not even as a minor member of a team. An unaccompanied woman wouldn't even be allowed to check into a hotel in Riyadh or Jiddah without government approval. (The only women who work in Saudi Arabia are teachers who teach only female students and doctors whose only patients are women.)

• Stay in one of the best hotels. Saudis feel that if your company thinks a great deal of you, it will provide you with the best accommodations. If you stay at a lesser hotel, Saudis will think that you're not a valuable asset to your company and will lose respect for you.

• Hire a car and driver. Renting a car is easy, but driving is very difficult because people don't pay attention to the basic rules of the road, such as slowing down or stopping at intersections. If you are driving, you'll be exhausted before you get to your meetings.

• Be punctual, but be prepared to wait. Don't show any sign of impatience.

• Have your business cards printed in English on one side and Arabic on the other. Add a phonetic transliteration of your company's name in Arabic, if it isn't well known. Present your card immediately, with the Arabic side up. Keep the cards of Arabic businessmen in a safe place, since many people have unlisted addresses and phone numbers.

• Don't feel obliged to have materials for your presentation translated into Arabic or to hire an interpreter. People at higher levels will know English. However, official business with the government and any documents relating to a joint venture must be in Arabic.

• Use metric measurements in any specifications.

• Don't load your luggage with copies of materials you plan to use. It's very easy to have things copied in Saudi Arabia.

• Note that the general rule is: Refuse first, then accept. This applies to an offer of coffee, going through the door first, etc.

• Expect to drink countless cups of coffee or tea—the minimum to be polite is two to three cups. (Cups are very small.) Tea is sweet and may have mint in it. Coffee is always extremely bitter. If you see something floating around in the coffee, it's cardamom, a spice. Always take the cup for either drink with your right hand. It's ritual to hand your cup to the server, and he will refill it. When you've had enough, shake the cup gently back and forth as you hand it to the server. That gesture signals him not to pour any more.

• Never begin talking business before a Saudi does. People want to know you well before they do business with you. Business may not be mentioned at all during your first two or three meetings. Plan on *much* more time than you think you'll need. If your dealings should take about a week, plan on at least two to three weeks in Saudi Arabia. To make a good impression in conversation, prepare in advance by reading about Saudi history and especially about Abdul Azziz Ibn Saud, who united various provinces into the modern Kingdom of Saudi Arabia.

• Don't be surprised if a meeting is interrupted so that a Saudi can go to a mosque for prayer. The trip will add about half an hour to his prayer time, so you'll have to be patient.

• Note that the foreigners who are most successful in doing business in Saudi Arabia are those who balance subservience, flattery, and authority. Always begin by flattering a Saudi's business acumen before addressing any problems. Never discuss a problem in such a way that it would suggest that a Saudi is incompetent. It is very important to a Saudi to preserve appearances and to maintain self-respect and honor.

• Realize that most decisions are made by a few people at the top. Give four or five copies of your materials to the man with whom you're dealing. He will distribute them to the appropriate people. Giving him several copies will ensure that you're not leaving anyone out.

• Don't expect Saudis to offer resistance to you as an outsider, even though they tend to be clannish. They will be genuinely interested in finding out what improvements you and your company can provide.

• Be sure to study your competition carefully. Saudis will often quote prices and terms other companies are offering.

• *Never* try to "con" Saudis. They instinctively spot phoniness and will lose all respect for you

• Keep in mind that Saudis are impressed by visuals, but they probably won't pay a great deal of attention to them. Don't "quiz" Saudis on them—"Do you remember when I showed you X?"

• Be aware that time estimates won't be reliable. People will say what they think you want to hear, so avoid questions that require a "Yes" or "No" answer. Don't say, "Can this be delivered on June 15?" Ask "When can this be delivered?"

• Don't ever expect to meet privately with someone. There may be many people in the room who have nothing to do with your business, and there may be constant interruptions. Sit as close as possible to the person with whom you are meeting. It's acceptable to whisper in his ear if you don't want others to overhear. When it's time to sign a contract, you will probably be afforded more privacy.

• Be aware that Saudis may take months to make a decision and then rush to conclude a deal.

• Expect to work with a Pakistani, Yemeni, or Egyptian during the paperwork phase of your dealings. Paperwork is left to immigrants.

• Present a modest gift after meeting someone two or three times. The gift should not advertise anything, nor should it be of great value. People appreciate electrical gadgets and desk accessories.

• Note that Saudis formerly did not have the habit of business lunches and dinners, but, since dealing with the West over the past fifteen years, they have adapted to the practice. Invite a Saudi to a meal in the restaurant of one of the best hotels.

• If you have gotten to know a Saudi businessman and want to invite him to a restaurant, suggest that he bring a friend. He will probably bring someone who has been educated abroad. If you know that there's a foreigner the Saudi would like to meet, ask him, "Do you mind if I bring so-and-so along?"

• *Never* suggest including a Saudi wife in a business meal.

HOLIDAYS AND SPECIAL OCCASIONS

• In addition to the religious holidays celebrated according to the Muslim calendar, Saudi Arabia celebrates National Day (commemorating the unification of the kingdom) on Sept. 23. Expect to find banks, businesses, government offices, and most restaurants and shops closed.

TRANSPORTATION

Public Transportation

• Don't expect to find subways.
• Realize that buses are divided

by a wall into the male section and the female section. Men enter from the front and pay the driver. Women enter from the rear and are supposed to leave money for their fare. There is no person to collect the fare, and there are no inspectors. Within cities the fare to all destinations is the same.

• Note that taxis are not metered, and rates are set by zones. If possible, determine in advance what the fare will be.

• A woman should not ride alone in a taxi unless she knows the driver, and she should have her destination written in Arabic to show the driver.

• Be aware that long-distance buses are comfortable and usually have one or two bathrooms. If the trip is long—e.g., the eight hours from Jiddah to Riyadh—there will be one or two stops for food.

• Keep in mind that there is only one train system operating between Riyadh and Dahran (a trip of four to five hours). There are two trains—with air-conditioning and food and drink—a day in both directions. Buy a ticket at the station. (There are no couchettes, because they aren't necessary for such a short trip.)

• If you've rented a car with a driver, and the driver has an accident, realize that you may be put into a police car and taken to the station for questioning. The police are simply taking you to someone who speaks English so that you can explain what happened.

• If you rent a car, always have license, I.D. card, and car registration ready to show at road checkpoints.

• Note that most street signs are in Arabic and English.

• Don't drink and drive, since drinking alcohol is illegal. You'll be sent to jail.

• Be aware that there are on-the-spot fines for such offenses as running a red light.

• Don't attempt to bribe the police.

• If you're in an accident, don't leave the scene. Be aware that if you stop to help someone else who's been in an accident you may be held responsible for the condition of the person if he sustains serious injury or dies.

• Realize that there are major hazards if you decide to drive in Saudi Arabia: (1) Saudis rarely slow down at intersections or indicate turns. (2) Roads are only two-lane, and there are many head-on collisions. (3) People and animals (camels, goats, and sheep) wander onto the street. (4) Many cars have no lights on at night. (5) There are no signs indicating construction or barriers.

• If you must swerve, swerve to the right.

• Remember that women—Saudi or foreign—are not permitted to drive. (Foreign women can drive within the Aramco compound in Dahran.)

LEGAL MATTERS, SAFETY, AND HEALTH

• To obtain a visa you need a telexed invitation from a host in Saudi Arabia sent to a consulate or embassy or a telexed invitation confirmed by the Ministry of Foreign Affairs. Foreign women receive visas only if they are dependents of foreign workers or if they have critical skills such as nursing, though foreign nurses' lives are as restricted as though they were in boarding school. You will also need some proof (baptismal certificate, letter from a clergyman) to show that you are a member of a church.

• Be aware that Saudi Arabia forbids the import of many items: pork; liquor; nutmeg (because of its hallucinogenic properties); vanilla flavoring (because of its alcohol content); pornography (which includes magazines with lingerie ads as well as books with famous paintings of nudes); Bibles; crucifixes; the Star of David; carvings and statues; any books on Saudi Arabia not printed by the Saudi Ministry of Information; books by Jewish authors.

• Keep in mind that there is total prohibition of the open practice of any religion other than Islam.

• Note that during Ramadan, when no eating or drinking is allowed during daylight hours, non-Muslims who are caught eating or drinking may be whipped or jailed.

• Recall that Mecca (Mohammed's birthplace) and Medina (the site of his tomb) are considered too holy for non-Muslims to enter. Don't try to go beyond any warning signs. You will be arrested immediately if you do.

• Expect your mail to be censored. In letters about your work, don't make any negative comments about the Saudi people, the country, Islam, or any adverse conditions you have encountered.

• Never try to bribe anyone. Such an attempt can lead to a jail sentence.

• Don't arrive at customs in an intoxicated condition. You may be arrested.

• Bring a copy of the prescription, signed by your physician, for any narcotics you're bringing in to the country.

• If you want a work permit, you will have to have an AIDS test. Results of tests done in the U.S. are acceptable.

• Any woman—Western or Saudi—on the street alone is considered a prostitute. However, if you have your neck and legs covered, wear a dress with long sleeves, have legs covered to the ankle, and a scarf covering your hair, there is less risk.

• A woman who goes out alone should walk with a purpose—straight to where you're going without dawdling or stopping.

• Be conscious that the religious police—called *matawain*—don't allow Western women to ride a bike, jog, have bare legs, or ride in a car with a man unless they are married. A woman not dressed properly (see above) may be hit with a camel prod by these police.

• Never drink tap water. Don't use ice cubes. Don't eat fruits and vegetables that cannot be peeled.

YEMEN

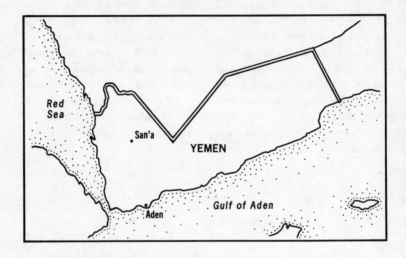

Red
Sea

• San'a

YEMEN

• Aden

Gulf of Aden

    Writer Naomi Sakr recommends Yemen to those who would like to see "the old Arabia before it is bulldozed into oblivion."

    An American anthropologist who visited Yemen reports: "Going to Yemen is like going back in time to the olden days when the virtues of dignity, respect, and kindness were important. It's very calming and soothing."

GREETINGS

• When introduced to someone, shake hands.

• Note that only two titles are important: *Qadi*, which is judge, and *Faqih*, which means religious scholar. Both are religious titles.

• Use first names when you meet a person. Yemenites don't really have last names. Their second name is their father's name, *or* people will be identified as "Father of ———" or "Mother of ———." Some examples: (1) In the name "Muhamed Hassan," Hassan is the father's name. Western equivalent: If your first name was Mary and your father's name was William, your name would be Mary William. (2) After people marry, they are identified as the father or mother of their first-born child. Abu Muhamed is the name for the father of Muhamed. Umm Muhamed is the mother of Muhamed.

• Remember that when men meet men friends and women meet women friends, they kiss one an-other on each cheek while shaking hands. Women friends may stroke each other's cheeks after kissing. Men and women are never together and never touch.

• If you're in a large group, expect to be introduced to a few people standing or sitting near your host. Introduce yourself to the others at the gathering.

CONVERSATION

• Don't discuss anything political, especially the Israeli-Arab conflict.

• Some good topics for conversation: positive comments about the country such as its beauty or the great weather. Ask questions about the other person's children. Seek advice about places to visit and good foods to sample.

TELEPHONES

- Don't look for public telephones. There aren't any. For local calls, go to the town's main post office, where you'll find coin-operated phones. You won't find telephone directories (there are none of those, either), but the staff at the counter will find numbers for you and will show you how to use the telephones.

- To make an overseas call, go to the Cable and Wireless Company (which is for overseas calls only). Estimate the time of your call, and pay in advance. If you speak for less time, you'll receive a refund. Loudspeakers announce —in Arabic only—which call is in which booth.

IN PUBLIC

- Keep in mind that foreigners are no longer allowed into mosques, except for some historical ones that may be entered when it's not a prayer time. Never go into a mosque without asking permission. Both men and women should remove their shoes before entering; women should be sure that hair, legs, and arms are covered.

- Foreign women should not travel alone in Yemen unless they speak Arabic.

- A gesture to avoid: the Western "okay" sign (index finger joined with thumb to make a circle); in Yemen it refers to female genitalia.

- Other gestures: (1) The whole hand up with the palm facing away from the body means "Stop." (2) The palm up, the thumb and index finger stuck out, and the other three fingers folded into the palm, with the whole hand moving from side to side is a general interrogative—"who," "what," "when," "where," or "why." (3) Flipping your hand down means "Come here."

• Acquaint yourself with the custom of chewing *qat*, an activity very important in the life of Yemenites. *Qat* makes people's minds alert and their bodies relaxed. It's also an appetite depressant. If you're invited to a "chew," buy your *qat* at the market and bring it with you. *Qat* costs from $40 to $100 per person and is bought by the wad. The long type is the most expensive. *Qat* is "officially" opposed by the government, though it realizes large tax revenues from its production and marketing. Religious authorities sanction the use of *qat*. (For a complete description of *qat* chewing, see the "Business" section).

• Don't be surprised to see Yemeni men wearing daggers all the time.

• Don't expect to bargain in Yemen as you would in other Arab countries. Grocery store prices are fixed, and even in the bazaars bargaining is rare. The quoted price is usually the final price. However, before you buy, make comparisons of prices in different areas of the bazaar.

• Remember that all sales activity stops during prayer time (five times a day).

• Don't bring video or movie cameras into Yemen. They are forbidden. Even if you manage to smuggle them in, police can confiscate them if they observe you filming. The only way to make a film is to have permission from the Yemen embassy in your country, an authorization that can take up to six months.

• Don't photograph military buildings and installations, checkpoints, communications stations, or airports.

• If you want to photograph a person, *always* ask permission first. Some people will try to break your camera if you take a picture without first asking. However, others (usually the younger generation, which has been raised on TV) will ask to be photographed.

• Look for public bathrooms in restaurants and hotels. Those in hotels are usually Western style, while those in restaurants are Turkish style (i.e., a hole in the floor). Bring your own toilet paper or tissues.

• Realize that some public bathrooms (for example, those at the airport) have signs only in Arabic. Wait to see which sex enters which door.

DRESS

• When choosing clothes for going outside, remember that Yemen is very dusty, the few sidewalks are in very poor condition, and there are few paved roads. Sturdy walking shoes are essential.

• For casual dress, men can wear short-sleeved shirts and pants, while women must be sure that their arms are covered and that skirts are no higher than mid-calf.

• For business, men should wear suits and ties as a sign of respect; women should wear suits or a dress with long sleeves and skirt to mid-calf or ankle length. Blouses or dresses should have a high collar.

• Both men and women should remember that it's *very* important to have the crotch covered. Women should wear slacks under their skirt. Men should bring a scarf to place over the lap when invited to dinner in a home.

• If you're a foreign woman invited to a meal, choose your costume carefully. Wear a long tunic over pants or slacks under your dress, since you may be sitting on the floor.

• Note that the only parties for which formal attire may be required are embassy functions. Men should wear a dark suit and tie, and women should wear a cocktail dress with long sleeves.

MEALS

Hours and Foods

• Keep in mind that Yemen is not a "food culture," where meals are central to life—as they are in France and Italy, for example. Meals are planned around the five-times-daily prayers, and people tend to "squeeze in" meals and to eat in a rush.

Breakfast: About 8:00 A.M. The usual meal is *ful* (cooked white beans) or eggs or fish or liver (it's always a high-protein meal). There will also be fresh bread (like large flat loaves of pita) and coffee, served with milk and sugar.

Lunch: About 2:00 P.M. Expect several kinds of bread to be offered throughout the meal—

e.g., flat wheat bread, sorghum bread, or sweet bread. The first course usually consists of vegetables, followed by potatoes, spaghetti, and bread. If the family is affluent, the last course will be chicken or lamb. During the entire meal, there will be *holba*, a dish made of fenugreek seeds (they are aromatic and mucilaginous) which have been soaked, crushed, and whipped into a sauce with chives, and then eaten with bread. At the end of the meal, everything that was served is mixed together and put into a dish that is kept warm on the stove. People keep eating this mixture for an hour or so after the end of the meal.

Dinner: A light meal served about 7:30 or 8:00 P.M. There will be bread and either leftovers from lunch, eggs, beans, or cheese. The beverages will be either tea or water.

• Note that alcoholic beverages are available only in hotels.

• Expect to find bottled water (mineral water) available everywhere, even in villages.

Beverages: None are served with meals. During the day, the drinks served are: *Qishr*, a tea made from coffee husks; tea flavored with cinnamon and cloves; Coca-Cola; Pepsi; bottled water.

• At breakfast, assume the drink will be coffee with milk and sugar.

Table Manners

• If you're invited to a meal, expect to be asked to lunch, since that is the main meal of the day.

• Should you come for a visit in a home before lunch, prepare to snack on mixed raisins and almonds, popcorn, or toasted seeds (e.g., pumpkin seeds), along with tea or soda.

• An invitation to lunch means that you're expected to stay for the afternoon—until the evening prayer time. It's the back-and-forth of conversation that's the important part of the visit. When you try to leave, people will press you to stay. Make up an excuse ("I'm expecting an important call at my hotel"), and then leave.

• At one end of the room, usually the end opposite the entrance, expect to see higher cushions or more cushions for the host and the guest of honor. If you are guest of honor, your host will lead you to these cushions.

• Realize that there are no tables and chairs. People eat on a mat or a plastic tablecloth that has been placed on the floor. Most foods are scooped up with bread. As a foreigner, feel free to ask for a spoon.

• Always eat with your right hand, as Yemenites do.

• Keep in mind that men usually eat first; then women and children eat—usually leftovers—either later or in another room.

• Don't expect conversation during meals.

• Note that as soon as someone has had enough, he leaves the table, washes his hands, and goes to the sitting room for coffee, where the men smoke a shared water pipe.

• If a wife accompanies a foreign businessman, she'll eat with the men. About an hour after coffee is served, she can ask to join the women. She must be sure to allow enough time for the women to have eaten the leftovers. However, if she doesn't speak Arabic, joining the women will be a waste of time, unless the family is Westernized and the women speak English. It's perfectly acceptable for her to remain with the men.

Eating Out

• Realize that there aren't a large number of restaurants in Yemen, primarily because Yemenites don't eat out. They want to be sure that the bread is absolutely fresh and the meat freshly slaughtered, and they don't trust restaurants.

• Don't look for Western-style restaurants in Yemen. Only hotels serve Western food—often poor imitations of Western dishes.

• In San'a, consider eating at one of the few foreign restaurants; they serve Lebanese and Vietnamese food.

• Note that restaurants usually serve lunch between noon and 4:00 P.M. and dinner from 6:00 to 9:00 P.M.

• Expect to find a single menu on the wall in Arabic, or menus handwritten in Arabic brought to the table. The best strategy is probably to ask the waiter what he recommends. Waiters speak English.

• Realize that many restaurants have poor hygienic standards. Never accept food that is not *steaming* hot when brought to the table. Never drink the water in the plastic jugs on the table.

• To attract the waiter's attention, clap your hands.

• A woman traveling alone should eat her meals in the hotel restaurant.

• Don't eat salads, raw fruits, and vegetables that cannot be peeled. Don't drink tap water or have a drink with ice cubes.

Specialties

• The national dish: *salta*—a hot, thick stew made of lamb or chicken, beans, chick-peas, lentils, coriander, and other spices, and served on rice.

• Two special breads: *khobz*—wholemeal flat bread; *malvz*—barley bread.

• *Zhug* is a hot dip made of pepper, chilies, cardamom, caraway, garlic, and coriander. It's eaten with bread.

• Some soup specialties: *shourba ful*—dried bean soup; *hulba*—a thick soup made of fenugreek, chilies, tomato, onion, garlic, chicken or lamb, lentils, rice, coriander, clarified butter, lemon juice, and salt; *shurba bilsan*—lentil soup; *shurba wasabi*—lamb soup; *chefont*—a green yogurt soup. Soups are usually served with thin Arabic bread, which is brushed with butter, fenugreek, and coriander paste.

• A typical dessert is *Bint al Sahn*—a sweet bread that is dipped into honey and clarified butter.

This will leave no doubt that your intentions are honorable—that you're not interested in amorous relationships.

• Keep in mind that in lower-category hotels, the toilets are the Turkish ("squat") type.

• Before accepting a room, check the taps in the shower to make sure that they work. Often there is a water heater, but it may not be properly connected.

• Remember that hotels in the middle price range usually offer double or triple rooms; single rooms are sometimes available.

HOTELS

• At the best hotels, you'll find the same level of amenities as at a top hotel in Europe—air-conditioning, room service, restaurants, and fax machines. Middle-range hotels will probably not have a restaurant but will offer simple, clean rooms.

• If you're a woman traveling alone, when you register at the hotel, use the word *"Insha'allah"* ("God willing") often. If people ask if you're a Muslim, say "Yes."

TIPPING

• Don't tip taxi drivers, but negotiate the fare before you get in the taxi.

• Don't tip gas station attendants.

• In tipping the following, give the same amount that you would in North America, since costs are so high in Yemen: porters at airports and hotels; waiters; the person who cleans your hotel room.

PRIVATE HOMES

• Visit around 3:30 or 4:00 P.M. You don't have to phone first. Just drop in. Leave before the evening prayer at sundown.

• Note that Yemenites will always invite you to a meal in their home if they're doing business with you or if they have met you socially. Once you have a relationship with a family, they will very likely ask you to be their guest for a few days.

• If you're staying with a family, prepare to be the source of entertainment. Be chatty and gregarious. Expect people to invite their friends over to see you and visit with you.

• Offer to help, if you wish, but you won't be allowed to.

• If you're staying in a home, remember that water is scarce. Ask your hostess, "How can I get water to wash?" In the city, people have bathtubs and showers, but in older homes, there may not be baths. In that case people go to the public baths once or twice a week.

• The *hammam* is both a public bath and a social center, especially for women. Try to go with a Yemenite—especially if you're a woman, since you'll be introduced to other Yemeni women. Women's hours are usually 9:00 A.M. to 7:00 P.M., and men's hours from 7:00 P.M. to 1:00 A.M.

Because modesty is important, men should wear underpants or swimming trunks and women should wear underpants. Everyone should wear thongs on their feet. Bring a bag, go to the changing room if you're a woman, or undress facing the wall if you're a man. Put your clothes in the bag, and give it to an attendant. You can put your clothes on a hanger in your cubicle, but they will almost certainly get wet. Don't bring valuables with you.

Have with you a bucket, soap, and black gloves that feel like loofahs—and that you can buy at a market or get from an attendant. Pay as you enter, and get soap and towels. Go to the central bathing area, where you will find individual cement cubicles with a shower and a wooden bench. An attendant will come around, pour water over you, wash you, and put henna in a woman's hair, if she wishes. Friends scrub one another—often with great vigor in order to slough off dead skin. Don't be surprised if you're asked to scrub someone's back. That person will then scrub yours. Don't stand behind anyone and slosh your dirty water at them. Floors are washed after each person finishes.

Gifts: Women enjoy receiving scarves, and men like solar-energy calculators and shirts and ties. People will also appreciate a book with photographs of your area. Give children video games, which you should buy in Yemen (machines are different from those in North America and Europe), and give little girls costume jewelry.

BUSINESS

Hours

Government Offices: Saturday through Thursday, 8:00 A.M. to 2:00 P.M.

Businesses: Saturday through Thursday, 8:00 A.M. to 12:30 P.M. and 4:00 to 7:30 P.M.

Banks: Saturday through Thursday, 8:00 A.M. to 2:00 P.M.

Shops: Saturday through Thursday, 8:00 A.M. to 1:00 P.M. and 4:00 to 9:00 P.M.

Currency

• The unit of currency is the Yemen *rial*, abbreviated YR; it is composed of 100 *fils*.
• Coins: 5, 10, 25, and 50 *fils* and YR 1.
• Bills: YR 1, 5, 10, 20, 50, and 100.
• Realize that notes are easy to distinguish, since the amount is given on one side in Arabic and on the other in English. Coins show their value only in Arabic.
• Bring cash rather than traveler's checks, since some money changers won't accept the checks. Don't worry about carrying large amounts of cash. Theft is virtually nonexistent in Yemen. If you're still nervous, use a money belt.
• Don't plan to use credit cards rather than cash. Only five-star hotels accept credit cards.
• If you arrive at the airport and find bank offices for changing money closed, ask your taxi driver to take you to a money exchange. (Money exchanges are open from 8:00 A.M. to 1:00 P.M. and from 5:00 to 8:00 P.M.) If you arrive at another time, ask anyone at the airport to change some money. Be sure to bring with you some bills —preferably dollars—in small denominations ($20 or under).

• Change money at money changers rather than at banks. Some
banks don't have exchange services, and, even if they do, you
will have to wait for a very long
time. Money changers usually give
better rates than banks. An additional advantage is that, unlike
banks, money changers are open
in the evening. Money changers'
offices, clearly marked with signs
in the Roman alphabet, are found
in major towns near the main
square and in the market sections.

• Don't expect to be able to
change money outside San'a, Ta'izz,
or Hodeida, the three largest cities
in Yemen.

Business Practices

• Remember that it takes a long
time to accomplish anything in
Yemen. Add two weeks to your
proposed stay in Yemen to allow
for the unknown.

• Note that Yemen's government does not require firms to
have a local agent, but such agents
can be useful in moving bids and
contracts through the country's
bureaucracy.

• If you have a staff, an agent,
or a contact in Yemen, ask them
to make appointments about two
weeks in advance. Otherwise,
you'll have to make your appointments a week in advance.

• Keep in mind that business

people are allowed to bring in to
Yemen samples of products, sales
promotion equipment, and brochures.

• To acquire contacts, go to
Yemen and meet with people in
the expatriate community. Ask at
your country's embassy for a list of
foreign businesses in Yemen, visit
their offices, and tell them that
you would like to speak to someone regarding contacts in the field
in which you want to do business.
Other sources of contacts: The
American Institute for Yemen
Studies and also the French or German Institutes—all in San'a; the
Cultural Affairs Officers at your
country's embassy.

• Avoid making business appointments during the months of
April through August (because of
the heat) and during Ramadan.

• Try to schedule your initial
business meeting between 10:00
A.M. and noon. Office hours are
usually in the morning. The lowest echelon people arrive about
7:30 A.M., while those at the top
level arrive about 9:00 or 10:00
A.M. They usually sign papers and
then leave. The morning hours
aren't a good time for discussion,
because of the chaotic atmosphere
of people coming and going. Most
business is done at afternoon "*Qat*
chews." (See below.)

• Bring business cards printed
in Arabic on one side and English
on the other.

• Always be on time, even though important Yemenites with whom you have appointments may be late. The person you're waiting for may not show up at all, but don't think you have wasted your time. (See below.) If people are apologetic about not showing up, you'll know they're sincere. Since men in the culture do everything outside the home—e.g., shopping, taking children to the doctor—they may not show up for an appointment, but they'll never tell you why. Example: A Yemenite didn't appear for an important appointment with American government workers. The Americans later learned that his son had died, but the Yemenite didn't tell them.

• Realize that while you're waiting for the appointment that may or may not materialize, you are being carefully scrutinized. If you show signs of impatience, treat people badly, or complain, you won't be successful. The tea boy may be humbly dressed and wearing flip-flops, but you should treat him with the same respect as you would someone from the upper echelon. People, including the tea boy, are looking for clues on how you react. They're testing your patience, as well as your respect for the culture, for authority, and for all types of people. The more gracious and regal (but not haughty) you are, the better your chance for success will be.

• Be sure to hire a *Yemenite* interpreter, if your business counterparts aren't fluent in English. An interpreter from another country may not be familiar with Yemeni Arabic, which is quite different from other Arabic. You want someone who speaks the language with the exact nuances people are used to. Seek an interpreter through your hotel or through the expatriate community.

• Remember that Yemen doesn't have a "chit chat" business culture. People get down to business right away, so you should feel free to state your purpose briefly and concisely.

• Be aware that *qat* and the chewing of *qat* is an essential component of business life in Yemen. Many Yemenites chew the mildly narcotic *qat* from early afternoon to sunset. (Yemenites don't chew in the morning, because that's regarded as shameful, nor do they chew alone.) During the *qat* chewing sessions, business is discussed and visiting businessmen may be invited to join. It's okay to decline, but that inhibits your chance of success. If you do chew *qat*, you'll be overwhelmingly accepted, and people will be amenable to doing business with you.

• To chew *qat*, wad about 100 grams into one cheek. Yemenites usually spit out the bitter juices periodically. After 15 minutes the chewer experiences a sense of alertness and heightened awareness, which lasts about two hours. After the initial stimulation, the chewer becomes euphoric. There follows a period of listlessness and depression.

• Keep in mind that almost all business is conducted in a home during *qat* chews. Many foreigners erroneously think that Yemenites don't work. Not true. Working is just arranged differently; if you want to "fit in" and succeed you have to take the *qat*-chewing sessions seriously. For example, don't be upset if a business appointment is cut short because the Yemenite has an appointment to attend a *qat* session.

• Don't expect Yemeni business people to take you to a restaurant, and you can't reciprocate for an invitation by inviting them to a restaurant. The only way to reciprocate is to invite them to a *qat* chew in your office. If you don't have an office, ask an acquaintance, perhaps the person with whom you're doing business, where you can hold a *qat* chew. Add that you would like to provide the *qat*. (Typical Yemenite businessmen go to *qat*-chewing sessions daily.)

• A typical *qat* chew begins about 3:00 P.M. By 4:00 P.M., everyone is talking—often about business—in an animated fashion. People smoke a water pipe and drink bottled water. At around

5:00 P.M., people sit very passively. A calm hush falls over the room. (This time is referred to as the "hour of Solomon," because it is associated with wisdom.) Then people spit out the *qat*, wash out their mouths, and pray. During the prayers, sit quietly. The "chew" is usually held in a special room—lined on three sides with cushions—at the top of the house. The windows are low, so that everyone can look out at the countryside. (Women chew *qat* in less luxurious surroundings). No food is served until several hours after a *qat* chew, because chewing *qat* dulls the appetite. There will be water.

• Note that *qat* is not medically addictive, but it is psychologically addictive.

• Foreign women should note that they have a good chance of succeeding in Yemen, especially if they speak Arabic. Yemeni women are very secluded, so Yemeni men are used to treating them with kindness, tenderness, and respect. Since foreign women are not family members, they will assume a status somewhere between that of a man and a woman. They will be accorded the same kindness and respect as Yemeni men give to Yemeni women.

HOLIDAYS AND SPECIAL OCCASIONS

The following are national holidays. You will find banks, business and government offices, shops, and restaurants closed. Plan to eat in your hotel restaurant. For dates of religious holidays celebrated according to the Muslim calendar, check with Yemen's embassy in your country.

Holidays: Labor Day (May 1); Correction Movement Day (June 22); Revolution Day (Sept. 26); National Day (Oct. 14); Independence Day (Nov. 30).

• Remember that when any holiday falls on a Wednesday or a Sunday, Yemenites take a long weekend, so you'll find shops and businesses closed on Thursday or on Monday. (Friday is the weekly holiday.)

TRANSPORTATION

Public Transportation

• Note that in cities and major towns, there are large buses, as well as black-striped mini-buses that go along certain defined routes. Buses are usually not very crowded. Generally, a mini-bus will become a private taxi if you are the first to get in, and if you mention a destination that is not on the route. Agree on a price before you get in.

• Remember that city taxis and short-trip service taxis have black stripes. Long-trip service taxis have stripes colored according to the destination. In a service taxi, the cost is per person. (Women should buy space for two people so that there will be space between them and another person, and they should sit next to the door.) Usually service-taxi fares are fixed, but a Westerner may be charged more.

• Be aware that short-trip service taxis run along definite routes on major streets and stop along these routes.

• Long-distance service taxis leave from terminals and don't leave until they are full. (While buses go only on asphalt roads, service taxis will go on non-asphalt roads as well.) When the car is full (eight passengers), fees are collected, and all passengers' names are written on a list. Sometimes the collection and listing takes place at an office a few kilometers away from the starting point.

• Keep in mind that names of destinations of buses are marked only in Arabic. Seats are not reserved. You'll find a bus number (in Arabic) on the front bumper of the bus. The same number (in Arabic) will appear on your ticket.

• Expect to find intercity buses running between San'a, Hodeida, and Ta'izz.

• When taking a long-distance bus, purchase your ticket at a bus terminal. Ticket offices open 30 minutes to an hour before the bus departures. They close as soon as the bus has left. You can't buy your ticket in advance, not even a few hours before departure. For a ticket on a crowded route, arrive at the terminal an hour before the ticket office opens, especially on weekends.

agent (be sure to have an International Driver's License). However, if you have never driven a four-wheel-drive vehicle, don't rent a car—hire a driver. (This course is especially economical if there are a few people to share the cost.) Further, there are no reliable maps, and tracks in the lowlands change drastically with the climate. Finally, there are large, unpopulated areas in Yemen, so there may be no one to help you if you get stranded. (Only the roads between San'a, Hodeida, and Ta'izz are paved.)

• Remember that there are no signs in English, so travel alone is very difficult, unless you read Arabic.

• Be aware that most towns have night curfews; therefore, you should avoid travel outside towns at night. (Check the times of the local curfew when you arrive.)

• Don't forget that there are *extremely* heavy fines if you are in an accident, especially one in which someone was killed.

• Read the section on "Desert Driving" in the chapter on "Customs and Manners in the Arab World" to learn the special precautions you should take.

Driving

• You can rent a car either through a major hotel or a travel

LEGAL MATTERS, SAFETY, AND HEALTH

• Understand that nothing that could possibly be construed as pornography is allowed in the country. (An art book with classical paintings of nudes might be regarded as pornography.) Something else that will be confiscated at customs is any controversial book—e.g., Salman Rushdie's *The Satanic Verses*.

• Note that when you arrive at customs, you must show your passport and visa, tell where you are going, and state the purpose of your visit. You will then receive a tour permit. (The word for this permit in Arabic is *tasree*.) There is no fee for the permit, which can be obtained at the General Tourist Corporation in San'a or at its branch offices in Ta'izz and Hodeida. Staff at all branches speak English. In applying for the permit, list the towns you plan to visit, including towns and villages at which you want to stop en route to other towns. Immediately after you obtain the permit, make several photocopies, since soldiers at some checkpoints keep the permit.

• Give a copy of your tour permit only if it is requested. First offer your passport. Don't try to bribe soldiers to allow you to go to a place not listed on your tourist permit. They won't accept your offer.

• Expect to find roadblocks along every major road and around every major town. All travelers must stop at checkpoints manned by soldiers and show their I.D. card. Yemen is run by a military government. Yemenites have permanent access only to certain areas. In order to visit other towns, they must have special permission from authorities—as must foreign visitors.

• Realize that you cannot export anything over 40 years old, except with permission from the General Tourism Corporation.

• Be aware that alcoholic beverages are prohibited, except to non-Muslims, who are allowed to bring one liter into the country.

• Don't be surprised to find customs at the airport very time-consuming. Every bag, including handbags, is opened. If possible, choose a line where there are only foreigners; there you will finish sooner.

• Women should feel free to take a taxi at night.

• Women should understand that Yemen is not a dangerous country. If there is a problem, people are generally very helpful.

• A woman should follow her "gut instinct." If you get in a taxi and don't feel comfortable with the driver, tell him to let you out. If you think that someone is following you, go into a shop or hotel. If someone grabs you, walk away, and try to find a taxi. You probably won't be in danger of rape, theft, or mugging, but you may be verbally harassed or touched, especially if you don't dress properly and behave discreetly. Don't flirt. Don't smile at men. Don't make eye contact with men.

• Remember to drink only bottled water or soft drinks. Don't eat raw fruits or vegetables that cannot be peeled.

• Realize that milk is safe, because it's pasteurized, and that Yemen's eggs are imported from Denmark. Feel free to eat the shrimp (which are large and delicious).

• Don't swim or even wade in shallow streams, ponds, or rivers, because of the danger of the parasitic disease bilharzia.

• Note that prescriptions are not required in pharmacies, but if you take a specific drug regularly, bring it with you. You might also want to bring toilet paper or tissues, since toilet paper is difficult to find. In Yemen, people always wash with water after going to the bathroom. Women will find sanitary napkins available, but not tampons.

Key Words and Phrases - Arabic
⚜

PRONUNCIATION

The following Arabic phrases are in the Cairo dialect.

h = strongly aspirated h
kh = the *ch* sound in the words Bach and loch
ʾ = a glottal stop, a gulp-like sound formed in the back of the
throat, used in the colloquial New York pronunciation of
the word *bottle*

GENERAL WORDS AND PHRASES

Hello (literally, may peace be with you)	as-sah-láh-moo ah-láy-kum
Hello (in response; literally, and on you peace)	wi-ah-láy-kum is-sah-láhm
Good morning.	sah-baĥ el-kháy-reh
Good night.	tes-baĥ áh-lah kháy-reh (to masc.)
	tes-bah-ĥee áh-lah kháy-reh (to fem.)
today	in-nay-háhr-dah
tomorrow	bok-rah
Good-bye.	maʾ ahs-sah-lah-máh
Good-bye. (in response)	Ahl-láh is-ahl-máhk
I would like	ah-náh ah-wiz (masc.)
	ah-nahów-zah (fem.)

I have	to-leh-eh-zehm ah-nah ahn-dee (masc. & fem.)
I need	ah-nah ah-wiz (masc.)
	ah-nah ow-zah (fem.)
I don't like	mish bah-heb (masc. & fem.)
Help!	el-hah-oo-nay
cold	bahr-dahn (masc.)
	bahr-dah-nah (fem.)
hot	hah-rahn (masc.)
	hah-rah-nah (fem.)
How much is it?	bee-kahm
It is too much.	dah rah-lee ah-wee
Where is ———?	fayn
Where are ———?	
a bathroom	doh-ret el-mye-yah
the restaurant	el-maht-ahm
the hotel	loh-kahn-dah
the post office	el-bohs-tah
the station	el-may-hah-tah
the bus	oh-toh-bees
the train station	mah-hah-tet is-sik-ka el-ha-deed
a market	sook
a hospital	mus-tahsh-fah
a doctor	dok-tohr
a bank	bahnk
a taxi	tahk-see
a telephone	it-teh-leh-fohn
the police station	mahr-keez ish-shor-tah
the embassy	is-seh-fah-rah
the gas station	may-hah-tet bahn-zeen
a garage	gah-rahzh
the pharmacy	ahg-zah-kah-nah
the mosque	ig-gah-meh
the museum	el-maht-huff
the airport	el-mah-tahr

left	ish-shee-máhl
right	el-yee-meén
straight ahead	ah-lah-tool
At what time is ———?	is-sah-láh
What time is it?	is-sáh-a' kahm
Yes.	aye-wah
No.	la'
Thank you	shoo-kráhn
You're welcome.	el-ah-foo
I'm sorry.	ah-nah áh-sif (masc.)
	ah-nah ahs-fah (fem.)
Excuse me.	es-mah-lee (to masc.)
	es-mah-hee lee (to fem.)
Please speak slowly.	min-fáhd-luk et-kahl-lim ah-lah mah-lahk (to masc.)
	min-fáhd-lik et-kahl-lí-mee áh-lah mah-lik (to fem.)
Do you speak English?	en-tah beh-tit-kahl-lim en-geh-lee-zee (to masc.)
	én-tee beh-tit-kahl-lí-mee en-geh-lee-zee (to fem.)
Glad to meet you.	tah-shar-rúf-nah
How are you?	iz-zyé-yak (to masc.)
	iz-zyé-yik (to fem.)
I'm fine.	el-háhm-do lil-láh (literally, thanks to God)
What is your name?	en-tah ís-mahk ay (to masc.)
	en-tee ís-mik ay (to fem.)
My name is ———.	ah-náh ís-mee
Professor	oo-stéz or pro-fes-sór
Doctor	doc-tór
Engineer, Architect, Attorney	moo-háhn-dis
Mr.	say-yeéd (or monsieur)
Mrs.	zów-gah (or madame)
Miss	mademoiselle

a man	ráh-gleh
a woman	shef
a girl	bent
a boy	oo-áh-lahd
to eat	eh̄-kol
to drink	ash-ráhb
to go	ah-róo
to see	ah-shóof
I am sick.	ah-náh aye-yáhn (masc.)
	ah-náh ay-yah-nah (fem.)
I am tired.	ah-náh tah-báhn (masc.)
	ah-náh tah-báh-nah (fem.)
I am thirsty.	ah-náh aht-sháhn (masc.)
	ah-náh aht-sháh-nah (fem.)
I am hungry.	ah-náh gah-áhn (masc.)
	ah-náh gah-áh-nah (fem.)
I am lost.	ah-náh tah-yéh (masc.)
	ah-náh tie-hah (fem.)

AT THE HOTEL

twin beds	bis-ree-ráyn
a double bed	bis-réer doób-leh
hot water	máye-ah sókh-nah
a shower	dyush
a room	óh-dah
with a bathroom	bee-h̄am-máhm
air-conditioned	moo-kye-yáh-fah
a television	teh-leh-viz-yóhn

TELEPHONING

"Hello"	ah-lóh
collect call	Use the English term.
credit card call	Use the English term.

AT THE PHARMACY

deodorant	moo-zeel ler-ree-hah
toothpaste	mah-goon is-nahn
antacid	malh fow-wahr
laxative	mohs-hill

RESTAURANT

the menu	el-lis-tah
the check	el-heh-sahb
large	ki-beer
small	soo-raye-yahr
a little	shway-ah
a lot	k'teer
a fork	shoh-kah
a knife	sik-kee-mah
a spoon	mah-lah-a' soo-raye-yah-arh
a glass	kub-bah-yah
a cup	koo-pah-yah
a plate	tah-bah
fried	ma'-lee-yah
grilled	mash-wee-yah
roasted	may-ham-mah-rah
well-done	mis-teh-wee-yah kwaye-yis
rare	nohs-see-wah

MEATS AND FISH

lamb	oo-zee
beef	uh-gah-lee
chicken	far-kha
fish	sah-mahk
lamb chops	ray-ash dah-nee
shrimp	gahm-bah-ree

VEGETABLES

tomato	to-mah-tuhm
potatoes	bah-tah-tis
eggplant	bid-in-gahn
okra	bahm-yah

FRUITS

melon	but-teekh bah-lah-dee
banana	mohz
oranges	bohr-too-ahn
grapes	aye-nub
dates	bah-lah

OTHER FOODS

rice	roz
bread	aysh
butter	zib-dah
sugar	sook-karr
eggs	bayd
soup	shor-bah

BEVERAGES

beer	bee-rah
wine	nee-beed
mineral water	mye-yah mah-dah-nee-yah
tea	shaye
coffee	ah-wah
with milk	bil-lah-bun
orange juice	ah-seer bohr-too-ahn
soda	wah-hed

DAYS OF THE WEEK

Sunday	el-hud
Monday	lit-nayn
Tuesday	it-tah-laht
Wednesday	lahr-bah
Thursday	el-kha-mees
Friday	ig-gohm-ah
Saturday	el-huhd

The following is a transliteration of the Gregorian (Western) calendar used for business purposes:

January	yah-nah-yer
February	fig-rye-yer
March	mah-ris
April	ab-reel
May	mah-yoo
June	yo-neh-yah
July	yo-leh-yah
August	ah-ros-tos
September	September
October	October
November	November
December	December

NUMBERS

1	wah-hed		17	sah-bah-tah-sher
2	et-nayn		18	tah-mahn-tah-sher
3	ta-la-ta		19	tes-sah-tah-sher
4	ahr-bah-ah		20	aysh-reen
5	kham-sah		21	wah-hed wi aysh-reen
6	sit-tah		22	et-nayn wi aysh-reen
7	sahb-ah		30	tah-lah-teen
8	tah-mahn-yah		40	ahr-bay-een

9	tes-ah	50	kham-seen
10	ah-shah-rah	60	sit-teen
11	heh-dah-sher	70	sahb-een
12	et-nah-sher	80	tah-mah-neen
13	tah-laht-tah-sher	90	tes-een
14	ahr-bah-tah-sher	100	may-ah
15	khah-mahs-tah-sher	1000	ahlf
16	sit-tah-sher		

TELLING TIME

noon   id-doh-reh
midnight   noss el-layl

For 1:00 to 11:00 use numbers listed above.

Quarter past, add *wee-rah-bah* to the number.
Half past, add *wee-nos* to the number.
Quarter of, add *teh-leh-tah el-lah* to the number.

ARABIC NUMERALS

It is important that you learn to recognize Arabic numerals (read from left to right, like ours)—this will prove a great help when shopping or catching numbered buses.

RESPECTFUL PHRASES

There are certain phrases that travelers should use to show that they understand and respect the social customs of Arab countries:

God willing—used in the sense of "I hope so."	in-shah-ahl-láh
When you step in front of someone	moo-tah-ah-séef
With great pleasure.	bee-kúl soo-roór
If you admire something or someone, i.e., someone's children	ma³-shah-al-láh
Have a good time.	in-shah-rée
Have a good trip (go in safety) —used by a host when a guest departs.	mah-ahs-ah-lah-mah
God keep you in peace—used when a person is leaving a house.	ahl-láh is-ah-máhk
Congratulations.	mah-brúk
Welcome.	ah-lahn wah sah-lahn

Key Words and Phrases-Hebrew

श्ल

A large percentage of Israelis do speak English, but the following phrases may be useful in certain situations.

PRONUNCIATION

ch = the sound the the Scottish word lo*ch* or the German name Ba*ch*

GENERAL WORDS AND PHRASES

How much is it?	kah-mah zeh oleh?
It's too much.	zeh yo-tair meed-daye
Where is/are?	ai-fo
Is/Are there?	yaish
a bathroom	bait shee-moosh
a restaurant	mee-sah-dah
the hotel	hah mah-lone
the post office	hah do-ar
the bus station	hah tah-chah-nah
a bus	ou-toe-boos
the train station	hah tah-chah-naht rah-keh-veht
the market	hah shuk
the hospital	bait cho-leem
a doctor	ro-feh

the bank	hah bahnk
a taxi	mo-neet
a telephone	tai-lai-fon
the police station	hah tah-chah-naht meesh-tah-rah
the embassy	shah-gree-root
the gas station	hah tah-chah-naht deh-leg
a garage	moo-sach
the pharmacy	bait mehr-kah-chat
the grocery store	chah-noot
the synagogue	bait kneh-set
the church	hah knai-see-yah
the museum	hah mo-sai-oom
the airport	hah zdeh ti-oo-fah

left	smo-lah
right	yi-meen
straight ahead	yah-shav

At what time is ———?	bi-ai-zeh shah-ah
What time is it?	mah hah shah-ah

Yes.	cain
No.	lo
Thank you.	toe-dah
You're welcome.	bi-vah-kah-shah
I'm sorry.	ah-nee mis-tah-air
Excuse me.	slee-chah
Please speak slowly.	bi-vah-kah-shah da-bair li-ahd
I don't understand.	ah-nee lo mai-veen (masc.)
	ah-nee lo mi-vee-nah (fem.)
I don't speak Hebrew.	ah-nee lo mi-da-bair eev-reet (masc.)
	ah-nee lo mi-da-beh-ret eev-reet (fem.)
Do you speak English?	ah-tah mi-da-bair ahn-gleet? (masc.)
	aht mi-da-beh-ret ahn-gleet? (fem.)

How are you?	mah shlom-cháh? (masc.)
	mah shlo-maích? (fem.)
I'm fine, thank you.	tóv toe-dáh
What is your name?	mah shmaich (masc.)
	mah sheem-chách (fem.)
My name is ———.	schmee———
Good morning.	bó-kehr tóv
Good evening.	eh-rehv tóv
Good night.	líe-lah tóv
today	hah-yóm
tomorrow	mah-chár
Hello.	shah-lóm
Good-bye.	shah-lóm
I would like	ah-neé mi-vah-késh (masc.)
	ah-neé mi-vah-késh-et (fem.)
I need	ah-neé tsah-reéch (masc.)
	ah-neé tsree-cháh (fem.)
I don't like	ah-neé lo o-haív (masc.)
	ah-neé lo o-héh-veht (fem.)
Help!	hah-tzée-loo
a man	eesh
a woman	ee-sháh
a boy	yéh-led
a girl	yahl-dáh
cold	kar
warm	chahm
Mr.	mahr
Mrs./Miss	gi-véh-ret
Doctor (M.D., Ph.D.)	dóc-tor
Professor	pro-fés-sor
to eat	leh-eh-chól
to drink	leesh-tóte
to go	lah-léh-chet

to see	lee-rote
I am sick.	ah-nee cho-leh (masc.)
	ah-nee cho-lah (fem.)
I am tired.	ah-nee ah-yafe (masc.)
	ah-nee ah-yay-fah (fem.)
I am thirsty.	ah-nee tsah-meh (masc.)
	ah-nee tsmay-ah (fem.)
I am hungry.	an-nee rah-aiv (masc.)
	an-nee ri-ai-vah (fem.)

AT THE HOTEL

a single bed	mee-taht yah-cheed
a double bed	mee-taht foo-lah
hot water	mah-yeem chah-meem
a shower	meek-lah-chaht
a room	cheh-dehr
a private bathroom	shay-roo-teem prah-tee-yeem
air-conditioning	mee-zoo ach-veer
a television	tay-lay-vee-zyah

TELEPHONING

collect call	see-chaht goo-vay-nah
"Hello"	hah-lo
credit card call	*Use the English term.

*Israeli telephone operators speak English.

AT THE PHARMACY

deodorant	day-oh-do-rahn
toothpaste	meesh-chaht shee-nah-yeem
sanitary napkins	tach-bo-shote hee-gay-nee-ote
laxative	mi-shahl-shayl
anti-diarrheal medication	troo-fah neh-ged shil-shul

RESTAURANT

the menu	hah tah-freet
the check	hah chesh-bone
large	gah-dole
small	kah-tahn
a lot	hahr-bay
a little	mi-aht
a fork	mahz-taig
a knife	sah-keen
a spoon	kah-peet
a glass, a cup	koz
a bottle	bak-buk
a plate	tsah-lah-chat
fried	mee-too-gahn
grilled	tzah-lo-ah-lee
baked	al-fuy

MEATS AND FISH

steak	steak
chicken	oaf
fish	dahg
shrimp	gahm-bay-ree
shish kebab	shish kebab

VEGETABLES

tomato	ahg-vahn-yote
potatoes	tah-poo-chay ah-dah-mah
eggplant	chat-zee-leem
avocado	avocado
cucumbers	meh-lah-feh-fo-neem
vegetable salad	sah-laht yee-rah-kote

FRUITS

fruit salad	sah-laht pay-rote
watermelon	ah-vah-tee-ach
banana	bah-nah-nah
orange	tah-pooz
grapes	ah-nah-veem
grapefruit	esh-ko-leet

OTHER FOODS

rice	o-rez
bread	leh-chem
butter	chem-ah
sugar	soo-kar
eggs	bai-tzeem
soup	mah-rahk

BEVERAGES

beer	bee-rah
wine	yah-yeen
soda	gah-zoz
mineral water	mah-yeem meen-aye-rah-leem
tea	tay
coffee	kah-feh
milk	chah-lahv
orange juice	meetz tah-poo-zeem

DAYS OF THE WEEK

Sunday	yom ree-shone
Monday	yom shay-nee
Tuesday	yom shlee-shee
Wednesday	yom ri-vee-ee
Thursday	yom chah-mee-shee
Friday	yom shee-shee
Saturday	Shahb-bat

HEBREW PHRASES

The following is a translation of the Gregorian (Western) calendar used for business purposes:

January	yáh-noo-ahr
February	féb-roo-ahr
March	mayrtz
April	ah-préel
May	maye
June	yóo-nee
July	yóo-lee
August	ów-gust
September	sep-tém-behr
October	oc-tó-behr
November	no-vém-behr
December	day-tsém-behr

TIME

midnight	chah-tzóte
1:00	hah-sháh-ah ah-cháhd
2:00	hah-sháh-ah shyah-yeem
3:00	hah-sháh-ah shah-lósh
4:00	hah-sháh-ah ahr-báh
5:00	hah-sháh-ah chah-máysh
6:00	hah-sháh-ah shaish
7:00	hah-sháh-ah shéh-vah
8:00	hah-sháh-ah shmó-neh
9:00	hah-sháh-ah táy-shah
10:00	hah-sháh-ah eh-sehr
11:00	hah-sháh-ah ah-chad es-ráy
12:00 noon	hah-sháh-ah shtaym es-ráy
2:15	hah-sháh-ah shtáh-yeem vah reh-váh
2:30	hah-sháh-ah shtáh-yeem vah chái-tzee

2:45   hah-shah-ah shtah-yeem
                 arbah-eem vi chah-maish

NUMBERS

one	ah-chahd	seventeen	shi-vah es-ray
two	shtah-yeem	eighteen	shmo-nah es-ray
three	shah-losh	nineteen	tee-shah es-ray
four	ahr-bah	twenty	ess-reem
five	chah-maysh	thirty	shlo-sheem
six	shaish	forty	ahr-bah-eem
seven	sheh-vah	fifty	chah-mee-sheem
eight	shmo-neh	sixty	shee-sheem
nine	tay-shah	seventy	sheev-eem
ten	eh-sehr	eighty	shmo-neem
eleven	ah-chahd es-ray	ninety	teesh-eem
twelve	shtaym es-ray	one hundred	may-ah
thirteen	shah-losh es-ray	one thousand	eh-lef
fourteen	ahr-bah es-ray		
fifteen	chah-maysh es-ray		
sixteen	shaish es-ray		

About the Authors
🪬

We have written three other travel books—*The Travelers' Guide to European Customs and Manners*, *The Travelers' Guide to Asian Customs and Manners*, and *The Travelers' Guide to Latin American Customs and Manners*.

Writing this book has involved countless hours of interviews, as well as visits to exotic ports of call neither of us ever expected to see.

Elizabeth Devine lives in Marblehead, Massachusetts, and is a professor at Salem State College. She has edited reference books and has written travel books as well as travel and feature articles for such publications as *TV Guide*, *Boston Magazine*, *The New York Times*, and *The Chicago Tribune*.

Nancy L. Braganti has taught foreign languages in the U.S., Europe, and the Middle East. She has traveled extensively in the Middle East and North Africa. Ms. Braganti is currently studying Russian and serving as a volunteer mediator in the Salem, Massachusetts, area. She lives in Marblehead, Massachusetts, with her husband, Fausto, and her daughter, Tanya.

Order Form

If you're traveling to Asia or Latin America, you'll want to have a copy of Elizabeth Devine and Nancy Braganti's other books in this series. They can be ordered through your local bookstore or directly from the publisher.

To order, just send check or money order to: St. Martin's Press, 175 Fifth Avenue, New York, NY 10010, ATTN: Cash Sales. For information on quantity orders, discounts, and credit card orders, call the St. Martin's Special Sales Dept. toll-free at (800) 221-7945, extension 662. In New York State, call (212) 674-5151, extension 662.

Please send _____ copies of THE TRAVELERS' GUIDE TO ASIAN CUSTOMS & MANNERS (ISBN: 81610-3) @ $9.95 plus postage and handling charges of $1.50 for the first book and $.75 for each additional book to:

Name _____

Address _____

City _____ State _____ Zip _____

....

Please send _____ copies of THE TRAVELERS' GUIDE TO LATIN AMERICAN CUSTOMS & MANNERS (ISBN: 02303-0) @ $10.95 plus postage and handling charges of $1.50 for the first book and $.75 for each additional book to:

Name _____

Address _____

City _____ State _____ Zip _____

....